THE BRIG OWHYHEE, OF BOSTON

Shipmasters
of
Cape Cod

HENRY C. KITTREDGE

PARNASSUS IMPRINTS
Hyannis, Massachusetts

TO
MY WIFE

Contents

1. EARLY DAYS   3

2. THE COASTERS   14

3. THE NORTH-WEST FUR TRADE   40

4. NEUTRAL TRADERS   70

5. JOSIAH RICHARDSON   98

6. THE LIVERPOOL PACKETS   121

7. EUROPE, CHINA, AND THE EAST INDIES   142

8. THE CLIPPERS   162

9. MORE CLIPPERS   191

10. THE LAST OF THE CLIPPERS   221

11. NON-CLIPPERS FROM THE FIFTIES TO THE EIGHTIES   254

12. THE MEDITERRANEAN FRUIT TRADE   285

ACKNOWLEDGMENTS   295

BIBLIOGRAPHY   301

INDEX   307

Illustrations

THE BRIG OWHYHEE, OF BOSTON   *Frontispiece*

JOB CHASE, JR.   22

CAPTAIN WILLIAM STURGIS   46

THE ATAHUALPA IN MACAO ROADS   54

CAPTAIN JOSIAH RICHARDSON   104

THE S. S. PACIFIC RESCUING THE CREW OF THE BRITISH
    BARK JESSIE STEPHENS, 1852   126
      Photograph by L. B. Robbins

CAPTAIN ASA ELDRIDGE   134

THE SCHOONER AMERICAN BELLE   146

THE CLIPPER SHIP STAGHOUND   164

CAPTAIN JOSHUA SEARS   206

THE CLIPPER SHIP CHARIOT OF FAME   234
      Photograph by L. B. Robbins

CAPTAIN PRINCE S. CROWELL   246

Shipmasters *of* Cape Cod

Shipmasters *of* CAPE COD

I

Early Days

THERE is little in the appearance of Cape Cod today to suggest that it was once the home of sea captains. From Sandwich all the way to Provincetown, one rides past neat, low cottages with wide chimneys and long pitched roofs on the one hand, and solid, two-story houses with little porticoes on the other. No grizzled mariners in yachting caps and pea jackets stroll along the village streets, nor do giant clam shells from the antipodes, placed beside every other door-step, speak of voyages round the world. Here and there, to be sure, on the ridgepole of a barn, is a weather vane in the shape of a model bark; now and then you may pass a boarding-house with a nautical name — The Anchorage, The Captain's House, or The Ship-Shape Inn. For the rest, there is nothing to show that the houses were not built by lawyers or country doctors — hardly a hint of the part that the Cape played in the great days of sail.

But inside, the salty flavor of past years, arresting and unmistakable, dispels all doubt. Over the stove in the sitting-room hangs a picture of a full-rigged ship, framed after the Chinese fashion in black wood carved into elaborate filigree. In a corner stands a camphor-wood writing-cabinet brought from Canton, and in the next room is a painting of another vessel, com-manded, like the first, by the grandfather of the owner of the house. Stored away in a closet is a box full of the Captain's letters from foreign ports. They tell of bargains struck between Dennis captains and San Domingo wreckers; of African fever in Prince's Island and cholera in Singapore; of lads who at nineteen commanded ships on China voyages and sounded their way through the uncharted channels of the North-West Coast, for sea otter. Envelopes sent from Shanghai *via* Marseilles to waiting wives in Chatham hold letters that give glimpses of life on the China Coast, of crews deserting in de Galle, and of gay dances in Hong Kong. They tell exultant tales of beating the clipper fleet to San Francisco in the fifties, of new records home from Calcutta, and of mandarin coats bought in Hong Kong for Cape Cod wives.

There are log books too, their leather bindings stained with the salt water of three oceans, that hold, beside their terse entries of latitude and longitude, the unadorned tale of weary weeks of calm in the Pacific, of head winds across the Indian Ocean, of blinding snowstorms in the North Atlantic, and of typhoons that swept ships clean in the China Sea. They tell of grain-carriers with choked pumps and of schooners clawing off lee shores or carrying corn to starving Ireland. In the attic, it may be, is a chart-chest pushed back under hand-hewn oak rafters; in it are charts of courses pricked off as straight as a steamer's wake between San Francisco and China and as crooked as the Meander in the mazes of the Malacca Straits.

In another house, framed, perhaps, of Russian fir which its builder brought back from Archangel for want of a better cargo, is an account-book of the owners of little local packets that made weekly trips between Brewster and Boston. Here, too, is a foxed old journal, that paints a lurid picture of Revolutionary France and sheds new light on customs officials at the Cove of Cork. Other letters tell of months of waiting for a cargo in Manilla, of addressing Sunday Schools in San Francisco and Lord Mayors' luncheons

4

in Southampton; of going to church in Calcutta; of celebrating the Fourth of July in Bremerhaven and of being held up by a Japanese festival in Nagasaki. Coasting skippers write of swapping barrel staves for mahogany in the West Indies, of carrying flour from Baltimore to Boston for five cents a barrel, and of limping into St. Thomas dismasted by hurricanes.

If you are privileged to read these letters and to turn the musty pages of the log books and the journals, Cape Cod will vanish, and you will be in a very real sense transported from port to port round the world. When you have finished, you will have gained some idea of the humor and piety and vigor and resourcefulness that these men learned on their voyages. This book is an attempt to tell something about these voyages and so to give an idea of the quality of the men themselves.

Some such undertaking is called for in fairness to the Cape, for, though maritime Massachusetts has, on the whole, fared well at the hands of the historians, Cape Cod has received but shabby treatment. A host of writers have sung the praises of Salem; Boston and her merchants stand revealed in the publications of the State Street Trust Company, and her great shipbuilder, Donald McKay, has had justice done him in a sumptuous volume by his grandson; one lively and scholarly volume has dealt with the whole story of Massachusetts seafaring; the fishermen of Gloucester have been thrice immortalized; Marblehead and Kingston sailors have been honored in a book apiece. Innumerable little volumes deal in detail with the life and achievements of this shipmaster or that. But where, in all this salty literature, are the men of Cape Cod? Lost, many of them, or forgotten; and the rest are scattered through a hundred volumes and usually with nothing to show that they were born on the Cape.

Two of its towns, to be sure, have come off better than the rest. Barnstable has its Francis Sprague and

Brewster its J. Henry Sears; but neither of these writers, useful as their work has been, has tried to exhaust the possibilities of even his own town. The purpose of this volume, therefore, is to present the maritime case of Cape Cod as a whole. So far as the author is concerned, it makes no difference whether a man was born in 'High Barnstable,' with what has been called 'its native aristocracy of lawyers and clipper-ship commanders,' or way down among the rolling hills of Truro, whose sons were the first to follow sperm whales to the Falklands. If he was a captain in the merchant service, he is material for these pages.

Captains aplenty there were, in all conscience, but strangely enough even local historians have been at small pains to name them. For the most part they prefer generalities, and generalities, be they ever so truthful, are too easy to be of much use. Here, for example, is a characteristic passage from Frederick Freeman: 'A large proportion of the male inhabitants of the Cape are, as is well known, early addicted to the seas.... Perhaps no portion of the globe, of similar extent, has furnished so many able commanders of ships.'

Again, H. C. Thatcher, Esq., a distinguished Boston merchant and loyal son of the Cape, announces that he can remember fifty captains who lived along the main street of Yarmouth within a space less than two miles. Daniel Webster, who was lured to Sandwich annually by the yellowlegs and plover, bears further testimony to the salty character of its inhabitants in a letter which he wrote to a friend in Dennis: 'I was once engaged in the trial of a cause in your district, in which a question arose respecting the entrance into the harbor of Owhyhee, between the reefs of coral rock guarding it on either side. The counsel for the opposite party proposed to call witnesses to give information to the jury. I at once saw a smile which I thought I understood, and suggested to the judge that very probably some of the jury had seen the entrance themselves. Upon which, seven out of the twelve arose and said they were quite familiarly acquainted with it, having seen it often.'

Writing in 1809, the Reverend John Simpkins, whose word we must believe, asserts that more masters and mates in the merchant service hailed from Brewster than from any other Cape town; and he adds that three quarters of the men of Brewster followed the sea. A century ago, J. G. Palfrey thus paid rhetorical tribute to the sailors of Barnstable: 'The duck does not take to the water with a surer instinct than the Barnstable boy. He leaps from his leading strings into the shrouds. It is but a bound from his mother's lap to the masthead. He boxes the compass in his infant soliloquies. He can hand reef and steer by the time he flies a kite.' Among recent writers none speaks with more authority than Carl Cutler in *Greyhounds of the Sea*. 'In the matter of men,' he says, 'no similar area produced more deep-water masters of outstanding ability than Cape Cod.'

All this is interesting but hardly convincing. It is fair to ask for a few names with which to leaven so many generalities. Who were some of the fifty captains of Yarmouth, and what vessels did they command? What nimble Barnstable boys were those who leaped gaily from their cradles to the mastheads of ships? And who were the seven salty jurors who knew so well the entrance to the harbor of Owhyhee? In the following pages, some of the voyages of Cape men will be examined in an attempt to answer such questions as these and to discover, so far as may be, what sent them to sea in the first place, and by what talents they rose to fame once they had left dry land.

The first twenty years or so of the history of the Cape (1640–1660) may be scanned almost in vain for any trace of a sailor. And naturally enough, for at that tender age the crooked peninsula was little more than a child of Plymouth, and the Plymouth men — landsmen all in the Old Country — had had enough salt water to last them for a long time. Furthermore, the pioneers who first came from Plymouth and Lynn and Scituate to settle on the Cape had plenty of troubles ashore without going to sea for them. They were thankful to be on dry land once more and were determined to stay there. So, like the farmers and herdsmen and mechanics they were, they set to work clearing the land and building houses, with no time and no wish to venture farther from shore than the clam-flats or the creeks where the eels abounded.

In this posture affairs remained while the first generation of children grew up on the Cape. By that time the towns had begun to develop from struggling outposts of progress, whose very existence was precarious, into going concerns, secure and increasingly prosperous. Sandwich, Yarmouth, Barnstable, and Eastham were experiments no longer; they had succeeded; and other towns followed fast. The citizens began to take their farms for granted and to look out thoughtfully across the Bay. Thomas Huckins had already looked there in fact, and by 1660 was bringing rum from Boston to the taproom of his tavern in Barnstable in his own vessel. But he was by no means a professional sailor. His time was well occupied in performing the duties of selectman and deputy to the General Court as well as presiding over his hostelry. Voyages to Boston were, with him, only incidents in a busy life. Yet by making them he helped to break the bonds that still held most Cape men to the shore.

Another consideration, too, began to turn the settlers' minds seaward. The soil, though still adequate and far richer than it is today, grew gradually thinner as the forests that protected it were hacked down. This energy of the woodchoppers, who felled acres of woodland with wanton disregard for the comfort of generations to come, was in fact a blessing in disguise, for by discouraging men from farming, it forced them to sea, where in the years to come they were to fulfill a prouder destiny than ever grew out of the most fertile furrow. But the beginnings were small

and tentative. The young merchant marine of Cape
Cod did not leap, like Dr. Palfrey's Barnstable boy,
from the cradle to the shrouds. It felt its way seaward
bit by bit like a cautious bather, and was at first no
merchant at all and hardly marine either, for shore-
whaling and short cruises for fish were its earliest
limits.

But it is not the purpose of this volume to follow the
rise and fall of either whaling or fishing. Each is a
science apart, entirely distinct from the merchant
service, and quite worthy of a volume of its own. Yet
they had their effect on merchant sailors, for by showing the settlers that the sea was not always the grave
of those that sailed on it, they encouraged men who
cared neither for boiling blubber nor for salting codfish to use it as a highway for trade. So, one by one,
Cape men turned their backs on their flocks and their
farms and followed the fishermen to sea. The change
had to come, of course. No man can live month after
month and year after year with the sea at his very
door, its surf pounding in his ears in winter and its
sunny surface dancing before his eyes all summer,
without at last accepting its invitation — or taking up
its challenge. The dullest must finally become in-
quisitive and, wearying of the sight of his own barn-
yard and woodpile, dissatisfied with the sure comfort
of his winter hearth, must at last head out to sea, where
every moment is big with adventure and expectation
sits upon the dial's point.

But the first Cape Cod seafarers knew nothing of
these fine fancies. They were hard-headed men to
whom the sea, now that they had grown used to it, appeared as a ready means to a material end; and they
gratified their unrealized desire for adventure and
their fully realized desire for profit by pushing off in
little vessels and returning with miscellaneous cargoes.
So it happened that by 1700, the Cape was in a small
way producing merchant captains.

Little time need be spent on these early Cape sailors.

The important thing about them is that they went to sea at all, not what they did when they got there. An anecdote or so about one or two of them, like Joseph Atwood, of Chatham, and Isaac Freeman, of Eastham, will suffice to show what sort of seafaring was going on at this period. Captain Atwood was master of at least three vessels: the schooner Isle Sables Galley, the sloop Falmouth, and the snow Judith. He made foreign voyages in all of them between 1740 and 1750, but the most interesting is one in the Judith in 1749, for it shows that owners even at that early date were fond of sitting safely in their counting-rooms, writing out orders for their captains to follow in far countries.

The Captain was about to embark on a voyage from Boston to Nova Scotia, south to Honduras, across to Amsterdam, and back again to Boston. He took with him the following orders from his owners to cheer him on the way: 'While you are loading [in Honduras] you must keep a good lookout lest you be overpowered by Spaniards, and as you are well fitted for defense [an eighty-ton vessel!] we expect you to make a manly defense in case you are attacked.' But Atwood was too good a Yankee to run risks for nothing. He retired with what was for those days a fortune, and built himself a gambrel-roofed house in Chatham that is today one of the finest specimens of Colonial architecture on the Cape and is still called the old Atwood house.

As a matter of fact, Spaniards, even when their vessels bristled with cannon and their decks were thronged with men, were not always so formidable as they looked. Captain Isaac Freeman, of Eastham, for example, had little trouble in bluffing one of them that he fell in with off the Azores. It was in 1748, the year before Atwood made his first voyage to Honduras, and Freeman was in command of the Boston ship Bethel, letter-of-marque, carrying fourteen guns and thirty-seven men. He bore down on the big Spanish ship — the Jesus Maria y Joseph — with her twenty-six guns and one hundred and ten men, stuck half a dozen

Early Days

Quaker guns through his bulwarks, put caps on sticks
to make his decks look crowded, slung lanterns in the
rigging, and closed in on the enemy with what he describes as 'A serenade of French Horns and Trumpats.'
The Spaniards surrendered without a shot, and Freeman's men were kept hard at work until daylight tying
up prisoners whom they subsequently landed in Fayal.
'I believe,' wrote Captain Freeman in a letter to his
owners, 'it first Instance of such a prize taken by so
small a Force without firing one Gun on either side but
however assure you I esteem it much better than
Fight'g.' One of Captain Freeman's sailors, Samuel
Eldredge, came home, if tradition is true, with as much
gold as he could 'back' across the Cape from the Bay
shore, where he landed, to East Harwich, where he
lived.

One more story of these early days is good enough to
tell — the more so as it is a mystery that remains un-
solved after a hundred and fifty years. Captain Joseph Doane, Jr., of Chatham, was off the Back Side of
the Cape in a schooner in 1772 and there sighted a vessel flying distress signals. Coming alongside, he found
that she was the schooner Abigail, Thomas Nickerson,
of Chatham, master, outward-bound from Boston; and
a grim spectacle she presented. Her deck was smeared
with blood; Captain Nickerson, his cousin, Sparrow
Nickerson by name, and his brother-in-law, Elisha
Newcomb, lay murdered on deck; chests were smashed
open and rifled; a rum barrel with its head stove in
stood almost empty; and only one man of the crew,
Ansell Nickerson, of Chatham, was left alive on board.

According to him they had been overhauled the
night before by a piratical topsail schooner which sent
four boatloads of men on board. To save his own life,
he had lowered himself over the taffrail on a rope and
kept out of sight under the vessel's counter. The pirates killed everyone on deck except a thirteen-year-old
boy named William Kent, whom, after helping themselves to the contents of the lockers and nearly finish-

11

ing the barrel of rum, they had carried off with them. There had been some discussion, so Nickerson said, as to whether or not they should burn the Abigail, but they left her as she was and put back to their own vessel, which was soon lost in the darkness.

This story sounded plausible enough to Captain Doane. He carried Nickerson back to Chatham and reported the occurrence to Edward Bacon, Esq., of Barnstable. Bacon sent a copy of the report to the Governor and straightway rode to Chatham to cross-question Nickerson. Apparently he was not satisfied with the result of the examination, for he had the man locked up in the Barnstable jail until further evidence should be forthcoming. Two frigates scoured the Sound in vain for any trace of the pirate, and Squire Bacon's suspicions increased. He sent his man in custody to Boston, where he was tried by a special Court of Vice-Admiralty for murder on the high seas. The trial lasted for two weeks and rocked the town. John Adams and Josiah Quincy, Jr., were counsel for the defense, and finally Nickerson was declared not guilty. Such, so far as they are known, are the facts in this strange tale of the sea. Let each decide for himself what happened or let him unearth more evidence if he can.

Fishing, which had already done much to set the merchantmen afloat, now pointed out for them another sort of business. Trips for cod had for years been taking men to the Labrador Coast and the Bay de Chaleur, up among the haunts of the wild fowl. Here, as the fishermen dried and salted their cod on the bleak provincial beaches, they saw at certain times of year millions of birds moulting and hardly able to fly. Feather beds were softer than corn-husk mattresses; so some of the fishermen decided to give the cod a rest for a season and take a cargo of feathers instead. So profitable did this business prove that 'feather-voyages' became immensely popular. They were easier than fishing trips, too, and smaller vessels would serve than were needed to withstand the rugged water of the Grand Banks.

Two brothers of Barnstable, Josiah and Edward Childs, were among the men in the eighteenth century who followed this cruel business for a time. The helpless birds were killed with brooms made of bundles of spruce branches. They were then stripped of their feathers and left to pollute the air of the rocky Labrador islands. The Childs brothers, after a few years at this work, switched to the more estimable business of trading with the Carolinas, for what reason nobody knows. Certainly it was not that the demand failed or that the supply gave out, for as late as 1825, Captains Barnabas Wixon and Ezra Howes, of Dennis, were going on feather-voyages in the sloop Phœbe with no apparent difficulty in making up cargoes. But it is a pleasure to note that the Childs brothers did abandon the unsavory practice and headed south on their later voyages.

The captains that have been mentioned during this early period were by no means great figures, but if we are to judge their success, not by what they themselves achieved, but by the kind of foundations they laid for those that were to follow, their work was well done. They led the way, not always by the shortest route and never in record time, from Labrador to the Falklands and east to the ports of Europe, a small cruising ground, compared to the limitless flights of their successors, but yet broad enough for them to test the strength of their wings in North Atlantic blizzards and to learn something of the ways of West India hurricanes. And by showing that these, for all their fury, might yet be survived, the Colonial captains encouraged their sons and grandsons to fare farther across uncharted seas until they had reached the China Coast and found it just as easy to come home the other way.

2

The Coasters

EVERY war spells ruin for the shipping of the country
where the fighting takes place, and the Revolution
was no exception. Colonial merchantmen everywhere
were either paralyzed for the duration of the war or
were snapped up by the King's ships if they took a
chance and tried to slip through the British blockade.
Trade was at a standstill; vessels began to fall to pieces
from disuse. The suffering, everywhere acute, was
doubly hard on the Cape, for the British, quick to see
the strategic value of Provincetown Harbor as a base
for naval operations, took possession of it without any
opposition — or any chance of opposition — from the
handful of fishing shanties that in 1775 comprised the
town. A detachment of His Majesty's Navy, including the celebrated Somerset, sailed in and made themselves entirely at home there, sallying forth often
enough to spread terror among the Cape villages by
menacing cruises up and down both shores of the
virtually defenseless peninsula.

Such tactics not only killed all trade on the Cape
but, what was worse, ruined the vessels. Seven years is
too long a time for any sort of craft to be kept out of
water; by the time Cornwallis had surrendered, the
brigs and schooners that lay shored up on the beaches
of every Cape village looked like phantoms indeed.
With seams opened, planking warped and paint blis-

14

tered, they were enough to discourage any but determined sailors from going to sea again. But the
Cape had some determined sailors, who, as soon as
they could get their bearings and some new vessels,
did go to sea again, on all sorts of voyages: short trips
to Boston on local packets; miscellaneous coasting
ventures; and cruises on the other side of the globe —
types of seafaring which were all well under way before the country was five years old. The trips of the
packets between Cape towns and Boston were picturesque and useful, but they hardly qualify as seafaring. Of the long voyages, more anon. The coasters
are our present concern.

The gulls that sail over the beaches of the Cape are
not more numerous than were these coasters in their
day — sloops, brigs, and schooners, that before the
days of steam bore the burden of our coastwise commerce. From Halifax to New Orleans, from Savannah
to Portland pier, they carried the cargoes that are today the lading of a thousand freight trains. To cat-
alogue them all and to name their captains would be
like trying to name and number the gulls that are
their symbols. The best that can be done is to select a
few — like the ornithologist who, with his aluminum
bands, labels what gulls he can, that he may follow
them in their flight. All but a few of the Cape men
who commanded coasters are dead, and with them too
often have died the tales that they told. What follows,
therefore, is a meager gleaning of a vanished harvest.

One of the earliest of them, Captain Benjamin Hallett, of Osterville, who ran a freight sloop between
Boston and New York, is a picturesque figure to begin
with, for he was many things besides a coasting skipper. He was a soldier in the Revolution, a sailor on the
frigate Dean, and the father of twelve daughters and a
son. After the war he came home to Osterville and began his career as a coasting captain, proclaiming his
pride in his family by naming his vessel the Ten
Sisters. But he did more for his daughters than that;

every time a new one was born, he added a room to his house, until he had a veritable mansion — the largest in the village. Neither his experiences in the Army nor in the Navy killed the Captain's piety, for he carried religion along with cargoes to the water-fronts of Boston and New York and raised the first Bethel flag for seamen's worship in both these cities. There being, as often as not, no minister on hand at the meetings which preceded the raising of these flags, Captain Hallett himself led the prayer and the hymn:

> Ye sons of the main, ye that sail o'er the flood,
> Whose sins, big as mountains, have reached up to God,
> Remember your short voyage of life soon will end;
> Then come, brother sailor, make Jesus your friend.

> Look astern on your life; see your wake marked with sin;
> Look ahead; see what torments you'll soon founder in.
> The hard rocks of death soon your keel will beat out —
> Hard a lee, brother sailor; 'tis time to heave about.

Though Captain Hallett has been called a pioneer amongst Cape coasters, he was by no means alone in the business even at that early date. The year 1804, which found him in the prime of life, was a busy one for all Cape harbors and skippers. With proper loyalty, most of them traded to and from their own towns, piling the local docks with every sort of merchandise from cotton to pine planks. Here, for example, is the cargo list of the sloop Polly in which Captain Simeon Higgins, of Eastham, left Boston in 1783: 1 crate, 1 tierce of crockery ware, 2 boxes of pipes, 4 chests of tea, 2 tons of steel, 1 bundle of frizzing irons, 4 bags of shot, 5 boxes of chocolate, 5 crates of nails, 5 barrels, 1 trunk, 1 ton of hollow ware, 1 hogshead of brandy, 1 bag of indigo, 1 bag of pepper, 2 kegs of spirits, 1 box of glass, 6 looking glasses and 3 tierce of 'goods.' Sometimes, instead of carrying general cargoes, captains specialized. Nathaniel Lewis, of Falmouth, brought his schooner Minerva home from St. Lucia in 1804 with forty-five puncheons of Jamaica rum under her hatches. Forty-five puncheons meant about five

The Coasters

thousand gallons; so it is safe to guess that the Captain's friends were glad to see him.

The men who took these little craft up and down the coast were by no means fair-weather sailors. Cape towns needed provisions in winter as well as in summer; so January, February, and March saw coasters at work as well as May, June, and July.

The journal of Captain Nehemiah Smith, of Eastham, who left Boston in January, 1810, in the schooner Polly, bound for Richmond with a cargo containing vinegar, herring, apples, and salt fish, gives a good picture of what winter coasting might be:

Thursday, Jan. 18.... Hove to.... Increasing gale.... Snow and hail. At 10 A.M. reefed a balance mainsail.... At 12.00 were not able to take in or set sail for ice, being obliged to lay in that dismal situation.... The most distressing gale we ever experienced. Shipped a sea, stove our quarter-board, broke our tiller and, we expect, damaged our cargo.

Friday, Jan. 19. This day begins with dismal weather for to behold in our situation. Severe gale, with our vessel almost sunk with ice and leaking bad. Middle part nothing better but more ice.... At 2.00 A.M. shipped a heavy sea in our foresail... and carried our foremast overboard with bowsprit and all the sail and rigging with them. A shocking scene for to behold, expecting the sea to be our grave... expecting every moment our mainmast to go, as we had no stay to support it, but kind providence preserved us in our distress.

Saturday 20th Jan. First part squally with snow. At 5.00 P.M. bent our jib, beat off ice and set ballance mainsail.... A Heavy sea.

For the next week they had a succession of gales from the S.S.E. Then on January 28, when they were close up with Cape Henry and hoping to weather it, another blow struck them, and they had to anchor. The journal continues:

Sat. Jan. 27.... Fresh gales.... Laying to anchor.... Pitching bows under and ice making fast. Expecting every moment to drift.

Sun. Jan. 28.... Wish for a wind that would carry us to a safe harbor, but look in vain. At 11.00 A.M. weighed anchor, but the wind so light and scant, found it impossible to pass the Cape.

Jan. 29.... It seems to be determined that we shall not pass the Cape.... God only knows what another 24 hours will bring about. Our wood gone and not much water on board, but we must wait with patience. So ends this day.

Wed., 31*st Jan.*.... We were so anxious to find a safe anchorage, we weighed anchor for the 5th time in hopes to weather [Cape Henry] but it was impossible for us to gain.... How our situation will terminate, God only knows. No wood — but little water.

Fri. 2nd Feb. 1810.... All the appearance of a heavy gale, which we found to our sorrow, laying on a lee shore without mast or sails to help us, nothing to depend on but our cables and anchors. At 6.00 P.M. the gale came on to our sorrow and still increasing till midnight, when it seemed impossible for us to ride. We had a number of heavy seas pour upon us, but we still praying for our vessel to ride, knowing that if we should go on shore on that dismal night, the sea running like mountains, we must all perish, but thanks to God we held on till morning.... We see no chance but we must sink as we lay. The people on shore, looking for the wreck, not expecting to see a man alive.... Latter part... gale... and severe cold, making ice very fast. So we end the day.

Sat. 3rd Feb..... Wind more moderate.... We begin to have some hopes of turning the Cape, but the wind still continuing ahead with severe cold and cloudy with a heavy sea. Nothing of importance happened this day.

At this point the journal ends. Captain Smith finally worked the Polly up to the false Cape, but for want of adequate headsail, and being logy with ice, she would not handle, and finally went on the beach. Here such of her cargo as remained unspoiled was sold at auction. That her owner, Benjamin Bangs, of Brewster, did not regard Captain Smith as in any sense responsible for the wreck is shown by the fact that before the year was out, he put him in command of the schooner Albert, in which the Captain distinguished himself in foreign trade.

The War of 1812 almost paralyzed the coasting trade, as it did all our commerce. Because of the British blockade, trips to Boston and New York became such wild work that most Cape skippers — particularly those who owned shares in their commands — preferred to stay at home and growl about the treachery of the Administration rather than run the risk of having their vessels scooped up by Commodore Ragget in the Spencer, which, together with the Majestic, had been assigned to the duty of patrolling the Cape shores. Coasting trips, instead of continuing as part and parcel of life, now became rare and wildly adventurous enterprises; and so effective was the work of the British that few even of those who did try to slip through the blockade came home with their cargoes. Some of these venturesome spirits were deep-water shipmasters, who, their wings clipped for the moment, turned coasters until better days should come.

Two such were Captains Winslow Knowles and Matthew Mayo, both of Eastham, who in 1814 succeeded in getting past the Spencer and into Boston in a whaleboat full of rye. The story of their return trip, as told by the Reverend Enoch Pratt, is perhaps colored with a touch or two of proper jingoism; but Pratt, writing in 1844, was near enough to the event to be accurate in the essentials. The two captains swapped their whaleboat in Boston for a larger craft and set sail for Eastham with a miscellaneous cargo. Off Plymouth they were picked up by a schooner camouflaged as a fisherman, which the British had taken and armed, and from her the two were put on board the Spencer. Their ransom was set at three hundred dollars, but since they did not have the money in their pockets, Captain Knowles was allowed to go to Boston to collect it. At this point he vanishes from the story; cash, it would seem, was scarce even at the capital.

After a dull week on board the Spencer, Mayo was

made pilot of the schooner that had captured him, with orders to patrol the waters of the Bay. Three officers and twenty men went with him, and the fun began. It came on to blow from the northeast and they anchored under the lee of Billingsgate, a safe enough anchorage but for the fact that Mayo, who saw an off-chance of capturing the schooner and her company, cut all but the last strand of the cable. It parted, letting the schooner go adrift in the shoal water between Billingsgate and the Eastham flats. She soon grounded; but still the Britishers seem not to have realized that they were being deceived, for they believed Mayo when he told them that the vessel had only hit the outer bar and would presently float over into deep water. They even obeyed him when he told them they had better go below lest they be seen and recognized as British by some of the townspeople who had begun to gather on the beach. An added inducement was a gimlet which he slipped to the sailors with the suggestion that it might be useful in case they felt like tapping a keg of West India rum that was among the ship's stores. Then Mayo, left alone on deck, improved his time by throwing overboard all the arms except a brace of pistols which he had stolen from one of the officers.

The tide was on the ebb, and the schooner, instead of floating over any bars, heeled gently over on her bilge until even the befuddled sailors below realized that something was amiss. The officers, too, at last aware of the trap they had been led into, ordered all hands on deck to seize Mayo; but he dropped over the side and waded ashore. The local militia, splashing out across the flats, seized the schooner and her company, but so great was the Cape's antipathy to the war, and so keen its anxiety for the safety of the salt works along the shore, that the Britishers, after a brief sojourn in an impromptu jail, were allowed to escape. But even this gentle treatment failed to smooth their ruffled feathers; Ragget soon afterwards came swoop-

The Coasters

ing into the Bay with the Spencer and collected twelve
hundred dollars from the town as balm for their injured feelings.

Disastrous though it was, the War of 1812 did not
last long enough to ruin vessels so completely as the
Revolution had done; and after it was over, business
everywhere picked up with extraordinary speed. The
fortunes of Job Chase, Jr., of West Harwich, illustrate
the matter clearly. From 1800 until about 1840, he
was one of the largest owners of coasting vessels on
the Cape — a merchant whose name was known from
Saco to South America. Business was steady with him
from 1805 up to 1812; even in spite of the war, he had
a vessel or two at work in 1813 and again in 1815. In
the course of the next two years, his fleet began to
grow and he began to prosper. Furthermore, by dealing in everything from sheep's wool from Nantucket
to mahogany logs from San Domingo, Chase contributed as much as any man in his generation to the
prosperity of the mid-Cape. Coasting skippers from
Orleans on the one hand and Yarmouth on the other
applied to him for commands, while Baltimore firms
wrote to ask the privilege to act as his agents, and
Boston politicians urged him to swing Harwich into
supporting Samuel Lothrop for Governor.

By 1830 a whole fleet of Chase's vessels were sailing
coastwise, almost all of them ringing the changes on
the name Hope. There were the Hope's Lady, Hope
and Phœbe, and New Hope, all schooners, and all at
work between 1806 and 1821. Others of the same
period were the Hope, the Hope for Peace, Old
Hope, and Hope and Polly. Later, in the twenties and
thirties, came the schooners Hope and Susan, Hope for
Success, Hope's Delight, Delight in Hope, Hope Mary
Ann, Hope and Hannah, Superb Hope, Lovely Hope,
Mount Hope, and the brig Lady Hope. But, as if to
show that, whatever faith he may have pinned to the
name Hope and its varieties, he scorned superstition,
Job Chase, Jr., carved other names on the quarter-

boards of three of his vessels — the Leonidas, the Rosebud, and the Amazon.

The Chase family founded something very like a maritime dynasty. Old Job Chase, Sr., had started the ball rolling during the last years of the eighteenth century; his son, having carried the business on and greatly expanded it, admitted the third generation into partnership by making his sons captains and joint owners of his best schooners. Two of the boys, Job, 3d, and Sears Chase, were sailing between the West Indies and New York in 1822 and 1823, Sears bringing mahogany from San Domingo in the Lovely Hope. A third son, Jonathan, made regular trips with passengers and freight between Darien, Georgia, and New York in the brig Amelia Strong, in which both he and his father owned shares. A fourth son, Ozias, died on a voyage to the Carolinas; a son-in-law, Isaiah Baker, was a distinguished mackerel-catcher and inventor of the purse seine on the one hand, and a South American trader on the other, always in Chase vessels. Still another of Chase's captains was a nephew, James Chase.

Now and then Chase took a flyer in foreign trade. In 1809, Captain Nathan Nickerson took one of the fleet, the schooner Polly, from Baltimore to Lisbon to the tune of $2211 freight money; and some twenty years later, Captain Isaac Kelly went to St. Petersburg, and back by way of Bremen and Tampico, taking on board at Cronstadt 'sixteen measures of Vodky' against the rigors of a North Atlantic crossing. But for the most part Chase depended not on any single long voyage with large profits, but on a multitude of short trips, each yielding a small return. Chase's fleet was, in truth, a fleet of tramps *par excellence*. Any port where there were cargoes or rumors of cargoes was a magnet for his skippers.

Of necessity Chase gave his captains complete discretionary powers in deciding where to go and what to do. Captain Jonathan Small, for example, discouraged at finding freights from Baltimore to Boston only five

JOB CHASE, JR.

cents a barrel, dropped down to Wilmington, North
Carolina, and picked up a load of lumber for the Bar-
bados. Job Chase, 3d, carried staves and shingles,
geese and turkeys, from the Carolinas to Martinique
and Guadeloupe and sold molasses in Baltimore on the
return trip. Nehemiah Harding was carrying coal and
flour from Richmond to Newburyport. Nehemiah Kel-
ley, turning his schooner Leonidas into a passenger-
carrier for the trip, took a group of young ladies from
Havana to New Orleans. Nathan Nickerson, in the
meantime, was trying to sell a cargo of salt fish in
Boston, and James Oliver was in the Carolinas, loading
shingles for St. Thomas with an idea of picking up salt
for New York somewhere in the Salt Keys.

The beginning of the end of Job Chase's business
came when his son Jonathan wrote from New York in
1836, 'I think it is about time to quit owning as you
now own.... I don't like the management altogether,
and there appears to be some jealousy.' The Chase
fleet gradually diminished during the following years,
and with its passing a lively business faded from Harwich.

While Job Chase and his sons were carrying cargoes of all kinds in and out of a dozen ports, a highly
specialized coasting business was going on briskly
farther up the Cape. Sandwich, never much of a seafaring town, nevertheless since 1800 had been taking
wood to Boston in a fleet of some thirty schooners,
owned chiefly by citizens of the town and almost always commanded by them. It would be hard to imagine a safer run than that between Sandwich and Boston, but since the demand for fuel was greatest in
winter, the little vessels were kept at work in the full
force of New England gales when many of their sisters
were cruising in balmier latitudes.

One of the Sandwich wood-carriers, Captain Josiah
Ellis, of the schooner Almira, started for Boston in the
middle of January, 1826, with a crew of only two, his
son Josiah and a seaman named John Smith. They

23

were almost up with Plymouth when the weather changed from one of those soft, overcast winter days which occur so frequently on the Cape, to a cold northwester, as clear and hard as a diamond. The wind came up ever fiercer and colder, putting Plymouth, which, though close at hand, lay dead to windward, out of the question as a shelter. Ellis let the mainsail, already a sheet of ice, come down by the run; furling it was out of the question; there it lay, with spray from every wave freezing to it until it became a solid heap of ice that threatened to lay the vessel on her beam ends. The other sails, deluged with spray, froze too and blew away. The clothing of the three men was first soaked and then frozen stiff. They hove to, went below and huddled round the cabin stove; but the Almira listed so badly that they did not dare to stay there.

To cut a long and tragic story short, the schooner was blown back across the Bay, until early in the morning she struck the sand close to the Dennis breakwater, which was a smother of surf. The three men were forced on deck, for the waves now made almost a clean breach over the vessel and filled the cabin with water. Volunteers from the town manned a boat and tried to row off to her through the surf and slush ice. Their boat was swamped, but they tried again. This time they got through the breakers and pulled off close enough to the Almira to shout encouragement. To go aboard her was impossible; the boat would have been smashed to pieces. Smith was the first to surrender. He crept forward and, seating himself on the windlass, was encrusted with ice in ten minutes and froze to death. Captain Ellis was the next to go; he too sat down and went the way of Smith. But the tide by this time had risen, and a great roller carried the wreck clear over the breakwater and high on the beach. The rescuers reached young Josiah in time, and, wrapped in hot blankets, he was thawed back to life in a Dennis kitchen.

The Coasters

As has been shown already, many coasting skippers owned a share or two in their commands, but the happiest were those who owned their vessel outright, and who, when the fancy struck them, could hoist sail and go on short trips, peddling local products to neighboring ports. Chatham and Harwich were centers for these maritime free lances, who called themselves 'corn-crackers' and their voyages 'corn-cracking,' and who looked upon their cruises as pleasant interruptions to the dull routine of farming or carpentering. Corn-cracking needed but little preparation — only time enough to get together a cargo of salt codfish and a few bushels of corn and salt. Warren Nickerson, of East Harwich, was a good example of this kind of care-free trader. He owned enough of the fifty-foot sloop Morning Star to enable him to do about as he liked with her, and in the forties, whenever the mood was on him, he would say to his son, 'Come, boy; it's time for a change; we're going corn-cracking.' And away they went, nosing in and out of Stonington or New Bedford or Providence until the hold was full enough to send them home. From one such trip Nickerson sailed back with a cargo consisting chiefly of yard goods, but with suspender-buttons, brass buttons, pocket-combs, writing-paper, and hooks and eyes as well, to say nothing of twenty-five dollars' worth of miscellaneous hardware and doubtless other merchandise of which there is no record.

By this time — the thirties and forties — halcyon days on the Cape had begun. Business of all sorts was booming; bridges and breakwaters were being built; banks and insurance companies were being incorporated; fisheries were in full swing; the caulker's mallet made music in a dozen small shipyards. Even cloth factories were started by a few misguided enthusiasts, and all this meant big business for the coasters. The number of vessels that had supplied the Cape with all that it needed during the first fifty years of our independence, was now inadequate. The fleet, already large, became a veritable flotilla, while the tonnage of each vessel grew in proportion. Fixed lines of good-sized freight schooners found plenty of work on both sides of the Cape; but the South-Siders on the whole had the better of it — in particular the men of Chatham and Hyannis, which now became hives of prosperity. Some of the skippers of these places, by the time they had grown tired of beating their way through the intricacies of Monomoy Shoals and of giving Peaked Hill Bars a wide enough berth for safety, had money enough in the bank to stay ashore and let others sail their schooners for them.

One of the best known of these merchants was Captain David Godfrey, of Chatham. By the time the War of 1812 was declared, he had learned enough seafaring to qualify as an officer on the privateer Reindeer, commanded by Captain Nathaniel Snow, of Truro. After the war, Captain Godfrey, together with a group of Cape merchants, among whom was George Lovell, Esq., of Osterville, started the Dispatch Line of packets between Boston and New York, perhaps the first regular service between these ports — an achievement for which he was dubbed Commodore. He left Chatham for New York in order to be nearer his ships. Captain Joshua Baker, of Hyannis, was another retired skipper who turned merchant about this time. Early in life he had commanded coasters — notably the celebrated topsail schooner Pequot; but she was no more than a preliminary hurdle to his vaulting ambition, which led him to forsake Hyannis for Boston, where, a senior partner of the firm of J. Baker and Company, he took his place among the many Cape shipowners of the capital.

Yarmouth, meanwhile, was sending schooners out of Bass River in all directions, on one occasion, at least, with important consequences, for the coasting trade south during the fifties was not lacking in signs of the times. A Virginia law, for example, required that every north-bound vessel not owned in the state should be searched for runaway slaves before leaving Virginia waters. The local pilots were made inspectors; the charge for inspection was five dollars for ordinary vessels and two dollars for coal-carriers. The money went half to the inspector and half to the state treasury for a fund which was used to pay rewards for the recapture of runaway slaves. If a vessel sailed north without being inspected, the captain or owner was required to pay a fine of five hundred dollars, and pending payment, the captain was to be held in the state or bail himself north by giving bond for one thousand dollars. In default of this, the vessel herself was to be seized. This law, which was passed about 1856, netted the State of Virginia $137,000 during the first year of its enforcement.

Because the charge for inspecting each vessel was small, Yankee skippers had submitted to it rather than go to law. But not so Captain Levi Baker, of Yarmouth, a veteran of twenty-five years' experience in the southern coasting trade. In July, 1856, he was in Norfolk with the schooner N. C. Hall, of which he was master and part owner. Having taken a cargo of corn and fruit for New Bedford, he lay at anchor at Hampton Bar to take on more fruit. While he lay there, a pilot boat hailed him and asked where he was bound, but sent no inspector on board. That night the wind came fair. Captain Baker, deciding that he had cargo enough after all, weighed anchor and stood out to sea, expecting that some of the pilot boats that always cruised about there would board and search him before he cleared the Virginia Capes; but no pilot appeared. His cargo was perishable; he could not return without loss. He therefore put to sea.

A month later, the N. C. Hall was back in Norfolk, this time under a new captain, as Baker was detained at home. She was seized by state officers and chained to the dock for having left Virginia on her previous trip without being searched. When he heard this, Captain Baker went to Norfolk to obtain her release. Here he found that the fine with costs had reached the sum of $700, but since the vessel was worth $3000 and was in danger of being ruined by worms if she lay in those waters much longer, he was inclined to pay the money and get her back. However, lawyers and merchants — some of them Virginians — both assured him that the law was unconstitutional; he therefore went to every official in any way connected with the business to deliver the required bonds and release his vessel until the affair could be settled. His one idea at the moment was to get her away from the worms. But no official would take any steps toward releasing her, on the ground that only the Circuit Court in session had power to accept such bonds. But this court would not convene for six weeks, during which time the schooner would be virtually ruined.

After trying in vain every possible scheme for releasing her — including a petition to the Governor of the state — Baker abandoned his vessel (which was later condemned and sold for $750 by the Virginia Court). Returning home, and, feeling himself in a sense the representative of the coasting interests of Massachusetts, he petitioned the Massachusetts Legislature for money to carry the case to the Supreme Court of the United States. His petition was granted, and the state appropriated $2500 to test the constitutionality of the Virginia law.

It is time now to look farther afield in the coasting trade, and to follow a few of the many Cape men whose voyages took them to the West Indies, at once the most picturesque and the most dangerous of all branches of coasting. Yet successful voyages were so profitable that owners and captains alike continued to run the gauntlet between hurricanes at sea and yellow fever on shore until long after the Civil War. Few were the villages on Cape Cod seventy-five years ago whose general store did not bear, among other signs, a board with the label 'W. I. Goods' — our ancestors' euphemism for rum and molasses; and these 'W. I. Goods,' more often than not, had been brought into the town by its own citizens, either indirectly *via* Boston or direct from the Jamaica docks. Harwich, Chatham, and Orleans were particularly enterprising in this business, as they were for that matter in every branch of coasting, but all the Cape towns had men who at one time or another had cruised among the plague-ridden islands of the Caribbean, some of them never to return.

In 1853, for example, Captain John Allen, of Harwich, took his schooner Cosmos through a West India hurricane, emerging with little but her hull intact. Even the Captain, a man experienced in those latitudes, called the storm 'tremendous.' He put the Cosmos under bare poles, but even so she was blown on her beam ends, and would have filled if Allen had not cut the lanyards of the fore shrouds and let the foremast go. With it went the main topmast, jib boom, and bowsprit. Thus eased, the schooner righted and, when the storm subsided, the Captain took her into St. Thomas under jury rig. There he found seven other wrecks, thanks to which the local ship chandlers had jacked up their prices until Captain Allen had to pay three hundred dollars for a single mast. It took three weeks to refit, and the Captain's son died of cholera in the interval. As though this were not enough, Captain Allen himself caught the disease; so did his mate and some of the crew. Ashore the death-rate was between forty and fifty a day. But the courage of the Captain rose above all these hardships. He drew on his owners for enough money to bury his son and pay the doctor; then, only partially recovered from his own sickness, he continued the voyage, loaded at Jacmel and started for Boston. But he was too ill to finish the voyage. The schooner put into Harwich, left Captain Allen there, and sailed into Boston under a new commander.

Captain F. M. Percival, of Orleans, knew both fever and wreck in the course of his West India voyages. In 1853, while in command of the schooner

Clark Winsor, he came down with yellow fever at Port au Prince, and while he lay in bed on shore, fighting a pitched battle with death, his mate improved the opportunity to absorb Jamaica rum to his heart's content, paying for it with money which he got by selling the ship's stores. It is no surprise to learn that he too took the fever, as did all the crew.

Captain Percival recovered and two years later was navigating the same waters in the same vessel. After another bout with yellow fever, he cleared from Gonaives for Boston, but off the island of Inagua he was carried off his course by the tricky currents that sweep between the islands. The Clark Winsor broke her back on a coral ledge and began to go to pieces. The Captain and crew made their way to Inagua in a boat and all except Captain Percival took passage home on a Bangor brig. The Captain stayed behind and, sick as he was, began the melancholy business of hiring wreckers to salvage what they could of his cargo and rigging at the rate of seventy cents for a dollar's worth saved.

Wreckers must have retired rich after a few seasons in those waters. A good illustration of their methods is their attempt to terrify young Edward E. Crowell, of West Dennis. In 1843, Crowell was mate under Captain Orrin Lewis on a voyage to San Domingo. All hands fell sick with yellow fever, the Captain and most of the crew died, and young Crowell, then just twenty years old and still shaky from his own bout with fever, was left with his first command. This was the kind of thing that West India wreckers dreamed of. Suavely they approached the young Captain and told him that it was hopeless for him to try to navigate the Crooked Island passage without a pilot, but that they had the very man for the job, an expert, who would take the vessel through for one thousand dollars. Crowell, however, had other uses for his money. He hired a crew and sounded his way through the passage a mile at a time for forty-five days. Then, with his troubles safely behind him, he cracked on sail and brought home his cargo of coffee. Without wishing to paint these San Domingo wreckers in more lurid colors ·than they deserve, it is fair to ask whether — with the best intentions in the world — they would have found the passage too intricate even for their skill, and would have piled Crowell's vessel up on a reef for salvage.

Even government officials in the West Indies looked on Yankees as fair game. While Captain John Kenrick, of South Orleans, was loading his schooner Three Friends with molasses in Cavanas in 1805, one of his sailors died. 'I have three more sick of the fever,' he writes, 'which leaves me one well man.... I am not well and should be pleased to get out of this damnable hole. The Commandant,' he continues, 'took the dead sailor's chest and clothes on shore and demanded the wages that were due him; but I shall not pay him one farthing, and I should like to know what business he had with the property of American Seamen or vessels.' This admirable firmness on the part of Captain Kenrick must have rejoiced the heart of his owner, William Coleman Lee, of Boston, for that gentleman, in giving the Captain his sailing orders, had stated his wishes with commendable candor. 'My one object,' he declared, 'is to make money with as little risk and as much dispatch as possible.'

As though hurricanes, fever, and land sharks were not enough to try the mettle of Yankee captains in the Caribbean, pirates infested these waters as well, and at least as late as 1822 did their share to discourage traders. In that year Captain Freeman Mayo, of Brewster, was taking a cargo of axes and nails from Boston to New Orleans in the brig Iris. With him were four other Brewster men — Sylvanus Crosby, second mate, Josiah Wing and Brewster Mayo, seamen, and Warren Lincoln, the twelve-year-old cabin boy. Off Cuba, the Captain sighted two vessels lying inshore of him; a look through the glass showed him that they were pirates. He set all the canvas the brig carried, but the airs were light, and the pirates came up on him fast, bending over long sweeps that sent their craft through the water even when the sails lay flat against the masts. After they had fired two warning shots at the Iris, Captain Mayo gave up the race and hove to. A boat put off from the pirate, and eight men came aboard the brig, their leader shaking hands ceremoniously with Mayo, who stood courteously at the gangway.

They took charge of the vessel, and after ransacking the cabin, the leader came on deck arrayed in the Captain's best shore-going clothes, and gave orders for the crew to stand in for the land. After tacking up and down the coast for a time, they brought the Iris into a bay which was the pirates' headquarters. Here they issued their ultimatum: unless the Captain dug up all the money on board, they would murder all hands. Mayo replied truthfully that there was no money to speak of on the brig, but that he would raise some if they would take him to Matanzas, about thirty miles away. They agreed to this, held the rest of the ship's company as hostages with the promise to kill them if the Captain was not back in three days, and took him in a small boat to Matanzas Harbor.

The Governor, however, was not interested; neither were the local merchants; but from the Yankee captains in port, Mayo collected three thousand dollars and a promise to raise volunteers among their crews to retake the Iris. The crews, however, were less willing than their captains, and the number who volunteered — thirty in all — was not large enough. Mayo decided to make the rounds of the merchants again in the hope of increasing his three thousand dollars. He had hardly reached this decision when the United States schooner Alligator came sailing along into the harbor. Captain Allen, the officer in command, instantly told Mayo to pilot him to the cove where the Iris lay; a sharp fight between the Alligator's crew and the pirate vessels resulted in the flight of the latter, but Allen was killed with a bullet through his head.

The Coasters

As soon as the pirates were gone, Mayo had himself rowed to his brig, where he found to his horror not a soul on board. Manning her with recruits from the Alligator, he sailed mournfully into Matanzas. What was his delight to find there all his ship's company smiling through bandages on board an American vessel! Under the vigorous leadership of Crosby, they had broken away from the Iris in a boat — albeit after a sharp scuffle with their guards in which most of them had received knife wounds — and, skirting the shore, had rowed the thirty miles to Matanzas. Back once more on the Iris, they squared away for Charleston, where the Captain bought a musket and a cutlass for every man and continued the voyage to New Orleans. Undaunted by this sanguinary episode, the young cabin boy, Warren Lincoln, continued to follow the sea, becoming captain of the brig Draco and the bark Mary. After retiring, he ran a general store in Brewster until his death in 1900.

A more successful West India trader was Captain Lorenzo Dow Baker, of Wellfleet. After a number of years in general coasting, Captain Baker in 1870 made his first trip to the tropics, as captain of the beautiful clipper schooner Telegraph, which was loaded with mining machinery for Ciudad Bolivar, on the Orinoco River. His return cargo for New York was bamboo from Jamaica. While loading there at Port Morant, Baker had the bright idea of throwing in a few bunches of bananas to see how they would suit the New York palate. They went so well that the next year, still in the Telegraph, he brought a whole cargo of them from Port Antonio, and landed them in Boston in the spring of 1871 — the first bananas that had been seen in any quantity in the Bay State.

Here was the key to a fortune for Captain Baker. During the next ten years, he was either shipping or carrying bananas from the West Indies to Boston and Philadelphia as fast as the schooners could load. The Telegraph gave way to two new vessels, the Ruth N.

Atwood and the Eunice P. Newcomb, both of Wellfleet, and Baker sometimes commanded them, sometimes stayed in Port Antonio, collecting cargoes of bananas and other fruit to be sent in chartered schooners. The business prospered so mightily under his management that in 1881 he was offered the position as agent of the Atlas Steamship Line, whose vessels ran between New York and the West Indies. He accepted and sent his bananas by these steamers. Soon after, he formed a partnership with his brother-in-law, under the name of L. D. Baker and Company, which later became the Boston Fruit Company, and was finally incorporated. This company then merged with the Minor C. Keith interests in Costa Rica and became the United Fruit Company, with Captain Baker as managing director of its Jamaica division. Thus had the Captain in his little schooner Telegraph started a business that was to reach such proportions as to justify within thirty years the launching of the Great White Fleet of the United Fruit Company.

Even after the railroad had stretched its way town by town along the Cape, reaching Sandwich in 1848 and Provincetown in 1873, schooners carried the bulk of local freight, and a great part of the traffic between southern ports and northern markets was still over the water route. As time went on, the little two-masters of other days began to give way to the big three-, four-, and five-masted schooners, which, with the clipper ships, form the chief factor in America's contribution to marine architecture. And here again, Cape men were on hand to command them. Captain Samuel W. Kemp, of Wellfleet, after learning the ropes on fishermen and oyster-carriers, began in 1864 general coasting in his own schooners. He commanded and owned the three-masted schooner Charles H. Lawrence, and took her up and down the coast between Maine and New Orleans for ten years. Then his mate wrecked her while trying to work his way into Boston Harbor. Another Wellfleeter, Captain George Williams, was

given command of the new five-masted schooner
Fannie Palmer, launched about 1900 at Waldoboro,
Maine — one of the great fleet of Palmers that swept
grandly along the coast during the few short years of
their glory. Captain J. Clement Harding, of South
Chatham, had another of them, the five-master
Dorothy Palmer, and Captain William Nickerson, of
Provincetown, as if to prove that Provincetowners
were something besides fishermen, took the five-master
Arthur Seitz as she left the stocks at Camden, Maine,
in 1901. Captain Willis L. Case, of Hyannis, had,
among other commands, the four-masted schooner Independent, and Captain Myron Peak, of Barnstable,
the three-master Abbott W. Lewis.

These big vessels were tried from time to time on
trans-Atlantic voyages, but, though most of them came
home safely, their officers had few easy hours on
the way. The Lucy Gibson, a three-masted schooner
that went into foreign trade, met disaster in 1870 while
under the command of Captain Otis D. Chase, of West
Dennis, with another West Dennis man, Horatio W.
Chase, as first mate. The Gibson was run into at night
while on her way from Liverpool to Boston with general cargo. The schooner foundered in a few hours, but
before she sank all hands but one were taken off by the
Dutch brig Engelina, and carried to Falmouth, England.

The art of sailing these big vessels was, it need not be
said, very different from the trick of handling the little
two-masters that still carried coal and lumber along the
Atlantic seaboard. Both were high arts, but of different sorts. This distinction was never more amusingly
illustrated than in the experience of Captains Allen H.
Bearse and Franklin Bearse, both well-known deep-
water shipmasters of Hyannis, when they embarked
for California in the days of the gold rush. As was the
custom, a group of Cape men, the Bearses among
them, formed a company and bought the Shiverick-
built fishing schooner Elizabeth B. to take them to the

gold fields. Her skipper, Captain Almoran Bacon, of Hyannis, formed one of the company and was wisely kept in command for the voyage. Following the ways of the fishing fleet, Bacon, as soon as he got into deep water, held on in spite of half a gale that was blowing, until the lee rail was buried under green water. The wind freshened still more, but the Captain held her to it, though the water reached the hatch-coamings. At this point the Bearse boys came running on deck, their hair on end, and demanded of Captain Bacon in no uncertain language what he thought he was trying to do. Bacon told them to keep calm and he would show them something about carrying sail on a fore-and-aft schooner. He did, and the Elizabeth B. arrived safe in San Francisco. After two years he brought her back and went into stone-carrying between Quincy and Philadelphia.

Another lively figure, who in the course of his voyaging wound up in the California gold fields, was Captain Thomas Harris, of Barnstable. He had been a coasting skipper in his youth and took to deep water about 1840 in command of the brig Pico in the Russian trade. While in her he on one occasion took the crew from a sinking English ship at night, a delicate maneuver, but nothing compared with a later exploit of his while in command of the bark Perua in 1846. This time he encountered another British vessel in distress, but the weather was so bad that he could do nothing at the moment. So he stood by for forty-eight hours until it moderated; then he trans-shipped all hands from the sinking ship to his own vessel, a feat for which he was given a gold medal by the Admiralty.

During the gold rush, Captain Harris followed the fleet round Cape Horn in the old Pico and left her all standing on the beach at San Francisco while he and his son headed for the mines. After being used for a time as a restaurant, the little craft was gradually buried under the made land that pushed the shore-line seaward as the city grew. There she lies today, no

The Coasters

doubt, if anyone would take the trouble to dig for her. Returned from his wanderings, Captain Harris settled comfortably down at home in Barnstable and, in spite of being encumbered with the dignified office of Sheriff of the County, he never forgot that fun is the spice of life. 'It was a pleasure to watch him dance,' writes his young friend, Francis Sprague, 'for he showed us more fancy steps... than we had ever seen.'

Hardy though they were, these coasting skippers were not by any means the godless set of men that writers of fiction delight in depicting. Some of them, naturally enough, may on occasion have forgotten a commandment or two, and others may have found temporary tyranny a convenience in delicate situations. But many of them were pious members of the church and went to meeting regularly when they were ashore. A few, indeed, became parsons in later life, not in order to square their accounts with the Almighty but because they had heard the call. Young S. S. Nickerson, the Chatham boy whom Alpheus Hardy thought too young to command the Heroine until he learned where he hailed from, became a minister after retiring from the sea. Captain Joseph Hawes, who in 1804 commanded the sloop Nancy, did not, it is true, ever become a parson. But he came close to it, for he was first a schoolmaster and afterwards a deacon, and that in the days when the title meant something. Captain Thomas Dodge was for a time a sea captain; then he got religion and became a Methodist preacher in Truro. Later he moved to Chatham and in 1861, while a member of the Legislature, distinguished himself by shouting 'Amen' at the close of Andrew's famous speech on the duty of Massachusetts. And, as Shebnah Rich so aptly puts it, 'when Dodge shouted Amen, it was no uncertain sound. He could make more noise in the pulpit with less religion, and spoil more Bibles, than any man I ever heard.' Be that as it may, he qualifies as a man of God. So does Simeon Crowell, of Yarmouth, who went to sea about 1790 and soon be-

37

came captain of the schooners Rosa Wing and Rambler. Whether it was his experience in the coastwise trade or his natural piety that led him into the ministry, does not appear, but after leaving the sea at the age of thirty-six, he was ordained a Baptist minister at his own house in Yarmouth and he continued in that calling until his death in 1848.

Lest it be supposed, however, that seafaring in some occult fashion led at last to the pulpit, it may be as well to mention an incident that occurred in Phinney's store in Barnstable one afternoon about forty years ago. Though business was comfortably slack, conversation was lively, a posture of affairs not unprecedented in that hospitable emporium. Suddenly, by one of those happy accidents that come once in a lifetime to make glad the heart of man, the front door opened, and a local coasting skipper hobbled in, leaning heavily on his cane. Since he was famous as being the most eloquent and versatile swearer in the village, the group round the stove looked expectant. But their hopes, high though they were, fell far short of the event, for at the same moment another figure came in at the back door. To most of them he was a stranger, but to Mr. Phinney he was well known as a visitor from Centerville, and as a mariner whose vocabulary was as sulphurous as the other's. Phinney saw his chance. As the two captains approached each other, he stepped, as it were, to the front of the stage, and with a sweeping gesture announced, 'It is a pleasure to introduce you two gentlemen: Captain ——, the profanest man on the North Side of Cape Cod; Captain ——, the profanest man on the South Side.' The two veterans gripped hands under an aura of deepening blue, the recollection of which has not yet faded from the memories of the lucky onlookers.

But the captains have gone — deep-water shipmaster and coasting skipper alike — and so have the vessels they sailed. Railroads, of course, were the great factor in their decline, for after the Civil War, New England was as busy driving spikes into railroad ties as it had been driving trunnels into the timbers of ships, and every spike was a nail in the coffin of the merchantmen. But another change in the methods of transportation also struck deep into the sinews of coasting. Barges in tow began, in the nineties, to take the place of schooners. The great advantage of this new style of cargo-carrying was that enormous quantities of freight could be taken on a single trip, and it arrived regularly, provided the weather was good. Coasting captains, seeing their livelihood threatened by this ugly innovation, were quick to point out that such clumsy catamarans were helpless in rough water; and there was truth in the assertion. But their objection was partly answered in 1909 when work was begun on the Cape Cod Canal, the new waterway that today eliminates the dangerous route outside the Cape.

There was now little room for the schooners or work for their captains. A few, to be sure, like Fred West, of Harwich, stepped from the tidy decks of their schooners to the great grimy hulks that, fettered one behind another like slaves in a chain-gang, were pulled from port to port by struggling tugs. But most of them, seeing that their race was run, went back to Chatham or Harwich or Hyannis, where they settled down in other trades.

3

The North-West Fur Trade

WHILE the coasting skippers, with their short voyages and quick profits, were keeping their owners in small change, other Cape men, their minds filled with the long thoughts that are proper for youthful nations, were pricking off courses round the world and piling up bank accounts for Boston merchants. England, to be sure, following the blind policy that had lost her the Colonies, barred her ports to Yankee vessels; but shipowners had enough to do at home for the moment without going to sea. Erecting a government is not a task to be achieved in a day. Yet east winds still blew the old salt smell into the nostrils of New-Englanders, keeping them restless for far horizons; nor did their struggle to stabilize an inflated currency or to meet unprecedented governmental problems ever drive from their minds their old trust in the sea and the ships. The Cape, saltier even than Boston, and looking always to Boston as its metropolis, was ready with a host of captains eager to square away in any direction as soon as the merchants should beckon to them.

They had not long to wait. Before 1790 the owners were ready, and Cape men flocked to Boston to take over their new commands. As early as 1783, Captain David Lawrence, of Barnstable, had the distinction of being the first man to show the Stars and Stripes on a merchantman in the old port of Bristol, England, and

with him as first mate was a friend from Yarmouth,
Joseph Hawes. Local historians, in fact, with entirely
proper pride, claim for their towns a number of men as
being the first Americans that ever sailed into one sea
or another. Captain Isaac Clark, of Brewster, who
went trading to Elsinore at least as early as 1795, and
who had the ship Financier in Cronstadt in 1800, is said
to have taken the first American vessel into the White
Sea. At all events, he was at Archangel so early that
he had to wait six months for the arrival of the first
American Minister before he was allowed to discharge
his cargo. His neighbor, Captain Isaac Foster, in
command of the ship George Porter, was trading with
Archangel almost as early as Clark; and another Cape
man, Captain Ebenezer Sears, of Yarmouth, was, we
are told, the first American to take a merchant vessel
round the Cape of Good Hope.

It might not be easy, perhaps, to establish the
claims of these early navigators; one wonders whether
a Salem vessel or two may not have beaten Sears round
the Cape of Good Hope, or whether an earlier American flag than Clark's or Foster's had not startled the
Russians in Archangel. But there is no doubt about
the next Cape man to distinguish himself — Captain
John Kendrick, of Harwich (now South Orleans),
whose ship Columbia was the first American vessel to
beat westward round the Horn, and whose brig Lady
Washington was the first Yankee to put in at a
Japanese port. Kendrick's claim to fame, however,
rests not on these exploits, noteworthy though they
are, but on his having led the way to the North-West
Coast — Oregon, Vancouver Island, and the Queen
Charlottes — in search of sea-otter skins for the mandarins of Canton. His voyage was financed by a group
of Boston, Salem, and New York merchants, who had
read the account of Captain Cook's third voyage, and
guessed that, in spite of the risk, there would be big
profits in the trade, once it was established. They
bought the eighty-three-foot ship Columbia, scanned

the list of eligible master-mariners, and invited John Kendrick to command the expedition. He accepted, and, accompanied by the sloop Lady Washington under Captain Robert Gray, set sail from Boston October 1, 1787. With him were his two sons, John, Jr., and Solomon, John as one of his mates, Solomon before the mast.

The plan was to fill up with sea-otter skins on the North-West Coast by swapping trumpery articles for them with the Indians, carry them across the Pacific to Canton, trade them for China goods, and square away for Boston by way of the Indian Ocean and the Cape of Good Hope. Certainly the merchants who conceived such voyages were not lacking in enterprise, nor were the captains who sailed for them lacking in courage. But as it turned out, his owners might have selected a better man for the business than Kendrick, for it was Gray, not the Harwich captain, who really founded the trade. Kendrick was forty-seven years old, and had proved himself an able commander on the privateers Fanny and Marianne during the Revolution. But, though nobody knew it, the peak of his energy was past. He spent six weeks at the Cape Verde Islands, when, according to Gray, five days would have been enough; wasted another week at the Falklands, getting ready to round the Horn, and finally, after a terrific beating off this dread Cape and in only ten days less than a year after leaving Boston, he dropped anchor in Nootka Sound, close to Vancouver Island. Gray, in the little Lady Washington, had beaten him there by about three weeks. Winter was at hand; it was too late to cruise about for skins; they accordingly put up a building on shore and went into winter quarters — gladly enough, no doubt, for all hands must have had as much seafaring as they wanted for the moment.

The next spring Kendrick and the Columbia lay comfortably at anchor while Gray in his sloop sailed here and there, buying otter skins for strap iron from the natives. By the end of July, he had enough to make up a cargo for the Columbia, and was ready to start for China. But Kendrick was in no hurry, nor were there skins enough for both vessels. He, therefore, turned over the command of the Columbia to Gray, who promptly set sail for Canton with young Solomon Kendrick still on board, leaving the Captain and his other son John on the Coast to collect a cargo in the course of the summer.

Complications arose, however, for a Spanish expedition under Martínez arrived from Mexico, built a fort, and took formal possession of all territory bordering on Nootka Sound. Kendrick in this emergency showed himself to be more astute as a diplomat than energetic as a trader. By tactful work he succeeded in getting permission from the Spanish commander to continue trading. So friendly, indeed, did the two become, that young John, who apparently did not share his father's fondness for the quiet life, joined the Spanish expedition, spent the next few years trading and fighting, and finally faded from sight in the mists of the Pacific.

This summer was, in fact, not an entirely uneventful one, for Kendrick in the course of his trading visited the Queen Charlotte Islands, where he showed that whatever his skill in handling Spanish agents, his methods with the Indians were not calculated to promote friendship. He fell far short, indeed, of following the excellent advice he had given to Gray: 'Treet the Natives with Respect where Ever you go,' he wrote. 'Cultivate friendship with them as much as possibel and take Nothing from them But what you pay them for according to fair agreement, and not suffer your peopel to affront them or treet them Ill.' Though the details of Kendrick's own adventure can never be known exactly, there remains little doubt that his methods on this occasion were both cruel and unwise. Here is about what happened.

He anchored in Barrel's Sound, off the Queen

Charlotte Islands, and after a few days of trading, found that the Indians had stolen, amongst other things, some freshly washed linen. This so enraged him that he seized the two chiefs, removed one of his cannon from its carriage, clamped a leg of each chief into the sockets thus left empty, and threatened to kill them if the stolen property was not returned. There was nothing for it; the Indians produced the linen — most of it, that is; what was not forthcoming they were compelled to pay for through the nose in otter skins. Not content with this, Kendrick forced them to hand over their whole supply of skins at his own price. 'When they had no more,' the narrative continues, 'the two Chiefs were set at liberty.'

Having thus obtained a cargo, the Captain set sail for Canton in the fall, but stopped at the Hawaiian Islands, where, ever on the lookout for new merchandise for China, he went nosing about from island to island until he found sandalwood growing wild on Kauai. Leaving three of his crew there to cut it, he continued his voyage to Canton, spent a year and two months there, during which he rerigged the Lady Washington as an hermaphrodite brig, contracted a fever on the one hand and a debt of four thousand dollars on the other, and was off for the North-West Coast again in the spring of 1791. It was on this voyage that he showed the American flag in Japan, where, if reports are true, he was hospitably entertained. Thence, with almost incredible folly, he headed again for the Queen Charlotte Islands. Naturally enough there was a fight; the natives sprang a surprise attack on the Lady Washington in the midst of apparently friendly trading, but were repulsed with heavy loss. The scrimmage must have been lively, though, while it lasted. One native, armed with a marlinspike fixed in the end of a club, brandished it over the Captain's head, ready to bring it down at a signal from his chief. Other Indians had got possession of the keys to the gun-chests, and for a few moments things looked bad for the

44

The North-West Fur Trade

Yankees; but the officers, some of whom had gone below for some spare muskets, appeared on deck at this moment, and the fight was virtually over. The Captain received a scratch from a native dagger, the only wound that any of the brig's company suffered, but the Indians did not get off so easily. The white men, in the words of Hoskin's *Narrative*, 'immediately opened, and a constant fire was kept up as long as they could reach the natives with the cannon or small arms, after which they chased them in their armed boats, making the most dreadful havock by killing all they came across.'

Leaving the waters of Barrel's Sound dotted with dead and wounded Indians, Kendrick headed south for his old stamping ground off Vancouver Island; but the Spanish fort guarded the entrance, and Martínez, if he was still there, had apparently forgotten his agreement to allow Kendrick to trade. At any rate, he was advised to look elsewhere for his otter skins, and he took the advice. By August he had a cargo, but Gray, who had arrived again from Boston in the Columbia, found him, instead of heading for Canton, living at ease in a big new house that he had built on the west coast of Vancouver Island, well out of the way of the Spaniards. Not until the fall did he set sail for China. Once more he stopped at the Hawaiian Islands, and once more left men on Kauai to cut sandalwood — a commodity, by the way, which found great favor with the mandarins, and which, thanks to Kendrick's experiment, was to prove a valuable item in the trade of China-bound Yankee merchantmen that had never yet rounded Cape Horn.

This time he stayed nine months in China, and had started for the North-West Coast again when he was dismasted by a typhoon and had to put back to refit. It was six months more before he had the Lady Washington to his liking; but he finally left for good in the spring of 1793, taking, though he did not realize it, his last look at the China Coast. After another summer with the sea otter, he headed again for Canton, but got no farther than the Hawaiian Islands. Life in these balmy latitudes suited him quite as well as in the Orient. Here he met the great Vancouver, dined with him on board the Discovery, and apparently told him, in an expansive moment, of the sandalwood on Kauai. At any rate, when Kendrick went there soon after, he found Vancouver on the spot. The next summer saw Kendrick again on the North-West Coast, and the next winter found him once more among his beloved Islands. About New Year's, 1795, he met a Captain Brown of the British Navy there. The vessels exchanged salutes. By some grim error the Britisher's cannon was pointed directly at the Lady Washington, and Kendrick, who stood on deck, was instantly killed.

Such was the dramatic end of a picturesque career. Kendrick, though he lacked the stability and perhaps the business acumen that led some Cape men to establish themselves behind mahogany desks in Boston when they had wearied of far voyages, was nevertheless an expert and fearless sailor, well deserving his title of the 'Navigator' with which later generations honored him. His was a roving nature — a combination of explorer and trader. He saw nothing remarkable in taking the Columbia round Cape Horn, or in sailing five times across the Pacific in a forty-foot sloop. He had a sharp eye for new trade and extraordinary skill in picking his way to it through uncharted channels, but he preferred to let others carry the proceeds home, while he continued to follow his fancy on the other side of the world. He could dig crude gold out of the remote corners of the earth, where many would have sought for it in vain, but he had no talent for minting it into the currency of a nation. Seven years on the Pacific had obliterated his thoughts of home. Such bonds as tied him to the place of his birth were no match for the magnet of far horizons, the exotic fragrance of palm-fringed islands or the license of the China Coast. Yet three generations of sailors spoke

CAPTAIN WILLIAM STURGIS

his name with pride. 'I was intimately acquainted with him in Canton Bay in 1791,' writes Amasa Delano, 'and I also knew his character afterward.... He was a man of extraordinary good natural abilities and was noted for his enterprising spirit, his good judgment and superior courage. As a seaman and navigator he had but few equals. He was very benevolent and possessed a heart filled with as tender feelings as any man I was ever acquainted with.' Another distinguished mariner and merchant, William Sturgis, writing some fifty years after Kendrick's death, says, 'Were I required to select any particular event in the commercial history of our country to establish our reputation for bold enterprise and persevering energy in commercial pursuits, I should point to this expedition of the Columbia and the Washington.'

Sturgis was, in fact, the next Cape man to distinguish himself in the North-West fur trade. His father, also named William, died in the West Indies after his vessel had been captured and robbed by 'piratical privateers.' Young William was at that time only fifteen, but he had already left the Barnstable farm where he had been born, spent a year in a private school in Hingham, and was at work in Boston in the counting-house of James and Thomas H. Perkins, merchants in the Oregon fur trade. His father's death left the family in slender circumstances; William was earning little or nothing; it was almost inevitable that he should follow in his father's footsteps and go to sea.

Unlike many young sailors, Sturgis was wise enough not to jump into the forecastle of the first ship that would take him. He went to work instead studying navigation under a good instructor until he had mastered it. Then he applied to the Perkinses for a berth. It so happened that one of their ships, the Eliza, was fitting out for a voyage to the North-West Coast and China under Captain James Rowan. Small though she was, the Eliza was signing on a crew of 136 men in case of Indian attacks; it was therefore

no difficult matter for Sturgis to get his name added to
the list, and away he went, one year after his father's
death and three years after Kendrick had been killed,
headed round the Horn and north for Oregon.

During the voyage, in spite of the terribly cramped
quarters, Sturgis did three things unusual for a boy of
sixteen; he kept a log, read Ossian, and practiced
navigation. His log records the position of the ship
from day to day, quite in the manner of an experienced
officer, and he checked his observations from time to
time against Captain Rowan's lunars. Some of the
'remarks' show young Sturgis's character vividly and
present an admirable picture of life on board a North-
West fur-trader. The most significant of them begin
some three months after the Eliza had left Boston and
was off Cape Horn, experiencing the sort of weather
that has tried the souls of many a veteran.

> *Nov.* 19 [1798].... It would be an amusement to an in-
> different spectator to observe the Woefull looks of our
> crew when we have one of our Dismal head Winds, and
> to see how soon they clear up when it changes, and we can
> well say that not only our feelings but likewise our looks
> depends on the Wind, so one may easily judge how often
> they vary.

Then, after two more days of dirty weather:

> *Nov.* 21. The Wind and Weather continue the same but
> I have got so inur'd to bad Weather and a head Wind that
> they have but a small effect on my ease, and were our
> Forecastle not so wet and disagreeable, I should enjoy
> myself as well here as I ever did on shore.

And this he wrote in spite of the fact that he was
very anxious to see the Sandwich Islands and was
terribly worried for fear that, if the Eliza was held up
too long by head winds, Captain Rowan would decide
not to stop there. A pleasant incident was their catching four albatrosses on baited hooks and making 'a
nice sea Pye of them.' In spite of everything, the
Eliza did stop for a week at the Sandwich Islands,

where the young sailor had his chance to see the sights.

It is no wonder that Captain Rowan had his eye on so discerning a lad or that he selected him to act as a liaison officer between the Indians and the whites in carrying on their trade for sea otter when they reached the Coast. And Sturgis, though he had absorbed from veterans on the way out much of the traditional fear and distrust of the natives, now showed a quality which always stood him in good stead — independence of judgment and readiness to change an opinion if circumstances warranted it. He soon found, in his dealings with the Indians, that they were ready to do as they were done by and that much of their legendary savagery was owing to outrageous treatment by free-lance traders like Kendrick. He studied their language with the same diligence that he had shown in studying navigation and mastered it sufficiently not only to carry on trade but later to discuss with them in friendly terms such abstract topics as the universal folly of mankind.

But in spite of his friendliness toward the Indians, Sturgis was too good a Yankee not to use every means in his power to drag from them the secrets of their own trade in skins, for the natives got much of the fur that they sold to Rowan by barter with other tribes, who, they hinted, had a limitless supply that could be bought at a low price. Nor was he so foolish as to suppose that every Indian was like every other. His opinion of certain chiefs, and of the more northerly tribes in general, is clearly shown in his journal:

[*Apr.*] 10*th* [1799].... In the afternoon part of them [an Indian tribe] arrived with their Chief whose name they pronounced Eternity. He is a fat impudent fellow, and withal very pompous in his opinion of himself, telling us he was as great as ye Sun and the greatest chief on the Coast — We told him we knew that before we came to Chatiqua; that Cow and Cunneau dared not come to attack him alone; therefore both meant to come together, as they told us that by uniting their tribes they should be a match for him — this lie we told him to retaliate for his boasting: he believed the whole we told him and he looked as if he wished the devil had them for having so great an opinion of him, which would give him more fighting than he had a stomach for.

[*Apr.*] 13*th* [1799].... There are two ledges of Rocks that lay off the South Point of this passage, which make it dangerous for strangers: the Natives being such villains they would be glad to even Pilot a vessell on them for the sake of Plundering her and Cutting the throats of the Crew, to be revenged for the People they have had killed in the fruitless attempts they have made on several vessells.

[*Apr.*] 24*th* [1799] [Concerning Northern tribes]... they are daring and insolent in the extreme: to awe them it is allways best to keep men in the tops: this we found was the best thing that could be done to let them know that their lives cou'd be allways at our disposal, and that the least insolence cou'd be immediately punished with death — one man in a ships top they look upon with more terror on acct of his height and the knowledge they have of the distruction that can be scattered from a Blunderbuss, than they do of twenty on her decks: one is sufficient to keep them in Order, for if he is in his station when they come along side they will keep their eyes the whole time they stay, as attentively fixed upon him, as a pious congregation will upon a fervent minister.... They are deceiving Crafty and daring: more so, I believe than any tribe on the Coast... and thus (returning thanks to Heaven that I do it so safely) I leave them.

It went sorely against Sturgis's Yankee thrift to see the prices which Captain Rowan sometimes paid for skins. Under the date of April 6, 1799, he writes:

.. We bought fifty sea Otter Skins though at the enormous price of three fathoms of Blue Cloth, a large Iron Pott and several other things as a Present.... The devil take this far fetched North West policy. for the soul of me I cannot see upon what principles it acts: if I had an inclination to sport away three fathoms of Blue Cloth and a Present for a Sea Otter's Skin, I think..., I wou'd have been content to have done it in some of the Sea Ports where it is common to do all foolish things of the same

The North-West Fur Trade

Nature, and where perhaps a hundred more Skins might have been got by it.

In the course of this voyage Sturgis was also learning things about owners and captains. His opinion of Captain Rowan's methods as a trader have already been shown; and now he found his Captain wanting in the essential virtue of loyalty:

> In fact [he writes], it seems that the Owners of a Ship are on the North West Coast of America held in allmost a contemptible light; and their right to give orders or even advice, as a flagrant Violation of the *delightfull privilidges* of Captainship — It was with great sorrow I found that Cap Rowan fell in with these self sufficient opinions and likewise expressed to me in strong terms his disapprobation of his owners conduct towards himself.... All of us contented ourselves, with taking no notice of such things except by silent contempt — well knowing how much it is in your power to refute as well as sincerely to despise assertions which were gendered by *self-interested rivals*, and had their nursery in the brain of folly.

So far Sturgis had prospered on his own merits; at this point his merits were re-enforced by luck. Even at that early date, there were more Yankee vessels on the North-West Coast than one would suppose. The Eliza had just missed falling in with Captain John Crocker, of Falmouth, who was out there in the ship Hancock; and now, as he anchored off the little Indian village of Caiganee, Captain Rowan found to his surprise that two other Boston vessels — the Despatch, Captain Breck, and the Ulysses, Captain Lamb — were there before him.

The crew of the Ulysses, aided and abetted by her two mates, had mutinied, weary, they said, of Captain Lamb's continued brutality, and had put him in irons. Captain Breck, of the Ulysses, had not enough assurance or enough men to jump in and break the mutiny; but with the arrival of the Eliza and her 136 stalwarts, the affair took on another complexion. Rowan and Breck joined forces, brought Lamb on board the Eliza

51

and held an informal inquiry, the upshot of which was that Lamb agreed to treat his men better and forget their mutiny if they would go back to work. Most of them consented willingly enough; but the mates flatly refused to serve under him, preferring berths in the forecastle of either the Eliza or the Despatch to a cabin under the quarter-deck of the Ulysses. This left Lamb with no officer higher than a boatswain. With the consent of the other captains, he offered a mate's berth to any man who could navigate. Young Sturgis saw his chance. He signed on as chief officer of the Ulysses at the age of eighteen. Though not a bed of roses, his new position was less disagreeable than he had feared, and lasted only half as long, for the Ulysses fell in with the Eliza at Canton, where his good friend Captain Rowan offered him the position of third mate for the voyage home. Lamb, with plenty of replacements to choose from in Canton, made no objection; so young Sturgis finished the voyage as an officer of the same ship on which he had started as foremast hand, arriving in Boston in the spring of 1800, after an absence of almost exactly two years.

After a short respite, Sturgis was off again for the North-West Coast, this time as first mate of the Caroline under Captain Charles Derby, of Salem. Derby was in such feeble health that Sturgis was obliged to assume virtual command soon after they reached Oregon. This, together with his duties as interpreter and manager of trade with the Indians, kept the young man jumping until the Caroline put in at the Hawaiian Islands on the way to China with her cargo of sea otter. Here Captain Derby gave up his struggle for health, officially turned over the command to his nineteen-year-old mate, and went ashore to die. Sturgis completed the voyage in so satisfactory a fashion that when he arrived at Boston, in the spring of 1803, after a three years' cruise, his owners kept him in command of the Caroline and sent him on another three-year voyage round the world, *via* the old route.

This voyage, which he finished successfully in June, 1806, placed him at the age of twenty-four in the position of being the leading Yankee captain in the North-West and China trade, not only because he brought his ships home safely, but because he continued to show extraordinary skill in handling thé Indians.

Such a combination of talents won quick recognition among Boston merchants. Theodore Lyman, who had two ships already on the North-West Coast and was fitting out another, the Atahualpa, for the same business, invited Sturgis to take her out ·to Oregon and on his arrival to assume full charge of the trade of all three vessels. After one season on the Coast, he was to load the Atahualpa and one of the other ships with all the skins that the three vessels had collected, and take them to Canton. Outward cargoes had changed greatly since the early days when bits of iron had been enough to dazzle the Indians. They had learned the value of other things as well, and this time Sturgis loaded the Atahualpa with blankets, cloth, greatcoats, firearms, cutlery, hardware, and trinkets — 'in short,' as he says, with 'everything that you can imagine and some things that you cannot imagine.' Keys, too, exerted a peculiar fascination over the Indians. On one occasion, Sturgis took all he could collect from the Boston locksmiths, and got so many that the police grew uneasy until his purpose was explained. At another time he took out ten thousand brass and copper keys imported from Holland especially for the North-West trade.

Captain Sturgis returned from this great voyage two years later with a handsome profit for himself and his owners — so handsome, indeed, that he stayed at home for the next ten months to get acquainted with his family, whom he had seen only at long intervals during the past ten years.

This was the Captain's last voyage to the North-West Coast and his last but one to China, for the next time that he sailed the Atahualpa out of Boston — April, 1809 — he headed straight for Canton with three hundred thousand Spanish dollars in his cabin to invest in a return cargo. Young Daniel C. Bacon, of Barnstable, was with him as mate. The financial side of this voyage was simple enough compared to the earlier negotiations that Sturgis had put through, but complications of another and more violent sort lay in wait for him. He anchored in a calm in Macao Roads, about seventy miles south of Canton, and Bacon went ashore. While he was away, a fleet of sixteen pirate craft, under the notorious chieftain Appotesi, swarmed down on the Atahualpa.

The ship was not heavily armed, but Sturgis, without consulting his owners, had taken along a few cannon, and he set to work with these, trying to keep the pirates from getting close enough to throw firebrands on board — one of Appotesi's favorite methods of attack. The confusion on deck may be imagined; some of the crew were serving the guns; some, flattened behind the bulwarks, were taking pot shots at the enemy with muskets; others were kept rushing from one part of the ship to another, putting out the fires that had started. Sturgis, meanwhile, stood on deck beside a powder-barrel, a cigar clamped in his teeth, ready to blow the Atahualpa to eternity if the pirates should get possession of her.

For perhaps half an hour the fight hung in the balance: sixteen to one was long odds. But Bacon, alarmed by the firing, came rowing off with his boat's crew, fought his way through the pirates to the side of the Atahualpa and climbed on board. These re-enforcements were enough to turn the tide; after another half-hour, the ship was clear, and Sturgis, taking advantage of a light breeze that sprang up, worked her up under the guns of the Portuguese fort at Macao, whence she made her way to Canton, though not without more trouble, for Appotesi returned to the attack after the Atahualpa had left the protection of the

THE ATAHUALPA IN MACAO ROADS

shore batteries. This second fight, however, was not
so serious as the first; the piratical ardor was apparently suffering from its earlier encounter with Yankee
sailors, and a few shots from the Atahualpa extin-
guished it altogether. It is an ill wind that blows nobody good. The Captain's cousin, James Sturgis, who
had come out as passenger on the Atahualpa and
throughout the last half of the voyage had been 'as
yellow as a sunflower' from jaundice, was completely
cured by the 'stirring remedy' of this memorable
fight. Appotesi was subsequently betrayed to the
mandarins, who executed him by a method of slow
torture known as 'the thousand cuts.'

The return voyage from Canton provided excitement of a different sort in the form of a race to Boston
between the Atahualpa and two other Boston ships,
the William, under Captain Emery, and the Mandarin, under Captain Nash. Sturgis got away two days
before Emery and one day before Nash; but during the
next four months or so they caught up with him, and
on April 13, 1810, all three vessels came booming into
Boston almost in sight of each other — a big day for
the merchants of the old town. Not so big was
Sturgis's reception by Theodore Lyman. Instead of
complimenting him on his quick passage, that gentleman charged him freight for the cannon he had used
against the pirates because they had been taken without owner's orders!

The Captain, now twenty-eight years old, had by
this time made money enough to start in business for
himself. He therefore formed a partnership with John
Bryant, a connection that lasted for over half a century, during a large part of which the firm Bryant and
Sturgis managed more than half of the American trade
between the West Coast and China. But the Captain's
experiences in the Oregon fur trade did more than
start him in business; on two occasions, at least, they
proved of real value to his country. When, some ten
years after he had given up the sea, the Russians laid

claim to most of the North-West Coast on the grounds of 'first discovery, first occupation and peaceable possession,' the Captain smashed their arguments by an article in the *North American Review*, in which he explained the whole history of that much-disputed territory and furnished the authorities in Washington with first-hand information without which they would have been hard put to it to answer their Russian rivals. Again, in 1844, when Oregon became a bone of contention between our Government and the British, Sturgis published a pamphlet which was widely circulated in both countries and which, 'by its judicial tone and manifest honesty,' went far toward pricking that absurdly rhetorical bubble of jingoism, 'Fifty-four-forty or fight.' 'Each has some rights,' said the Captain, 'which should be adjusted by compromise and mutual concession.' There spoke a man who was a hundred years ahead of his time.

The Indians, whose friendship Captain Sturgis had won and among whom he had spent so much of his time between the ages of sixteen and twenty-six, were seldom out of his mind during the long years at his desk in Boston. He talked about them, quoted them, and gave a series of lectures about them, in the course of which he referred to them as 'victims of injustice, cruelty and oppression, and of a policy that seems to recognize *power* as the sole standard of *right*.' Another passage from one of his lectures shows an eloquence of which Daniel Webster need not have been ashamed:

> When I call up the past [he wrote] and look back upon the trials and dangers of my early pursuits, it is with feelings that I should vainly attempt to describe. I have cause for gratitude to a higher Power, not only for escape from danger, but for being spared all participation in the deadly conflicts and murderous scenes which at times surrounded me. I may well be grateful that no blood of the red-man ever stained my hands; that no shades of murdered or slaughtered Indians disturb my repose; and the

reflection that neither myself nor any one under my command ever did or suffered violence or outrage during years of intercourse with those reputed the most savage tribes, gives me a satisfaction in exchange for which wealth and honors would be as dust in the balance.

Even on the floor of the State House, where Sturgis's quarter-deck voice might have been heard almost any year between 1814 and 1845, the Indians of the North-West Coast were with him still — on one occasion with amusing consequences. An opponent, in the course of a long harangue, had seen fit to drag in a number of quotations from the classics. Sturgis listened, smiled grimly, and when his turn came to reply, sprinkled his rejoinder with an equal number of sentences in the Indian dialect, which, he declared, were quite as germane to the matter as his worthy opponent's Latin and Greek, and quite as intelligible to the legislators! The Captain's interest in education and his feeling for the town where he was born are shown by his presenting Barnstable with a library which still continues as a source of culture for the community.

The last years of Captain Sturgis were in some respects his happiest. He had achieved wealth, esteem, and influence, and though the death of his only boy for some years virtually blotted the sun out of the sky for the old merchant, grandchildren were growing up and helping to fill the void. Let us leave him, surrounded by them in the twilight of a summer evening on the porch of his country house beside Horn Pond, where, looking out over the calm surface of the water to the trees beyond, he told them stories of his own youth among the Indians of the North-West Coast.

Daniel C. Bacon, who was Sturgis's mate when the Atahualpa was attacked in Macao Roads, was the next Cape captain to distinguish himself by China voyages and the North-West fur trade. Like most boys of his generation, Bacon left Barnstable to go to sea at the age of fourteen or fifteen, but unlike the rest, he made the journey to Boston astride an old white horse. His mettle showed itself while he and his mount were clumping through the outskirts of the city, where a group of youthful unregenerates hailed him as 'bushwhacker.' Young Bacon sailed into them with satisfactory results and resumed his ride to town. Of his first voyage before the mast, nothing is known, but by 1806, four years after he had left Barnstable, he was first mate of the ship Xenophon, trading between Philadelphia and Liverpool. Captain Moses Ingles, who commanded her, was anxious to retire, and heartily recommended Bacon as his successor, but the owners urged Ingles to continue in command for another year; so Bacon did not become her captain until 1807. The young man had clearly lost his 'bushwhacker' appearance, for his father, in a letter to him dated June 5, 1807, says that Captain Ingles 'gives you as good a character in public company as a father's wishes could aspire to.'

The Embargo of 1807 caught Bacon and his ship in Philadelphia with no prospect of getting clear. After weeks of idleness, which were as irksome to young Bacon as they were alarming to his father, whose parental letters at this time remind his boy that 'idleness is the mother of vice,' Bacon resigned his command and, in the spring of 1808, signed as first mate of the Atahualpa for a China voyage under Captain Sturgis. The part which he played in the fight with the Chinese pirates on this voyage has already been described. He was back in Boston in April, 1810, and after a month's rest was off for China again, in command of the same ship, for Sturgis had retired. On this voyage, as on the one preceding it, the Atahualpa went direct to Canton, without visiting the North-West Coast, a region which so far Bacon had never seen. His log shows that though his experience with Sturgis had taught him to take precautions in the China Sea, he had lost none of the native vigor which had led him into the brush with South Boston hoodlums on the one hand, and a life-and-death battle with Chinese pirates on the other.

June 1.... Employed making Boarding Knetting to keep out the Malays and Ladroons, but there is not much prospect of our wanting them for use in this five months unless we get more wind than we have had these three days past.

June 3.... I hope that the good people at home will remember us today at Church and pray that we may be blessed with a fair wind before the next twenty-four hours are at an end.

June 14.... Calms and hot enough to warm any old woman's blood. If we have no more wind than we have had since we Came out it will take us four years to make our passage.

Sept. 9.... At daylight we were abreast of the Town of Anjer.... Received from the Governor of Batavia a paper with questions concerning the political state of France and Holland which I answered as correctly as possible and sent them back again... and damn glad to get clear of him so easy.

The Atahualpa made good time, reaching Canton one hundred and twenty-six days out from Boston. After another four months spent in bargaining for a return cargo, Bacon set sail for Boston once more, dropping his pilot January 27, 1811. In company with him was the ship Trumbull, of Providence, Captain Page. Off Java Head, he came up with the Hope, of New York, Captain Chase, who had left Canton three days ahead of him. Bacon confidently expected to beat both these vessels home, but whether he did so or not does not appear. The long sunny days in balmy latitudes gave ample leisure for expansiveness in the entries of his log:

Feb. 22, 1811.... All sail out that is of the least use to drive us along toward the Yankee lasses.

Feb. 24, 1811.... It being Sunday it is possible some of the Barnstable lasses may by accident happen to think of us this evening after they have run through with the past weeks adventures.

Feb. 27, 1811.... All sail out, driving as hard as possible to get in before the other ships that sailed in company which I am pretty certain we shall do provided we have as favorable winds as they do.

March 4.... We have... a plenty of rain which washes the salt off and keeps us fine and fresh.

March 5, 1811.... It is so fine and smooth that I should like to have about forty or fifty pretty lasses on board for two or three hours upon a tea-drinking party, if there is any pleasure in them, but for my own part I had rather be excused any time than go to one of them.

March 12, 1811.... Saw a land bird which I think must be out of his reckoning or I must, but I think I shall find mine more correct.

March 18, 1811.... Commences with light breezes and a very heavy sea ahead so the ship [is] cutting some of her old pranks, diving flying boom under every other surge.

April 11, 1811.... Employ'd blacking ship to keep her [from] burning up for 'tis hot enough to burn any thing that can be caught on fire.

April 18, 1811.... Lively breezes and pleasant weather. Steering sails and top Gallant sails out to the breeze which makes the old Atahualpa dive through it merrily. If this breeze would continue, I would make the shortest voyage that was ever made from China.

April 29, 1811.... Light breezes from the Northwest and a cursed heavy sea which is enough to try the patience of any Country parson.

May 4*th*, 1811.... Hope, that soother of everything, still continues to cheer up our drooping spirits.

But the next day had a different tale to tell:

May 5, 1811.... The wind in the course of 1 hour hauled three times round the compass, it blowing a hurrycane all the time.... The wind flying round the compass in the manner it did and blowing so extremely heavy that the sea made a fair breach over us in every direction; we opened all our ports to let water off the deck; got out guns aft and every thing of any weight that we had on deck to keep her from going down head foremost, as I did not think it prudent to luff ship to the wind. At 8 it died away calm when the sea struck with more violence than it did before, but the old Atahualpa stood it bravely.

The North-West Fur Trade

About a week later they were in Boston. Here
Bacon received a happy and enthusiastic letter from
his father, congratulating him on his return and adding
this significant question in regard to his next voyage,
'How many Barnstable boys shall you Carry after
taking Mr. Asa Jenkins' and Jos. Crocker's Sons?
There is half the boys in town mean to go the next
voyage.' And well they might, and well might young
Jenkins and Crocker congratulate themselves on being
among the elect, for crews in those days were not made
up of the scum of the water-fronts of half a dozen
nations, but consisted of smart Yankee lads, such as
Sturgis and Bacon themselves had been, whose ambition made their time in the forecastle short indeed.
It was a dull lad who was not bunking aft while still
in his teens, and he might well have passed his few
years before the mast almost entirely in the company
of schoolmates from his own town. Officers, too,
blessed with nimble Yankees to make and shorten sail,
had small need of the bucko tactics that some of their
successors had to employ to get their men aloft.

Furthermore, voyages like those of Sturgis and
Bacon lent great prestige to all the ship's company.
Dana states the matter with authority: 'The style and
gentility of a ship and her crew,' he writes, 'depend
upon the length and character of her voyage. An
India or China voyage always is *the thing*, and a voyage
to the North-West Coast (the Columbia River or
Russian America) for furs is romantic and mysterious,
and if it takes the ship around the world by way of the
Islands and China, it outranks them all.' On just such
a voyage was Captain Bacon about to embark. He
took a six-months vacation after his second visit to
China, and in November, 1811, was ready to put to sea
again, sailing this time for Ropes and Pickman, in the
ship Packet, on a voyage that was expected to take
three years. As a matter of fact, it took two months
less than four years. The course was all that Dana's
definition demands for a voyage that 'outranks them

all,' and more besides, for the Packet, before heading round the Horn for the North-West Coast, was to cross to Liverpool for a cargo of coarse woolen goods and cheap hardware to trade with the Indians. From the Coast, Bacon's orders were to follow the old route of all North-West men, that is, Canton and home *via* the Indian Ocean and Cape of Good Hope. But his program was further complicated because he was directed to meet Captain Nye, of the brig New Hazard, somewhere between the Queen Charlotte Islands and the mainland, turn over to him whatever skins he might have collected up to date, and start in afresh to fill his own hold.

All went well. Though it was Bacon's first experience with Indians, he had no difficulty with them at any time; following the example of Sturgis, he learned their language, dosed them with medicine from the Packet's chest, acted as umpire in their disputes, and drove as sharp bargains with them as he dared. He became a firm friend of the Russian Governor — a fortunate thing, too, for just before he hoisted sail for Canton with a full cargo of furs, a Salem ship arrived with news that the War of 1812 was on.

Bacon played safe. He left half his cargo with the Governor for safe-keeping, did full justice to a farewell banquet given him by His Excellency, and headed for Canton. He slipped into port unmolested, sold his furs and bought tea, silk, sets of china, and nankeens with the proceeds, and was about to start out on the last leg of his great voyage, when the British clapped a blockade on the port. For a few days he hesitated; but he was young, hardly past the middle twenties, it was over three years since he had seen home, there was no knowing how long the blockade might last, and the delay was doing his cargo no good. On a black night with a fresh breeze, he slipped out past the Britishers with every stitch of canvas drawing, turned a deaf ear to the importunities of his pilot, who begged him to heave to long enough to let him get aboard his boat and put back, and stood out to sea. When far outside the blockading vessels, he lowered a boat over the taffrail, and dropped the terrified pilot into it, without luffing so much as a point. Then he let go the painter, leaving the Chinaman to get back as best he might.

Throughout the voyage Bacon kept a man at the masthead on the watch for His Majesty's frigates, but none were sighted. The Captain arrived in Boston safely with his cargo, early in September, 1815, only to find that the war was over. He had lost thirty-five pounds from worry between Canton and home, but his troubles were over, he had money in his pockets, and on board the Packet were six tons of China goods of his own, freight-free from Canton, bought with his allowance of seven per cent of the money he got for the otter skins, and as much of his thirty dollars a month wages as he had been able to save. It was a profitable voyage to his owners and to himself, and one of the most spectacular, both in length and variety, ever undertaken by a youngster.

Captain Bacon spent the winter at home in Barnstable, regaining his lost weight, and by the middle of May was ready for China again. He accepted Theodore Lyman's offer to take the brig Vancouver out to Canton from New York, supposing her to be sound and seaworthy. Lyman, to do him justice, supposed so too; but both men were grossly deceived by the New York shipwright who was to have put the old brig in shape. Her condition is well described in a letter from Bacon to Lyman written from Anjer Roads, September 10, 1817:

> I have at last arrived at a place where I am enabled to give you some information of the Brig Vancouver.... I took her for a vessel that had been properly Repaired and was fit to perform any voyage, and there is not a sound timber in her from the mainmast aft, except five small pieces of new timber which have lately been put in; all the Rest from the lower deck beams are pretty much en-

tirely gone.... Have got her along thus far by heaving over as much of the ballast as I dared to and carrying but little sail and frequently steering three or four points out of my course to keep her before the Sea.... What we shall be able to do with her I don't know, but if possible I mean she shall come back, but as for getting any freight it is out of the question altogether, for I would not put goods into her at five dollars pr. Ton if they could be carried in a good vessel at a hundred. Were I clear of her I would not engage to go in her at five dollars an hour, but with the Blessing of Heaven, I am in hopes to get along somehow or other.

The reference to freight is significant. The ideal return lading from Canton was a cargo composed partly of goods bought as a speculation by the owner of the vessel, and partly of freight consigned to others, of which there was usually an abundance awaiting transportation. Since no one but a fool would send freight in a rotten vessel, Bacon had no chance for any freight money on this voyage, a particularly heavy blow just at this time, for the Boston market was glutted with China goods, and merchants counted heavily on freight money for their profits. Lyman, as one of the principal China traders in Boston, felt this situation acutely. 'I am sorry to tell you,' he writes in reply to Bacon, 'that the market is so completely overstocked with silk goods that nothing I have can be sold for the cost in Canton and the import here.' The best advice he could offer Bacon was to sell the old Vancouver, if he could not get anyone to send freight in her; or if he should decide not to sell, to live economically in the meantime. He warns Bacon not to let 'the forward and teazing ship Compadore compel you to suffer him to put unnecessary articles of ship's provisions on board ship. *Live well, but live frugally.*' And again, 'I prefer to have a penny saved to two that is earned. No man can be poor if he is willing and knows how to save.'

Bacon, however, was constitutionally averse to

leaving a job half-finished. He was determined to get home with his command if there was an off-chance of keeping her afloat, even though he could not get any freight to carry. After having some repairs made on the Vancouver at Canton, he wrote his decision to Lyman: 'I believe she will come home safe, if we are not so unfortunate as to get an unlucky sea on board. I have taken a number of planks out of her sides which were entirely gone.' He adds gloomily that there were fourteen Yankee vessels in Canton, all trying to get freight, 'therefore, for the Brig, no person will put a dollar in her.' He loaded with tea and silk, trusting that by the time he reached Boston, some of the surplus would have been sold, and coaxed his frail command safely home across two oceans.

Between this voyage and the next, Bacon took a year off, which he spent in Barnstable, acquiring, among other assets, a wife. Then in the spring of 1819, he set sail for China for the last time, in command of another of Lyman's vessels, the ship Alert. Never was the folly of an owner's tying the hands of a captain more clearly exemplified than on this voyage. No owner — be he ever so shrewd — can foretell the future; if he is wise, he will leave a loophole in his orders, through which the captain may escape into the freedom of his own judgment. Lyman should by this time have realized that Bacon was not only a skillful shipmaster but a shrewd and trustworthy business man as well; but apparently he did not realize it; or if he did, he could not bring himself to the point of delegating any real authority. At all events, Bacon set sail, with strict orders not to buy any goods in Canton until October 20, unless they could be had below a given figure.

When he arrived, he found the price of silk well above this figure and steadily rising, with October 20 still three weeks away. 'Had I been at liberty to have contracted for Goods thirty days ago,' he writes, 'it would have been $20,000 to the voyage.... The prospect is as bad as it can be, for I cannot get a ton of freight... and goods advancing in price daily.' He finally bought a cargo of the old stand-bys, tea and silk, and with the final outburst to Lyman, 'God Knows I want to get clear of this place as much as ever any person did,' he cracked on all sail and roared back to Boston, where he arrived late in the spring of 1820. He lost no time in getting to Barnstable to make the acquaintance of an infant son whom he had never seen and who was undoubtedly partly responsible for the Captain's sudden distaste for Canton.

Barnstable, though a good place for a shipmaster between voyages, was not so convenient for a merchant and shipowner; since Bacon had decided to retire from the sea and become an owner instead of a captain, he moved with his family to Boston and embarked on his long career as a merchant. One more voyage, to be sure, he made. Years later, when he supposed that he had charted his last course, a daughter-in-law of Theodore Lyman was ordered to Cuba by her physician; but she refused to go unless Bacon would command the ship. There was nothing for it; the captain blew the dust from his sextant, polished up his glass, and took the old lady to Cuba in one of her father-in-law's vessels.

Life in Boston, however, was anything but dull. Bacon amused himself in what time he could spare from his desk, by building a summer residence in Barnstable, the celebrated Bacon Farm, which is still owned by his descendants; by lodging in his woodshed in Boston the Siamese twins, that one of his captains brought back from an Eastern voyage; and by attending the celebrated banquet at which the wooden head of President Jackson, stolen from the bow of the old Constitution, was brought in and placed on the table as a centerpiece.

The exploit of thus mutilating the figurehead of a naval vessel rocked the town to its foundations — not with horror but with glee. The Constitution had always been Boston's pride; and when in 1834 she was brought to the Charlestown Navy Yard for repairs, the citizens felt that the old war horse was coming back home for a rest. But they reckoned without Captain Jesse Elliott, Commandant of the Navy Yard. This worthy, doubtless through sheer stupidity, for it is inconceivable that he could otherwise have perpetrated such a blunder, ordered a full-length reproduction of President Jackson to be carved for her figurehead. Some believed that this was a bid for Western favor for the Navy, for Jackson was strong in the West. Others said that Elliott's idea was to remind the world that the President had opposed a scheme for breaking up the old frigate. But Boston Whigs, many of whom were seagoing direct-actionists, were quick to resent the placing of an effigy of a landlubber, whose views on national policy were widely at variance with their own, on the prow of their pet man-of-war. They may not have quite believed that it was 'defiling a national ship with a tyrant's image,' but some of them came pretty close to it. In the course of a heated diatribe against Jackson and the figurehead one morning in the counting-rooms of Messrs. Henry and William Lincoln, Captain Samuel W. Dewey, who was just back from a foreign voyage, declared that he would like to go over there and cut the head off the old image. 'I'll give you a hundred dollars if you do it,' said William Lincoln. 'Done,' replied Dewey; and the banquet was the result.

This episode would hardly have been included in the present narrative on the mere ground that a Cape-Codder was present at the dinner; but Dewey was a grandson of old Captain Benjamin Hallett, of Osterville, the pioneer coaster; so that Cape blood was represented at both ends of the affair. Not that it adds greatly to the reputation of either Dewey or Bacon; New York rhetoric, indeed, was vehement to the contrary, describing the sawing-off of the head as 'criminal and outrageous' and the dinner as 'a Pandemonian banquet,' at which was celebrated 'with licentious orgies, a violation of the law.' So be it. Perhaps Bostonian fibers were tougher and vibrated less readily with horror than those of their brethren in New York. Viewed from the distance of a hundred years, at any rate — a lapse of time that should help us to gain perspective — the incident becomes vigorous and picturesque, and it is a pleasure to find Cape men participating in it.

Merchants, if they were to prosper in the face of such competition as was rife during these busy years, had to keep abreast of the times. Bacon not only kept abreast of them but not infrequently was a jump ahead. In the late forties and early fifties, while the more conservative owners and underwriters were wagging their heads and pulling their beards in doubt at the sharp lines and towering spars of the first clipper ships, Bacon was contracting for one of them with Samuel Hall, of East Boston, who, with Donald McKay, was perhaps the greatest shipbuilder of that great decade. She was launched in 1851 and christened Game Cock, a name whose jauntiness was justified by her subsequent performances. Bacon became so enthusiastic not only about her, but about the superiority of American clippers in general, that the next year, while he was President of the American Navigation Club, he sent a challenge to British shipbuilders that remains one of the great sporting propositions of maritime history. Briefly stated, the terms were these: An American ship and a British ship, both carrying cargo, were to race from a port in England to a port in China and back for a purse of $50,000. There were almost no restrictions, beyond the stipulation that the vessels should be designed, built, and commanded entirely by citizens of the United States and Great Britain respectively. New vessels might be built for the race if desired; the Englishmen might name the size of the ships, provided only that they measure between 800 and 1200 tons, and might specify also the amount of cargo to be carried each way. Associated with Bacon in this challenge were such men as Thomas H. Perkins, John M. Forbes, and Warren Delano, Jr., but Bacon and Forbes were the active ones. Unfortunately, and greatly to the regret of many Englishmen as well as Americans, the challenge was never accepted.

In spite of his wide foreign interests and his manifold activities in Boston, Bacon never lost his affection for the Cape. He named one of his thirty vessels Barnstable, and whenever possible, got Cape men to command them. When Yarmouth began to show her heels to Barnstable in the local packet trade to Boston, Bacon supplied the money for the sloop Mail, a craft that well upheld the honor of the shire town. Such incidents were, for Bacon, the spice of his busy life as a merchant, a life which he led with varying fortunes until 1856, when he died of enlargement of the heart. His death was mourned by Barnstable fishermen and Boston shipowners alike; both had lost a friend, and New England had lost one of the pillars of its merchant marine.

4

Neutral Traders

NATURALLY enough, not every Yankee captain wanted
a voyage that might last three years and would take
him round the world, nor was every Boston merchant
gambler enough to depend for his return cargo first
on Indians and second on Chinamen. Some preferred
the more intricate chicanery of warring Europe to the
primitive frailties of Nootka savages. But if they were
looking for plain sailing in carrying on trade with
European countries, or expected the rights of neutrals
to be regarded, they were disappointed, for never,
perhaps, has there been so unsettled a period in European history as that between the years 1790 and 1815.

The French Revolution had rocked other thrones
than the Bourbons', and left Robespierre trying in
vain to hold the lid on the Reign of Terror. Napoleon,
aided by his sagacious brother Julian, rose like the
phœnix from the ashes of Revolution to find himself
at war with most of Europe; national perspectives
had everywhere gone glimmering; trade between
neutrals was legal in name alone; neither France nor
England hesitated for a moment to seize any Yankee
vessel, even when her papers showed her to be bound
for a neutral port. Spain, divided between those who
sympathized with the Bourbons and those who tol-
erated Napoleon's régime, sometimes bought American
cargoes and sometimes seized the ship instead. The

Neutral Traders

British Orders in Council, which declared a blockade on most of the western coast of Europe, was answered first by Napoleon's Berlin Decree, which declared a blockade on all ports in the British Isles, and second by his Milan Decree, which announced that all neutral vessels trying to slip through this blockade were fair game for French frigates. As though these measures did not make things hard enough for American captains, Jefferson, hoping to save his ships by keeping them at home, and believing that prompt retaliation would force both the French and the British to open their ports again, administered the *coup de grâce* to American trade with Europe by his Embargo of 1807, which forbade any Yankee vessel to clear for a foreign port.

Luckily not until 1807 were all these proclamations and decrees in force at the same time, or American merchants would have been paralyzed indeed; nor was any of them fully obeyed. Even after the Embargo, American captains continued, from time to time, to jockey cargoes out of the country *via* the Maritime Provinces and to slip into foreign ports with them under the very guns of the British or French blockade; and before the Embargo, our ships squared away for Europe as blithely as if it had been a friendly and honest world. This was natural, too, for their captains at first knew little or nothing of actual conditions in Europe; they supposed, naïvely enough, that wars were no concern of countries not engaged in them, and not until the captains returned with other tales to tell did Boston merchants realize the extremes to which lost perspectives can drive even civilized nations. But because these same captains so often managed, in spite of everything, to make their voyages pay, the owners continued to send them, time after time, into the hornets' nests of European ports.

The Cape captains who found themselves involved in such complications were many; but to tell of their voyages in detail is impossible. Too often have tidy

71

housewives among their descendants burned their log books and their letters, and too often, in their own day, were their adventures taken for granted as unworthy of recording. There was, for example, Captain Daniel Howes, of Dennis, who took the schooner Harriet to Spain in 1792, and in the course of another voyage in 1796 wrote from Havre that he was ordered to St. Michaels and from there to Russia. He adds cheerfully, 'I have met with some acquaintance here and we enjoy ourselves upon the best that the country affords.' It would be interesting to know something about the experiences of Captain Freeman Foster, of Brewster, who during these ticklish times took the brig Rice Plant and the ship Ten Brothers from New Orleans to Archangel, and from the West Indies to Elsinore, or of Captain John Kenrick, of South Orleans, who in 1811 carried flour to Lisbon in the brig Constellation and, so the story goes, saw her burned there under Napoleon's Berlin and Milan Decrees. What are the stories that Captain Daniel Atkins, of Wellfleet, told to his daughters between voyages to Marseilles in the Araminta, the Pomona or the Leonore? He must have had something to say about these vessels, for he thought so highly of them that, if tradition is true, he named his daughters after them. Where are the records of Captain Stephen Sears, of Yarmouth, who was seized by the Spaniards while trying to sell a cargo of salt fish in the Mediterranean, or of Captain Samuel Rider, of Truro, who wrote from Virginia that his 410-ton ship, Liverpool Packet, was too large, and that he could have done better with a smaller vessel? Two other Truro captains, Nehemiah Harding and Jazzaniah Gross, were trading to European ports during these troubled years, but one may seek in vain for any account of their voyages. The same is true of two more Truro shipmasters, the brothers Ephraim and Henry Snow. Captain Ephraim, trading to Liverpool and Spain, crossed the Atlantic fifty times in the years following 1807 in the schooner

Neutral Traders

Ruth and the ships Mt. Vernon and Warren. His brother began foreign voyaging in the schooner Speedwell in 1811 and kept it up until about 1824. And what of their fellow townsman, Captain Obadiah Rich, who entertained the Reverend Timothy Dwight on his visit to Truro and who could find his way between Boston and Archangel with no more elaborate reckoning than a few chalk marks on the cabin door?

These men, and a host of others from Cape towns, were sailing up and down the Atlantic, and back and forth across it at one time or another between 1785 and 1815 — almost exactly the years that saw others from the Cape rounding the Horn for the Queen Charlotte Islands and Canton. But that is about all that can be learned of them. It remains for three or four among the number, who have left some information about themselves, to show us what manner of life they led in the disordered seaports of the Continent; and first and fullest among these narratives is that of Captain Elijah Cobb, of Brewster.

Cobb's father, Captain Scottow Cobb, died at sea, leaving a widow and six children virtually penniless. At the tender age of six, young Elijah went to work away from home. In 1783, when he was thirteen, he walked over to Orleans and embarked for Boston on the schooner Creture, hoping to find a berth in the forecastle of some ship. Here is his account of his first day in the capital:

> ... the first time I went down the long wharf, and stood gazing at a new vessell, wondering, and admiring her monstrous size, her great cables and anchors etc. — a gentleman stept from her deck and thus accosted me. My lad, do you want a voyage — where are you bound Sir — to Siranam — I am told Sir, that all flesh die, that go there — well my boy, to prove, that you have not been told the truth, I have been there 13 voyages, and you see I'm alive yet — well Sir, I should like to go, what wages will you allow me — do you know how to cook — not much Sir, but I can soon learn — well my boy, if you

73

think so I presume you will. I like your candour and will take you, and give you the customary wages of a boy; half of Seamens wages $3.40 pr month, but you must go immediately on board, and git dinner for the men at work — and thus I commenced my duty as cook and cabin Boy.

By the time they reached Surinam, young Cobb had collected enough in tips from the officers to take a flyer on his own account in the shape of a barrel of molasses and some boxes of fruit. These he sold on his return to Boston for enough to buy himself an outfit of sailor's clothes and to give his mother twenty dollars out of his twenty-one dollars of wages. Encouraged by so auspicious a beginning, Cobb went coasting to the West Indies and southern ports for some years, rising to the position of mate and master. When he was twenty-four, he married, and after a short vacation in Brewster, set sail for Cádiz as master of the brig Jane with a cargo of flour and rice. It was at the very height of the Reign of Terror in France, when Robespierre was at the top of his power. Cobb was worried about the Algerian pirates who were reported to be cruising outside the Straits of Gibraltar, but he had no notion that there was anything to fear from the French. What was his surprise, then, at being picked up off Brest by a French frigate and escorted into the harbor a captive. 'And here,' he writes, 'commences my first trouble and anxiety, as a ship Master — having under my charge, a valuable vessell and cargo, inexperienced in business — carried into a foreign port, unacquainted with the language, no American consel, or merchant to advise with — and my reputation, as a ship master, depending upon the measures I persued etc. etc.'

His papers showing that he was bound for a neutral port had been stolen by the French prize-master, and until he got them back, he could do nothing but live on shore and watch his cargo of flour and rice vanish before the onslaughts of the 'half-starved populace.'

Neutral Traders

In this posture affairs remained for six weeks, during which Cobb had written to the American *Chargé d'Affaires* in Paris and received for a reply the advice to be patient. At the end of the six weeks, he was told that his case had been tried and that the court had decreed the Jane to be indeed a neutral vessel; that he was entitled to have her back, that he should be paid for his stolen cargo, and should receive demurrage until he got his payment. Far from having had a hearing at the trial, Cobb had not even been notified that it was to be held. However, he supposed, in his inexperience, that all was now well — that he had only to collect his money and sail back to Boston: he was still naïf enough to imagine that Revolutionary officials meant what they said. In his own words, the verdict of the court 'gave a spring to his feelings.' His cheerfulness increased when, after three days of dickering, the agent of marine agreed to pay for the vanished cargo three times what it had cost in Boston.

But this was the young Captain's last cheerful moment for a long time. The law forbade any money to be carried out of France; the wretched populace had not themselves enough to eat or wear; so payment in merchandise was out of the question. What form, then, was the payment to take? After long debate, Cobb agreed to accept government bills of exchange, payable by the French agent in Hamburg sixty days after they had been delivered to Cobb in France. The agent promised that these bills should be forthcoming within two weeks. Cobb waited a month; then, convinced that most Frenchmen were thieves and that all of them were liars, he sent the Jane home in ballast in charge of his mate, while he prepared to carry his case to headquarters in Paris.

He got from the Minister of Marine an official copy of his claims on the Government, taking the precaution (for he was being rapidly educated in the ways of chicane) to have another copy of them recorded. The next problem was to get permission to travel to

Paris. The only means of conveyance were the coaches which carried national dispatches, and these were forbidden to take passengers. But Cobb's dander was up. He called on an official who was thought to be friendly toward Americans, with the request for a passport in the first place and written permission to travel with the national dispatch-carrier in the second. This gentleman, to quote Cobb's narrative once more, 'after a long demur with himself, and repeatedly feeling of his neck, to see how it would bear the knife... returned a favorable reply.'

Without more ado, armed with pistols and a blunderbuss, he boarded the government coach, which was made bullet-proof for fear of lurking bands of loyalists that had not yet been executed. More effective, no doubt, was the escort of a dozen armed men that accompanied it on horseback each night. After three days and nights of constant vigilance and anxiety, Cobb arrived in Paris. Here he was not surprised to learn that the authorities knew nothing of any court decree in his favor, nor had they received any document relating to it, though one had been posted to them some days before Cobb had left Brest. Nothing daunted, the young Captain pulled his official copy from his pocket and bade them look it over. Their reply was that if he would call the next day, they would let him know when his bills would be ready. But when he presented himself next morning, he was informed that unfortunately the document had been lost — that it 'must have been left upon the counter, brushed off, and burned among the loose papers.'

> This [Cobb writes] was too much, for my already perplexed, agitated, mind. I knew of no way, but to write back to Brest, for another set — and they, probably, would meet the same fate, as the two preseeding ones had. I was now fully-conveinced, that the whole was designed, for the purpose of procrastination and putting off pay day as long as possible — but it was a severe trial for me, in my inexperienced state. I consulted with our consul;

and with our minister at the court of France, but the only satisfaction was; git another set of papers, and we will guard against another loss....

At this point a lucky chance — the first that had befallen him since the capture of the Jane — pointed to a possible way out. A Frenchman whose acquaintance Cobb had made advised him to take his case direct to Robespierre, relying on the great man's friendliness toward Americans to get a favorable hearing. Cobb, ready to try anything, sat down immediately and composed the following note:

> An American citizen, captured by a French Frigate on the high seas, requests a personal interview; and to lay his grievances before citizen Roberspeire.
>   Very respectfully
>   E. COBB

Within an hour a messenger returned with the reply:

> I will grant Citizen Cobb an interview to morrow at 10 A.M.
>   ROBESPIERRE

After giving Robespierre a detailed account of all his troubles, Cobb was rewarded by the following: 'Go,' said Robespierre, 'to that office, and tell Citizen F. T. that... if he does not produce your papers, and finish your business *immediately* he will hear from me again, in a way not so pleasing to him.'

The name of Robespierre proved to be an open sesame. Cobb not only received his bills but apologies as well; the payment, it may be remembered, was to be in the form of bills of exchange on Hamburg payable in sixty days, and it may also be remembered that Cobb was to receive daily demurrage up to the time when the bills should be placed in his hands. If he took them now, his demurrage would stop. He therefore directed that they be sent to him in care of the agent at Brest, there to await his pleasure, while he with a light heart took some time off to see the sights of Paris.

The sights, to be sure, were grim enough. Cobb

stayed in the capital about three weeks, during which he watched a thousand persons mount the scaffold to the guillotine — Robespierre himself among them. The death of this mighty figure sent a fresh spasm across the already convulsed Continent, and brought Cobb's bills on Hamburg down to half their face value. He promptly decided to go to Hamburg in person in the hope of driving a better bargain; but his sixty days were as yet not nearly up; so the young man, ever desirous, like the Athenians, for some new thing, improved the interval by traveling about the country, until, still with three weeks to spare, he arrived once more in Brest. Here he received his bills from his old friend, the agent of marine, and set sail on a small vessel for Hamburg. After some further complications there, which he overcame by shrewdness and luck, he collected payment in full for the par value of the bills.

In due time Cobb was back in Boston, where, as soon as his adventures and the happy conclusion of them became known, he found himself hailed as the leading authority on the subject of ways and means for collecting debts in Europe. He was, in fact, the first Yankee captain who had traded with the French under the Reign of Terror, a circumstance which added enough to his prestige among Boston merchants to more than compensate him for all his troubles. Owners gave him no peace. Four days only did he have with his family in Brewster; then, his owners sent him off again to France, with orders to load with flour in Virginia on the way. This time he landed at Havre, where, finding that the Government had a monopoly on flour, he sold his cargo to authorized officials and was promised payment in forty days. He soon found that the quality of French promises had not changed since his previous voyage; after waiting in vain for ten weeks, he again sent his brig home and went once more to Paris, 'prepared,' as he says, 'for the seige and expecting a long one.'

He was not disappointed. Two months of persistency in the capital netted him one third of the sum in the form of silver ingots. He took a breather, during which he went to London and deposited this first installment to his owners' credit. Somewhat refreshed by the change of scene, he returned to Paris to see what he could do about the remaining two thirds. He got it in three months more, in the shape of forty thousand silver crowns. Here was an end of one kind of trouble, and the beginning of another, for the law still forbade any currency to be taken out of France. Cobb could not buy a return cargo with his money, for he had sent his brig home; bills of exchange on foreign countries were no longer trustworthy. His only resource was to try to smuggle his money home. To reduce its bulk, he quietly changed the forty thousand pieces of silver for three thousand Spanish doubloons. Then, to avert suspicion, he went to a village outside Havre and had two money-belts made, capable of holding about half of his coin. The other half he wrapped up in thirty packets of fifty coins apiece. He was now ready for the actual smuggling. He engaged passage for Boston on the ship Caroline, hid his thirty packages of gold on board some days before she sailed, bribed a steward to wear one of his money-belts, strapped the other round his own waist, and on the morning when the ship was to sail, blandly stepped on board. Eight French officials were on hand to search him, but they searched in vain, and Cobb and his gold arrived safe in Boston.

Here a blow of quite another sort awaited him. To quote his own picturesque language, he found that 'his partner in life's voyage had run him in debt for a Cape Cod farm.' Mrs. Cobb, it would seem, was herself a woman of parts; but the Captain liked the farm so well that he stayed at home for a year. Then in 1799, giving the French ports a rest, he took the brig Mary on a long voyage to Lisbon, London, Rotterdam, Copenhagen, St. Petersburg, and back to Boston. On his return he was given command of a new ship, the

Monsoon, with orders to take the bulk of his cargo to some appropriate port in northern Europe, but to stop at Ireland on the way and try to sell there some hogsheads of New England rum.

The voyage was destined to be an interesting one, and before it ended, Cobb had received some further lessons in foreign business methods. He anchored in the Cove of Cork, whence he made his way to the town to see how the authorities felt about landing the rum. He found them willing but timid, for the law forbade any foreign liquor to be imported. They promised to consult men higher up, however, and to let him know the decision in a few days. Cobb returned to his ship to find her in possession of customs officials and with the King's seal on her hatches. But the local collector, who had ordered this move, treated the affair in so blithe a spirit that Cobb took heart, and following his usual practice, went overland two hundred miles to Dublin for an interview with headquarters.

Here the officials told him, with a wink, that his ship was confiscated and would be sold at auction. So, indeed, she was; but nobody bid on her except Cobb and one of his newly made Irish friends. The friend opened proceedings with a bid of two shillings sixpence; Cobb raised it to five shillings, and the ship was his — a quick conclusion, which left the business in exactly the same position that it had been in when first he dropped anchor in the Cove of Cork. 'So that,' said Cobb to himself, 'is an Irish auction. Thus men grow wiser day by day.' But the affair was not yet ended. Irishmen, like other wise folk, have never been averse to good liquor or a good bargain. The final chapter of the business follows in Cobb's own words:

The collector, observed to me when about taking leave, Capt. Cobb, I must confess, I think your usage has benn something rough here, I shou'd not blame you, if you were to help yourself a little, in the way of smuggling. — no Sir said I, but wou'd you not be one of the first to make a prize of me therefor — oh said he, I should have

to do my duty — well Sir, said I, when you *Catch'em* you
Hab'em. God blesse you said he, and thus we parted, and
the next morn' I sail'd; matters were, however, so ar-
rainged, that between the cove of Cork, and the Scilly
Islands, that I hove overboard Eight hogsheads of N.E.
rum, and a pilot boat sheer'd along side, and hove on
board a small bag, which I found contained 264 English
guineas — and although I saw them pick up, and hoist on
board 8 hhds of rum, I *was satisfied.*

Cobb, after an unsuccessful attempt to sell the rest
of his rum in Guernsey, set sail for Hamburg, where he
found at last a good market for it, and returned to
Boston with so large a profit for all concerned that his
owners sent him there again almost immediately.
This time, however, he followed a different plan; for as
soon as he had sold his cargo and loaded the Monsoon
with Russian and German goods, he sent her home in
command of his mate and fellow townsman, David
Nickerson, while he stayed in Hamburg to negotiate
for another cargo against her return. Here the Captain enjoyed himself thoroughly for three months.
'Ther was,' as he says, 'no lack of *amusements*, to
please the eye, tast, or mind.' But at the end of that
time he received a letter saying that his wife had been
seriously ill, and a few days later he read in a newspaper that his brother had died. This was too much.
Cobb came down with an attack of brain fever, but
recovered and, when the Monsoon returned in the
spring, she brought news of his wife's improvement
that 'was a cordial to his lasserated feelings.'
On his next voyage to Hamburg, this time in command of the brig Sally and Mary, the Captain found
that the British had blockaded the port. His brig was
boarded by a detail from one of the King's ships, and
Cobb was taken on board to present his papers. Her
captain was a 'haughty, crabbed, self-willed Scotch-
man,' who, convinced that Cobb had been trying to
run the blockade, ordered him with his brig as a prize
to England. Fortunately this proved to be nothing

more serious than a delay, for the English found his papers satisfactory and sent him and his vessel on their way.

Hamburg being apparently out of the question, Cobb laid his course for Copenhagen, and on arriving there, told his experiences to a merchant whose acquaintance he had made on an earlier voyage. This gentleman explained that there were more ways than one of getting a cargo into Hamburg; it was necessary only to drop down to the German town of Lübeck, from which an inland canal, unguarded by any Britishers, let into Hamburg. Cobb, whose cargo had been specially selected for the Hamburg market, was quick to follow this tip, and found no difficulty in slipping his goods to their destination through the convenient back door suggested by his Danish friend, or in getting his return cargo out by the same route. One more lesson in the devious ways of European trade had been mastered.

In December, 1807, after a short vacation with his family, the Captain was again summoned to Boston to take the Sally and Mary to Malaga. He made the voyage in a little under a month, only to find that the British Orders in Council had beaten him there by one day. Here was a dilemma: fruit and wine would go sky-high in Boston, but there was a fine chance of being picked up by a British ship in the Straits of Gibraltar on the way. Cobb decided to risk it. He loaded with fruit and wine, timed his departure from Malaga so as to bring him off Gibraltar at night, and went booming along toward the Straits before a fresh easterly blow. But luck was against him; off the famous Rock the wind flattened, and unless it breezed up again before morning, he would certainly be seen and captured. The best chance was to slip into a neutral port and wait for another fair wind and dark night to run through the Straits. Before he could make harbor, however, a British frigate sighted him and sent a midshipman on board, who, when they reached port, brought him with his papers before the captain of the frigate — straight into the jaws of the Orders in Council. There was no getting the brig out without British clearance papers, and for an American neutral trader to get British clearance papers was like trying to get a letter of recommendation for civility from a man you have insulted.

Cobb went ashore for a chat with the American consul, who told him that he had not a chance. As he was leaving the office, he ran across an old friend, who, knowing the ways of the port, advised him to try the efficacy of a few well-placed coins. The Captain immediately acted on this suggestion, and in exchange for two ounces of gold, quietly placed on the counter before a British official, was given clearance papers for Boston. At sunrise next morning the Sally and Mary was on her way; her cargo of wine and fruit brought the expected high prices at home, and once more merchants wanted to know how it was done.

The Captain's next voyage, from Virginia to Cádiz with flour in the ship William Tell, was uneventful. He returned in ballast to Virginia, where he found orders for another voyage to the same place. While he was loading, news came that Jefferson's Embargo, which would paralyze foreign trade in every American port, was to go into effect in thirty-six hours. Cobb had, in that time, to clear one hundred tons of ballast out of the William Tell, stow upwards of three thousand barrels of flour, get his wood, water, and provisions on board, ship a fresh crew — the old one having received its discharge — procure clearance papers from the Customs House, and be on his way. That he did all this and beat the Embargo by two hours is sufficient evidence that he combined energy at home, were it needed, with resourcefulness abroad.

In Cádiz he received orders to bring back cash for his cargo. The Spanish authorities, unlike the French, made no objection; but before he was ready to sail, news came of the repeal of the British Orders in

Council and of Napoleon's Berlin and Milan Decrees. Shrewdly guessing that this would, in Cobb's own words, 'have a favorable effect, to America, in our Exchanges, and finding I cou'd buy British Government Bills, at a great discount,' he disobeyed orders and remitted his $72,000 cash to his owners' agent in England. He set sail from Cádiz for Boston on July 5, 1812, blissfully ignorant that war had been declared. Both the bliss and the ignorance were soon dispelled. The William Tell was first stopped on the Grand Banks by the armed British schooner Alphea, whose captain informed Cobb that a war was on and would have relieved him of the $72,000, had it been on board. While they were conversing, the English frigate Jason, camouflaged as an American, bore down on them. The schooner, which was bound for England with government dispatches, went on her way, leaving Cobb and his ship in possession of the newcomer. Cobb was allowed to remain on board with a prize-master and a British crew, while the other Yankees were transshipped to the Jason; both vessels then headed for St. John's. The prize-master turned out to be an agreeable companion, but once more Cobb congratulated himself on his decision to transmit his money to his owners' agents in London instead of bringing it home with him on the William Tell.

At St. John's he found twenty-seven other American prize vessels; so he had plenty of company. He wrote a letter to his wife, telling her of his adventures, and after a short and by no means unpleasant sojourn, he was sent home through an exchange of prisoners.

> Two days after [says Cobb] we arrived in New York, and dispersed to our several places of residence. — I took passage with my two mates, and Josiah Crosby, in a schooner for Bass River, we reached the river about suns setting, and being but about six miles from my family, I could not feel willing to sleep without seeing them — consequently myself, and my 1st mate, Mr. Berry each hired a Saddle horse, and started for Brewster, and I

reach'd my dwelling, and gave a knock, at your G. Mo-
thers, sleeping room window.

It appears she had been reperusing my Lengthy letter,
Amegining and revolving in mind all the horrors of my
situation in an English prisin, *after she had been in bed*, and
had not been asleep, when I knok'd at the window.

'Who is there?' said she — 'it is I,' said I — 'well,
what do you want'; 'to come in'; 'for what,' said she; before I cou'd answer, I heard my daughter D., who was in
bed with her say, why, *Mar it is Par*, this was aneogh, the
doors flew open, and the greetings of affection and con-
sanguinity miltiplied upon me rapidly.

Thus, in a moment was I transported to the greatest
earthly bliss, man can injoy viz to the injoyment of the
happy family circil.

The war put an end, temporarily at least, to the
voyages of Captain Cobb and a hundred other Cape
shipmasters. That Mr. Madison's war, as they called
it, found small favor among them is not surprising; but
the extent to which their hostility toward the administration carried them is somewhat shocking to a
generation which, having had a hundred years more in
which to learn the importance of the Union, regards
loyalty to the Government as a cardinal virtue. Cape
men, whether at home or in Boston, remained hot and
rebellious toward the war, not infrequently approaching actual sedition in the decisions reached in their
town meetings. The Barnstable County Peace Convention, composed largely of shipmasters who had been
thrown out of work, proclaimed that the war had 'origi-
nated in hatred to New England and to commerce; in
subservience to the mandate of the Tyrant of France.'

Captain Cobb, who stayed in Brewster throughout
the war, and who in 1814 was moderator of the famous
town meeting that convened to find an answer to Ragget's threat to burn the town, reluctantly handed over
$4000 to the English admiral as the price of safety.
And in Boston, Captain William Sturgis, of North-
West Coast and China fame, voted in the Legislature
in favor of a New England Convention at Hartford,

some of whose members went so far as to advocate the secession of New England from the Union if a new Constitution of their own drafting was not accepted by the other states. Frenchmen were not the only ones that had lost perspectives in the smoke of war! Luckily none of the rebellious Yankee schemes went far enough to do any permanent damage, though they must have given Mr. Madison and his friends some sleepless nights; and when the war was over, Captain Cobb, whose sojourn ashore had given him the title of Major, was once more ready for sea.

He made two or three more voyages to Europe in the ship Paragon, and then in 1818 embarked on a brand-new sort of voyage, the African trade, to Prince's Island in the Gulf of Guinea, one of the worst fever-holes recorded in the annals of seafaring. Though the slave trade was flourishing there at the time, Cobb kept clear of it. He loaded his ship, the Ten Brothers, with print goods, tobacco, trinkets, and salt beef, and brought back palm oil, gold dust, ivory, and coffee. The voyage was so profitable that Captain Cobb urged his friend and neighbor, Captain Isaac Clark, a retired veteran of northern European ports, to come with him the next time as supercargo. Clark was reluctant, but finally consented, and away they sailed on the Ten Brothers.

Two other Brewster captains were on the Coast with Cobb and Clark: David Nickerson, Cobb's former mate, now in command of the schooner Hope, and Joseph Mayo, a young captain of twenty-nine. The voyage, for all these men, became a dreadful tragedy. A more ghastly battle with fever and death has seldom been waged by Yankee sailors. Only Cobb lived to return home; Nickerson died during his return voyage; the others were buried at Prince's Island before they could set sail. The first of Captain Cobb's letters home, written when the fever had only begun to prostrate the party, contains some reference to business; in the later ones, trade is forgotten in grief.

Neutral Traders

My dear Freind

We are here and all well, thanks to the controler of every event, but under circomstances, must remain here two months longer, as we have a considerable part of our cargo still on hand, business is astonishingly altered since last voyage, the coast is crouded with vessells and goods of every discription, and the natives have nothing to buy with.... This comes by Esq. Clark, via the W. Indies, he will sail tomorrow; Capt. Nickerson is very sick on shore. ... He is however in the hands of a mercifull God, may his will be done, and the submission of the creture sincier....

Pars love to all his children, he earnestly pray that his life may be spared, and he permitted, once more to greet his little flock in health and hapiness....

Feby 7th Since the above to the astonishment of all Capt. Nickerson has so far recovered that we have taken him on board the ship, — Esqr Clark is very sick, the Boy young Kimbal is dead.

Feby 14th He is gone — Nickerson does not gain any Strength wishes to go to sea and try a change of air, he is sildom himself we have as yet kept the Esqrs death from him, — such senes of distress and death, is severely trying to me, May God preserve me — We all continue well except Capt. Mayo, he has had a slight fever, but is apparently doing well; I have had a smart attack of the Nervous head ake, but have got over it,

A schooner will sail for Boston in a day or two, will write more fully

Your as ever

Elijah Cobb

My dear freind

I wrote you 4 days ago by the Schooner Hope which I sent away under the care of John Dillingham 3rd he being the only one willing to undertake,... you may posibly git this letter first, it is therefore necessary to repeat that Esq. Clark has paid the dept of nature, it was my task to close his Eyes the 11th Inst after a sickness of 8 days —

87

Young Kimbal died 4 days before, Capt. Nickerson was very sick on board this ship, but his fever having turned, it was the advice of Every One to send him to sea, that a change of air would have a good effect; I accordingly did, but fear he never will reach America; we must however commit him and ourselves to a mercifull just God, who always acts for the good of his Creatures and happy would it be for us; if we could always bow with humble submission to his righteous dispensations.

Capt. Mayo has been very sick; his fever turned two days since, and the people here who are no doubt better judges than strangers say he is out of danger, he also has great currage, but he is very weak, and it will be a long time before he gits his strength, he is on shore, I am something unwell, and taking Medicine that I cannot see him to day —

Feby 20th Alas Alas, Capt. Mayo is gone; an unfavorable turn in his disorder was his passport to (I trust) realms of blessedness — I have ordered the ship amediately to sea; shall work up to the windward of these islands and pass away 3 or 4 weeks, untill the sickly season passes of. — I must then return and git pay for 3 or 4000 Dollars of goods trusted out... in orders for coffee — and had I foreseen the consequences; I would not have put it out of my power to have left altogether at pleasure altho we should have brot home half our cargo, but circomstancd as I am, we must take all reasonable precaution, and trust our lives and healths, to an alwise, aljust, and merciful God, who cannot err....

21 *Feby....* Amigination in this country works wonders; ... feel a sort of pleasing confidence that I am again, to be permited to visit my beloved family — to offer a word of consolation, to the afflicted freind of those entoomb'd in this foreign land, but in every instance, I trust I shall be anable to say in sincerety thy will be done.

Your
E. C.

PRINCE'S ISLAND 24*th April* 1819

MY DEAR SON

We are all well, shall tarry here a few days longer and then proceed for St. Thomases, where I hope to procure a considerable quantity of coffee, and then proceed as bifore mentioned, hope yet to reach Boston in all the month of July.

I expect before this, my letters (by the two schooners) filled with heart rending tidings to our Brewster freind have been received, my mental, as well as bodily distress, has been such, that I hardly know what I wrote in those letters (probably much incoherency) as they were dictated by the feelings of the moment, but I trust those scenes are not to return upon this voyage, the place is healthy, frequent turnadoes, with thunder lightning and copeous showers purifies the air, all nature smiles and the human form wears a cheerfull countenance in the place of the gastly visage, which so recently presented itself at all points. What abundant cause of greatfull praise to the supreem controler of every event both of time and eternity, more especially to us the living monuments of His mercy who for wise purposes (tho' hidden from our view) have been spared while so many have fallen around us. May we express our gratitude by keeping his commands....

Your Affectionate Father
ELIJAH COBB

Luck and robust health brought Cobb home in safety from this, his last voyage. The rest of his long life he spent in Brewster, where his quarter-deck voice might be heard in town meetings and on the platform of the local Lyceum. From time to time, also, it was heard in the State House in Boston, for there, like so many other retired Cape shipmasters, he served his district as Senator. For the rest, his life was that of a gentleman farmer, respected and perhaps feared. At the ripe age of eighty-one he was gathered to his fathers.

Though no other Cape Cod captain had so thorough a training as Cobb in dodging blockades and extracting money from bankrupt Europeans during this lively epoch, two of them had a pretty good taste of it. One was Jeremiah Mayo, of Brewster; the other Isaiah Crowell, of Dennis. Mayo's father, who was a blacksmith, had nine sons whose aggregate height was fifty-five feet. Five of them died either in foreign ports or at sea. Jeremiah, who ably upheld the family stature with a height of six feet, five inches, visited plenty of foreign ports, but was lucky enough not to die in any of them. As a matter of fact, it looked for a time as though he would never leave home, for his father wanted him to be a blacksmith, and at sixteen he was still at the forge, shoeing most of the horses in town. But in 1804, when he was fourteen, a summer fishing voyage to the Straits of Belle Isle netted him $225, and a trip to the Bahamas for salt under his neighbor, Captain Solomon Crosby, gave Jeremiah such a taste for the sea that the old gentleman's wishes, like the wishes of many another father, went down the wind, and the boy shipped before the mast in the ship Sally, bound for Marseilles. This voyage settled the matter, for Jeremiah was paid twenty-two dollars a month — two dollars more than any other foremast hand.

In 1805 he went again to the Mediterranean, this time on the armed ship Industry, Captain Gamaliel Bradford. They carried salt fish to Malaga, Leghorn, Alicant, and Marseilles, picked up a cargo of wheat in exchange, and headed with it for Dublin. Near Gibraltar the Industry was attacked by three lateen-rigged pirates. The fight lasted for two hours, and in the course of it Captain Bradford lost a leg and young Mayo received a flesh wound. The Captain was left in a hospital at Lisbon, and the voyage was concluded uneventfully.

By this time Mayo knew enough, in the opinion of his fellow townsman, Captain Kimball Clark, to go with him to Amsterdam as mate of the brig Salem. The captain made no mistake, for Mayo took the brig through the tricky waters of the North Sea from Amsterdam to Cádiz for salt and wine while Clark lay sick in his berth.

On their next voyage, while carrying salt fish to San Sebastian, the old brig, leaky and overloaded, be-

gan to spew oakum from her upper seams in an
Atlantic gale. Captain Clark, in despair, told young
Mayo to go ahead and try anything he could think of,
as they were all bound for the bottom anyhow.
Jeremiah first knocked the head out of a barrel of
cider and ladled out generous rations of it to the crew,
passing around plenty of biscuits with it, in place of
the salt fish on which the crew had been living since
the storm began. He then put the brig under a close-
reefed main topsail and lightened ship by throwing
three or four hundred quintals of codfish on deck,
where they were washed overboard as fast as they
struck. Thus eased, the Salem made better weather of
it, as she now rode high enough to keep her upper
planking out of water. They arrived in San Sebastian,
sold what was left of their cargo, and squared away
for Bordeaux, where Captain Clark sold the brig and
took passage home, no doubt sharing the views of a
later Yarmouth captain who proclaimed that 'any
man who would go to sea for pleasure, would go to hell
for pastime.'

But for Mayo the departure of the captain was the
chance he had been waiting for. The French owners of
the Salem loaded her with claret for Morlaix (though
her clearance papers read Tonnigen) and invited him to
take command. Since France and England were at
each other's throats, the trip was a risky one. Mayo,
supplied with his false clearance papers, headed north
for Morlaix and, sure enough, was picked up just outside Bordeaux by a hostile frigate; but her captain, deceived by Mayo's papers, allowed the Salem to continue her voyage. Arrived at his destination, Mayo
discovered why the Bordeaux merchants had been
willing to risk such a voyage: the claret brought about
four times its cost. Besides selling his cargo, the captain was shrewd enough to have the seams of his brig
smeared with pitch while she lay in port in order to
have a plausible pretext for having put in there in case
he should again encounter the King's ships on his re-

turn trip. It was lucky that he did so, for he was once more held up at sea, but satisfied the British officers by pointing to his freshly tarred seams and explaining that the claret he had left at Morlaix was neither more nor less than the price of the work.

This was not the end of Captain Mayo's experiences with English ships. For the time being, to be sure, he kept clear of them, making a voyage or two as mate of an American ship between Bordeaux and Spanish ports in 1808 and 1809, and then returning to Boston for a vacation. But he was soon at sea once more, coasting to the Carolinas and Virginia in the schooner Lawry, bringing home, as an item in one of his cargoes, a huge sea turtle which a Southern gentleman was presenting to Governor Sullivan. One reason for his sudden distaste for long voyages may have been Sally Crosby, a Brewster girl who had just become Mrs. Jeremiah Mayo. After a year or so, however, he took to trans-Atlantic work again and made enough voyages to Oporto, Vigo, Corunna, and Gotenburg to keep him busy up to the beginning of the War of 1812.

Early in the war, deciding that his success in bluffing Britishers in the North Sea might enable him now to run their Atlantic blockade, he accepted an invitation to make a voyage from Baltimore to Lisbon with flour. He got a crew together in Boston and started with them in a schooner for the Chesapeake, only to find a British squadron anchored there. There being no chance to run past into Baltimore, owing to lack of wind, Mayo armed his crew and sent them all below except one man, with orders to stay there until he summoned them. He then stepped to the rail to greet a boatload of marines from the Britishers. Seeing the schooner so lightly manned, they left a prize crew of only three or four on board and departed. Then Mayo began to pray for wind, so that he might get his schooner out of range of the enemy and then, ordering his men from below, might seize the prize crew and take the vessel into Baltimore. But luck was against him; the calm held, and the British sent off two boats to tow her in alongside them. The game was up; Mayo remained a prisoner on the frigate Ariadne for three days until he could ransom himself and his schooner. During his captivity, he made himself useful to the British surgeon by holding down a sailor whose leg had to be amputated.

At Baltimore, greatly to his disgust, he received orders from Ellis and Loring, his owners, to take no chances on running the British blockade, but to load his flour on wagons and bring it overland to New York. A more distasteful job never taxed the patience of an impetuous shipmaster, but orders were orders, and Mayo saw it through. From New York he went home to Brewster, where he spent the remaining years of the conflict joining with Captains Kimball Clark, and Elijah Cobb and other leading citizens in an anti-war chorus that was heard all the way to Beacon Hill. After the war, Mayo kept on for a few years in the European trade with a new brig, the Sally, which had been built for him at Newburyport. He had, it would seem, a talent for being on the spot when momentous events were taking place: in Paris he heard the shot in the gardens of the Luxembourg, that was the death-knell of Marshal Ney, and in Havre, a month after the battle of Waterloo, he was approached by friends of Napoleon with a request that he take the Emperor back to the United States on the Sally. This was precisely the sort of commission that appealed to him, for he had a great admiration for Napoleon and liked nothing better than playing hide-and-seek with the British at sea. He accepted enthusiastically, but Napoleon gave himself up to the English instead. About 1820, Mayo left the sea for good and he spent the last half of his life in Brewster, as storekeeper, farmer, packet-owner, president of the local insurance company and chairman of the Board of Selectmen. He died in 1867 at the age of eighty-one.

Three of the factors that hampered trade during

these troublous years — the British Orders in Council, Jefferson's Embargo, and the War of 1812 — were encountered by another Cape shipmaster, Captain Isaiah Crowell, of Dennis, and from all but the last he emerged triumphant. In 1808 he was lying in Marseilles, loading for Boston, when news came that the Orders in Council were on their way. Captain Crowell finished loading in a hurry, headed for the Straits of Gibraltar and got through before the jaws could close.

A similar experience, this time in eluding a mandate of his own Government, followed early in the spring of 1812, while Crowell was in Boston, loading for Lisbon. It was announced that Jefferson's final Embargo was on the way from Washington. Rather than lose his entire voyage, the Captain got away to Eastport with half a cargo and still one jump ahead of the dreaded decree. But his lead was too short for comfort. He stopped only long enough to get clearance papers for Lisbon, and then dropped over to the Canadian port of Campobello, where he made up the rest of a cargo and set sail for Spain. He arrived safely in Lisbon, but on his return was picked up by a British man-of-war and sent to St. John's, where he may well have fallen in with Elijah Cobb, who was sojourning there at very nearly the same time. This was the end of seafaring for Captain Crowell. The rest of his life he spent in Yarmouth as a director and president of the Barnstable Bank. From time to time, too, he followed the footsteps of so many other Cape shipmasters to the State House, for voters in those days did not find it necessary to discriminate against men who had been abroad.

Some of the devices which these captains had to resort to if they were to complete their voyages with profit would not, perhaps, stand the rigorous scrutiny of abstract ethics. A few tender souls may regret that Elijah Cobb felt called upon to smuggle rum into Ireland and gold out of France. Some will lament the lies which Jeremiah Mayo told the Englishmen who held him up in the North Sea; others will disapprove of his using false clearance papers. But the New England conscience was then, as now, an accommodating virtue which rarely interfered with profits. Smartness, in the Yankee sense of the word, readily excused such occasional irregularities; and smartness was itself a virtue. The shipmasters who have been mentioned were upright men according to workaday business standards. They become paragons of integrity when judged by the standards which one or two other Cape captains let themselves down to; for there is nothing in seafaring *per se* to turn unrighteous men to righteousness, nor is it to be expected that every one of the hundreds of Cape-Codders who trod quarter-decks was born with a set of rigid scruples.

One of the most picturesque of these unconventional traders was born in 1768 in that part of Eastham which is now in Orleans, close to the Harwich line. His name, for reasons which will be apparent, is withheld. In 1793 — the same year in which Elijah Cobb was rejoicing in his first command — he was captain of the schooner Sea Flower, engaged in the African trade out of Boston. What cargoes he carried nobody knows; but there is no evidence that he was a slaver and no reason to suppose that his trade was not in itself entirely legal. When he returned to Boston after one of his voyages, his owner, William Boardman, expressed great dissatisfaction with the profits; in his own words, he received 'very inadequate returns for the cargo he sent.' So great was his chagrin that he removed the Captain from command of the Sea Flower, and sent him for the next voyage as mate of the schooner Success, under Captain John Taylor. For some reason Taylor stayed behind in Senegal, and the schooner returned to Boston, *via* the West Indies, with our Eastham friend in command. Once more Boardman found his returns unsatisfactory, and stated that the acting Captain 'brought me back but a very small proportion of what he had said he left there,' only one hundred pounds' worth of cargo and no cash.

However, he preferred no charges, and all remained tranquil until Captain Taylor came back from Africa in a towering rage some four months later, vowing that his mate had robbed him.

Accompanied by a certain James Smith, Taylor made a bee line for the Cape to find him. While passing through Chatham, the two fell in with David Godfrey, who, on hearing what they were after, told them of a strange experience of his that might have some bearing on the matter. He had been looking out from his house toward the harbor one morning some four months previous and had seen a schooner come in under easy sail and run up gently on the beach. On walking down to the shore, he met the Captain — none other than our nameless friend — who told him that the schooner was the Success, from Africa *via* the West Indies, and informed him that he needed help in landing a heavy object. Always willing to oblige, Godfrey went back to his barn, hitched up his horse and drove down to the schooner, from which his new acquaintance dragged out a pillow-case apparently full of coins and 'very heavy.' They got it on board the wagon and took it up to Godfrey's house, where they turned it over to Mrs. Godfrey for safe-keeping, though not until the Captain had counted out twenty pounds in silver to take along with him. He had then gone back to the schooner and resumed his voyage to Boston.

In view of this picturesque incident, it is small wonder that Boardman had felt dissatisfied with the returns of the voyage, or that Captain Taylor, who declared that part of the money was his, had proclaimed that he had been robbed. To corroborate his tale, Godfrey took the two men to his house and showed them the pillow-case. Elated by this unexpected piece of evidence, they continued their journey to Eastham, where they procured from Squire Freeman a warrant for the arrest of the culprit.

Up to this point, the events are clear and entirely authentic, for both Boardman and Godfrey testified to them on oath in Boston, where their statements appear in the court records. But the trial in the course of which this evidence came out, instead of being a case brought against the mate by Taylor for robbery, was one brought by the mate against Taylor for slander, which makes it look as if the Eastham skipper realized the validity of the principle, 'the best defense is attack.' At all events, whether or not he was a knave, certain irregularities were manifest in his conduct. No mention had been made to Boardman, for example, of the sojourn of the Success in Chatham Harbor; nor was any satisfactory explanation of the pillow-case full of money ever forthcoming. He subsequently moved to Norfolk and is said to have died in New Orleans, mourned, no doubt, by his family, but unwept by the other citizens of the Cape.

These are a few of the captains who represented our young country in Europe while the North-West fur-traders, with their sweeping voyages, were dosing the Queen Charlotte Indians with physic and swapping sea otter for silk with the mandarins of Canton. Very different were the qualities called for by these two branches of trade, but the Cape produced men who rose to the top in both; merchants and governments consulted William Sturgis on questions pertaining to Oregon and China; owners waited on Elijah Cobb to find out how to make Frenchmen pay their bills. Both were important factors in spreading eastward and westward the prestige of an unknown nation; and thanks to their talents, our flag was respected in Europe and in the Orient before we were thirty years old.

5

Josiah Richardson

FOUR branches of commercial activity emerged during the forty years that followed the War of 1812: miscellaneous trade with Europe; the stern routine of the Liverpool packets; long voyages to the East Indies and China; and the thrilling era of the clipper ships. These periods overlapped, of course, and sometimes almost exactly coincided. European trade went briskly on, while the packets thrashed their way eastward and westward between New York or Boston and Liverpool; and the packets continued after the clippers had arrived. Some Cape men were, in the course of their lives, active in all four lines of trade. A good example of such a one is Josiah Richardson.

Captain Richardson learned his seafaring on voyages between our southern ports and Europe; varied the monotony of these by a leisurely voyage to the East Indies; rose to unrivaled distinction on the quarter-deck of the first extreme clipper ship, made two record passages in another, and afterwards, wearied of long voyages, employed his talents in the Liverpool packet trade. Captain Richardson's father, John, graduated at Harvard College about 1800 and came to Centerville to teach school. Here he fell in love with the Cape and with a Cape girl, married her, and bought a farm, on which he brought up a large family of children, two of whom, Ephraim and Josiah, became sea captains. Josiah first went to sea as cabin boy in

Josiah Richardson

1820 at the age of eleven. At twenty-one he was master of the schooner Hetty Thom, owned by Captain Samuel Frazar, of Duxbury, and the next year he made his first foreign voyage as captain in the brig Orbit, which he took from Boston to Cronstadt with general cargo. For the next nine years he sailed for his cousin, George Richardson, of Boston, in the brigs Owhyhee and Leander, principally to Marseilles and Cape Haytière, but varying the monotony by an occasional side trip to St. Jago and Rio de Janeiro, and a voyage or two to Russia, sometimes carrying logwood from Cuba to Cronstadt, and once buying rum from a British bark in mid-ocean to preserve the remains of a passenger who had died on board. By 1839 he was through with small vessels. He took command of the ship Chatham and for two years was hard at work in her, carrying cotton from our southern ports to Liverpool and Havre, sometimes stopping at Cuba on the way.

Then he took a rest, during which he married and moved from Centerville to Shrewsbury, where he was living in 1846, interesting himself in setting out fruit trees on the one hand and in his duties as deacon of the church on the other. A year later he was back at sea in command of the ship Walpole, carrying wheat from New York to Liverpool, and taking a fearful beating for a solid week in the North Atlantic. Extracts from his log give a good idea of winter weather in those latitudes:

> *Jan.* 20, 1847.... Latter part much harder squalls; snow, hail and rough high cross sea, breaking in upon the deck, taking away ports, staving doors... and other damage.... The ship laboring hard, we trying the pumps often. Ends a tremendous gale from the W N W with high sea.
> *Jan.* 21. Hard gale coming in squalls;... Hail, snow; wind blowing a hurricane during the squalls. At 3 P.M. sea very high and winds increasing.... Sea breaking in upon decks, keeping them full, carrying away monkey rails etc.... Winds and sea increasing to such a degree

that the sea would break in upon both sides of the ship, filling her waist full of water, the ports being swept away. At times the sea seemed to make highway over her, sweeping the decks. Brought the ship to the wind under close reefed main tops'l, but found it blew so hard that the ship would at times lay her lee yard arms three feet under water.... At 7 A.M.... sea and wind very violent and high, breaking over us, staving in part of the deck house forward.... Constantly trying the pumps but the water did not come to them.

Jan. 22.... Heavy gales from N.W. and rough sea. Squalls, snow and hail.... Trying pumps but could not get any water from them, the ship laying down so much upon her broad side the water would not come to them at all. Tried the bilge pumps, but they would not work — soon choked with wheat — at 12 midnight... sounded the pumps; found two feet water in the well room; pumped a few strokes and the boxes became choked.

Jan. 26.... Squally with rain, thunder and lightning. At 5 P.M. took a gale of wind from the S W in a squall... a rough sea breaking in upon the decks with great force, at times filling the waists full... an ugly cross sea running. At 8 A.M. found by sounding the pumps we had but sixteen inches water in them. Could not get the water lower as grain prevents. Ends squally, cloudy weather.

In spite of everything, Captain Richardson got the Walpole across in twenty-eight days — what there was left of her — and brought her home again. On arriving, he was delighted to learn that his owners had decided to send her out to Manilla. Nothing could have suited the Captain better; he had had enough of the Western Ocean for the time being and looked forward to a voyage in balmier latitudes. He pushed the Walpole along steadily, and wrote cheerfully to his wife from the Straits of Sunda, August 18, 1847:

Arrived at anchor here last evening. Our passage has been 95 d., rather short, as the vessels that sailed before us one fortnight have not yet arrived.

Two weeks later he was in Manilla, where it took him four months to make up a cargo. At last, loaded with sappan wood, hemp, manilla rope, rice, sugar, and buffalo hides, he headed for New York. On her return, the Walpole was once more set at work carrying cotton to Europe. Her owners urged Richardson to continue in command, and he accepted; but not all his experience could turn a dull market into a brisk one. Times were bad, and the Captain wrote to his wife from New Orleans, June 22, 1848:

> ... Chartered the Walpole... to take a freight of Cotton to St. Petersburg, Russia, at so low a rate the ship cannot make any more than to pay her expenses unless I obtain some freight home. As I am well acquainted [there] hope to obtain something for New York if not for Boston. Otherwise shall not make one dollar. Never saw such times in New Orleans. Am not in the habit of getting discouraged but must say business prospects look dark now.

His return from Russia to Boston was enlivened by the sight of a remarkable vessel which he describes in his log as 'a steamer with 4 masts, the fore and mizzen sloop rigged, the middle two square rigged.'

Up to this point Captain Richardson's voyages had all been made either in blunt-bowed brigs or in the clumsy apple-cheeked ships of the thirties and early forties, and for the excellent reason that these vessels were the best there were. Shipbuilding was still in its infancy when Richardson first went to sea, and it had no more than reached adolescence when he made his first voyage to Manilla in the forties. But the dawn of a new era was at hand. Foreigners had long looked upon our country as a land flowing with milk and honey — to say nothing of silver dollars — and immigrants from the old country had been flocking to it as fast as they could raise passage-money. The Liverpool docks were crowded with sturdy Irish peasants whose hopes for easy money across the Atlantic had brought them by hundreds from the moors and peat bogs of the Emerald Isle. But transportation had been woefully inadequate. Until 1840 or so, a crossing from Liverpool to Boston was, for a passenger, about as agreeable

as a six-weeks sojourn in a dungeon during an earth-
quake. But still they came, and Yankee enterprise at
last woke up to the fact that some of them, at least,
would be glad to pay for decent accommodations.

This idea had slowly been taking shape in the minds
of merchants for the thirty years during which Josiah
Richardson had been following the sea; and now, in
the late forties, Liverpool packets were being built
that contemporary authorities refer to as 'floating
palaces.' Stout and staunch and equipped with state-
rooms for the rich and steerage accommodations for
the poor, these vessels, in the language of one lively
writer, 'won laurels that were immortal.' The launching of a new packet ship was an event; her captain, a
lord of creation. Until the arrival of the clippers, no
nobler vessels were to be found anywhere on the seven
seas, and few were the merchant captains who would
not have risked their souls for the command of one of
them.

But a new and delicate task confronted the few who
won the coveted berths under the quarter-decks of
Liverpool packets. Any swaggering bully who was a
good sailor would do to carry cargoes, but carrying
cargoes formed only a small part of the duties of a
packet captain. He must be able to move graciously
among distinguished passengers, like a diplomat entertaining his friends; at the table he must hold his own
with the intellectual and the genteel; and with him the
nicest sort of seamanship must be instinctive. If he held
on in a blow until a spar was carried away or a topsail
was blown from the bolt-ropes, a host of eager tongues
would spread the news to wide-eyed listeners on shore,
who declared that a man who ran such risks was no fit
commander for a passenger ship. If, on the other hand,
he lengthened his passage by shortening sail, the critics
were equally voluble. He must steer his course with
the utmost nicety between safety and speed, and he
must be a man of iron as well, for the forecastles of
Liverpool packets were infested with the wildest

breed of sailors (barring pirates) that the sea has ever produced — 'Liverpool Irishmen,' who thought no more of knifing an officer than of tossing off a neat half-pint of whiskey. It is no wonder that of the many captains who believed themselves qualified to command these ships, few were chosen.

Of these few, Josiah Richardson was one. A new Liverpool packet, the Townsend, was launched in 1849, not a queen in her class, but a notable vessel, and when Captain Richardson stepped upon her quarter-deck, a new phase of his seafaring life had begun. That his ability as a sailor qualified him for the position is clear to anyone who has seen how he took the old Walpole through a week of the worst weather the Atlantic can provide, and that his gentility was equally marked will soon appear from his letters. The Captain was now among the aristocracy of his profession; life, so he supposed, had no higher honor to bestow. Sometimes, when east-bound freights were scarce in Boston and New York, he took the Townsend to New Orleans for cotton before crossing to Liverpool; sometimes he headed her north for St. John's, where she became a center of interest to the citizens of that seafaring town. And from both New Orleans and St. John's the Captain wrote to his wife letters that reveal his character clearly. One of them, written apropos of a friend whose frailty had proved no match for temptation, is particularly significant: 'The wicked,' he writes, 'indeed are like the troubled sea. The fruits of their lives blast and mildew on those around them, and their final end, Death Eternal. They know not the happiness of domestic bliss, mutual love, mutual happiness. Light is sown for the righteous and gladness for the upright in heart. The wicked grope in darkness; they flee where no man pursueth — there is no peace for the wicked. There is a moral majesty in virtue that the most lewd and abandoned are bound to respect.'

There speaks the deacon of the church and the shipmaster who had taken his vessel through Atlantic gales. Under such a man, passengers might sail with security. That the Townsend herself was no ordinary vessel appears from a letter which the Captain wrote from St. John's: 'I suppose,' he says, 'many hundred people have visited the Townsend, ladies and gentlemen, yesterday after the rain ceased. I went to the Episcopal church twice. The morning sermon, could not hear the preacher but a few words. In the evening it did better.'

Piety such as this is, to be sure, viewed askance by skeptics, who find it so often a flimsy cloak for avarice and cruelty that they discount it always. However accurate such observations may be in general, they apply in no way to the piety of Captain Richardson. In 1850, while he was loading the Townsend in Liverpool, he received word from the owners of the old Walpole, in which he still held a $10,000 interest, that she had been abandoned in the Columbia River by her captain and crew and would probably be a total loss. Here was a heavy blow to a hard-working shipmaster, a blow that no false piety could have withstood. The Captain wrote the bad news to his wife and then continues; 'It's past; no murmuring. Onward to the Christian. All is well at last. Nothing comes by chance; a kind, all-wise Father over rules all accidents and miscalculations of man, showing him his weakness and shortsightness and dependence.'

Such fortitude is the more impressive in view of the small amount of money that even the smartest packet captains received — thirty dollars a month and five per cent of the freight money. Though this looks good, so many ships were in the business that there was not always freight enough to go round. On the next trip after the one on which he learned of his loss, having loaded every ton of freight he could find in St. John's to eke out the light cargo with which he had left Boston, Captain Richardson wrote: 'Our whole amount of freight is £973... it will require as much

CAPTAIN JOSIAH RICHARDSON

management as I can do to make the Townsend pay her way.' A little calculation will show the importance of the loss of a cool $10,000 to a man who was sailing so close to the wind as this. Perhaps the lines of his favorite hymn helped his philosophy during these dark days, particularly the stanza in which the Lord explains his reasons for sending afflictions upon his children:

> These inward trials I employ
> From self and pride to set thee free —
> And break thy schemes of earthly joy
> That thou mayst seek thy all in Me.

In spite of their misfortunes, Captain Richardson warns his wife not to scrimp too much, remarking that 'it is best to live comfortable, if we die poor.'

But the lean years were of short duration, for by this time the first clipper ships had been launched, and the California gold rush was creating a demand for more. This is not the place to enlarge on the importance of this new type of vessel or upon the revolutionary effect it had upon marine architecture throughout the country. Suffice it for the moment to say that even the earliest clippers were to the lumbering merchantmen of previous decades what Robin Hood's gray-goose shafts were to the clumsy missiles flung by the crossbows of the Saxons. New-Yorkers had for a year or two been turning out medium clippers with success, but it remained for Donald McKay, of East Boston, to build the first of the extreme clipper ships, the vessels that were to become, during the next ten years, the glory of our nation and the envy and despair of all other seagoing peoples.

She was launched in December, 1850, and christened Stag Hound, and her lines, drawn by McKay himself, set the old-timers to wagging their heads and muttering jeremiads as they cast their eyes aloft to her towering masts and tremendous spars. Her owners were George Upton and Sampson and Tappan, progressive merchants of Boston who had allowed McKay to follow his own genius unhampered in designing and building this new vessel. Not only was she the sharpest clipper that had ever been launched, but she was the biggest American merchantman afloat. The question on every tongue was, who was to be her captain. No higher tribute to the character of Josiah Richardson could have been paid than her owners' invitation to him to command her. After twenty years of quiet, steady work in schooners, brigs, and ships, Captain Richardson, by this command, became overnight one of the most eminent shipmasters in the country, a man in whose hands lay the making of maritime history. 'I should think,' said the celebrated underwriter, Walter Jones, to him, 'I should think you would be somewhat nervous in going so long a voyage in so sharp a ship, so heavily sparred.' 'No, Mr. Jones,' replied Captain Richardson, 'I would not go in the ship at all if I thought for a moment she would be my coffin.' And away he sailed on the first day of February, 1851, to test the wings of his magnificent vessel on the 16,000-mile course to San Francisco, with freight which shippers had paid a dollar a cubic foot to get on board of her — a different story, indeed, from the meager cargoes of the forties.

The first few days of the voyage were uneventful, the crew — 'most of them stupid,' as the Captain remarks — being employed in setting up the rigging and back stays. The best brief account of the passage is contained in a letter, dated May 8, 1851, which Captain Richardson wrote to the owners from Valparaiso.

GENTLEMEN:
Your ship Stag Hound is at anchor in this port after a passage of 66 days, which I believe is the shortest but one ever made, and had it not been for the accident of losing some of our spars, I do not doubt that it would have been the shortest.
When 6 days out, on Feb. 6th, during a heavy gale from S W with rain and a rough sea, and while running

Josiah Richardson

under double reefed topsails, the main topmast broke, taking with it all three topgallantmasts; the gale increasing with a high sea, it took us seven days before we were able to get a main topsail upon her. We saved all the sails, yards and rigging, only cutting a few running ropes. The accident was owing to the rigging stretching and settling down around the mast head, caused by the warm rain, and perhaps, as the ship worked so remarkably well, that we carried on her a little harder than we ought, before the rigging had settled down to its place. We lost by this accident 800 miles at least.

The ship has yet to be built that will beat the Stag Hound; nothing that we have fallen in with could hold her in play at all. I am perfectly in love with her; a better sea boat or better working or drier ship I never sailed in. You have reason to be proud of her as she is about faultless.

In 21 days from N.Y. we were across the Equator; in 29 days we passed Rio Janeiro; in 49 days we were off Cape Horn; and in 66 days to this port; and under every situation the ship performed her part well and has proved to my satisfaction that she has no defect as a clipper; in fact I should not know where to change her hull to make an improvement.

I shall get a main-topmast, take in my water, and leave here on the 12th for San Francisco.

JOSIAH RICHARDSON

The accident described in this letter and the labor that was called for in repairing the damage, obviously took it out of the after-guard, for in his log under the date of February 15, Captain Richardson remarks:

2d mate sick. 1st mate unwell. Captain with a wound on his forehead made by spanker vang block last night.

But all troubles were forgotten in the fine passage of 112 days to San Francisco. One other incident occurred, the rescue of the crew of a Russian brigantine off the coast of Brazil. The following is a copy of an unpublished letter of thanks which Captain Richardson received from the Russian Ambassador long after

107

the event, for the Ambassador, not knowing where else to send it, addressed it to Daniel Webster, then Secretary of State, and Webster in turn mailed it to the Collector of Customs at Boston, who forwarded it to the Captain.

WASHINGTON, *December 29th*, 1851

MR. SECRETARY OF STATE:

A Russian vessel, La Sylphide, Captain Sundstrom, was wrecked on the coast of Brazil in the course of last spring. The Captain and eleven sailors appertaining to the crew, having taken refuge in a frail boat, without water and without means of subsistence, remained for three days in a most dreadful position, and it was when they had reached the culminating point of their suffering that they were met by an American vessel called Stag Hound. Captain Richardson, who was in command of said vessel, hastened to pick up these shipwrecked persons and supplied them with whatever clothing they wanted. He fed them on board his vessel during six weeks, and after landing them at Valparaiso, Captain Richardson positively refused to receive any pecuniary compensation whatever. The particulars of this act of humanity and disinterestedness have been communicated to the Emperor, and his Imperial Majesty has been pleased to authorize me, Mr. Secretary of State, to convey his thanks to Captain Richardson as well as to express his gratitude to that officer for the promptness with which he hastened to save and take care of these Russian sailors.

Having no knowledge of the place of residence of Captain Richardson, I venture to ask, Mr. Secretary of State, that you will make such inquiries as may be within your reach on the subject, and that you will cause to be forwarded to that brave sailor this mark of the kind appreciation which his Imperial Majesty entertains for an act which reflects so much honor on the Merchant Marine of the Union.

Be pleased to accept, Mr. Secretary of State, the assurance of my high consideration.

A. DE BODISCO

THE HONORABLE
DANIEL WEBSTER
Secretary of State

Josiah Richardson

The florid manner of this letter is in striking contrast with Captain Richardson's own account of the incident as entered in his log for Sunday, March 2d, 1851:

> Latter part squally with hail and rain, winds varying from N N W — N E in squalls. Took in studdingsails. At six A.M. discovered ahead small boat with 9 men in it Came up to it and they made a signal of distress. Took them on board. They said they were the Captain and crew of Russian brig Sylphide, loaded at Rio with coffee, bound to Helsingfors. Was upset in a squall four days previous; one man, the carpenter, was drowned.

After about a month in San Francisco, Captain Richardson set sail for Manilla on June 30, 1851, and arrived August 18. 'All well with tedious passage,' is his comment on this leg of the voyage. In a letter to his wife he is more particular:

> There is so much expected from clippers, unless a very extraordinary chance occurs, all are disappointed.... The sailing of clippers is attended with many extra cares and anxieties and of course not exempted from trouble. [In San Francisco] found friends of my early years at school. ... San Francisco must reform, break off from its iniquities, or God's curse will follow it.... My home to me is a very dear place; when away, it is business that calls me.

Three weeks in Manilla, this time, instead of four months, and the Stag Hound cleared for Hong Kong, arriving after a ten-days sail. The Captain writes cheerfully from Whampoa, September 26, 1851:

> Am happy to say, expect to sail from here from 6th to 10th Oct. for New York. Friend Howland, Sea Serpent, about the same time. Of course much anxiety will be felt and heavy bets made.[1] Time discloses the victor. Howland is very friendly and kind. Think very well of him and his family.... Have received letter from Messrs. Sampson & Tappan. They seem highly pleased that Stag Hound beat Eclipse, Sea Serpent, John Bertram... and

---

[1] The Sea Serpent was an extreme clipper. Though she was launched after the Stag Hound, she was the first to get away on her maiden voyage. Captain Richardson came up with her at Hong Kong.

all others since she has left New York. My cares are full as much as when in a smaller ship, but hope to get through with them all and deliver up my commission honorably to myself and satisfactory to my owners.... Am glad Sawtell has dug around the fruit trees.... If time will allow, shall have a painting of ship Stag Hound made here as a present for my wife, knowing you are so fond of paintings.

The Captain's next two weeks in China were hard ones. The Stag Hound became at once a center of interest, and he was almost worn out entertaining distinguished visitors on board. Here is what he writes to his wife:

CANTON, *October* 7, 1851

I am now nearly ready to sail for New York. Take steam tomorrow A.M. and tow all the way down to Macao. The Sea Serpent, Howland, sails in about three days. Of course there is much interest felt for the result of voyages. ... Nearly all of the Americans, English and French have visited the Stag Hound. The foreign Consuls — English, American — dined or taken tiffin on board.... You will know that in this climate, with all this company and my other duties, my cares are not light. I feel most worn down. It has been thus far far more a public station than was expected by me when I entered upon it. Thus far, as much and more than if she belonged to U.S. Gov't. The public say her equal never came into these waters. She is now all newly painted, gilt etc. Your painting of her looks well.... There is no quiet life here at all.... Am thin in flesh.

At the end of this letter Captain Richardson mentions the fact that he had on board $175 worth of presents for the family. Troubles he certainly had, but he was no longer obliged to bear them for nothing. It is also a pleasure to record that he did beat the Sea Serpent to New York by six days. Ten months and twenty-three days after she had sailed from New York, the Stag Hound arrived home, having, in the course of this voyage round the world, paid for the cost of building her and earned a profit of $80,000 besides. What so many had regarded as Donald McKay's dream had turned into the solid reality of dollars and cents. No wonder clipper ships were in demand!

Captain Richardson needed a vacation. He resigned his command and spent the next three months at home with his family. But talents such as his were not allowed to remain idle for long. Another of McKay's great clippers, the Staffordshire, wanted a commander. She was one of the few clipper ships to be built for the Liverpool packet trade, and she had been crossing the Atlantic between Boston and Liverpool for about a year, under the house flag of Enoch Train. McKay never believed in standing still: bigger and better was his watchword; so the Staffordshire measured 240 feet over all, as against the Stag Hound's 226, and was larger throughout in proportion. She was named for the English shire where the famous pottery was made that comprised a goodly portion of her westbound cargoes. On one side of her stern was carved an elaborate Staffordshire manufacturing scene; on the other appear Enoch Train's business offices at Lewis Wharf — hands across the sea at last; crossed swords would have been a likelier symbol a generation before. But the Atlantic Ocean was not a big enough cruising ground for such a ship as this. Train, who was tremendously proud of her, wanted not only to see what she would do on a trip round the world, but was also anxious to get his share of the fantastic freight rates to California. He invited Josiah Richardson to command her on this sweeping voyage. The Captain accepted, and on May 3, 1852, set sail from Boston for San Francisco with 120 passengers and a freight list thirteen feet long.

This was in more ways than one a triumphant voyage for Captain Richardson. In the first place, he had a fine chance to show his own skill as well as the sailing qualities of his ship, in a race with Captain Judah P. Baker, another Cape man who hailed from Brewster, and who cleared from Boston in the clipper ship

Shooting Star on the same day that Richardson did, both bound for San Francisco. The Shooting Star, though much smaller than the Staffordshire, was sharper and one of the fastest in her class. Both vessels had been launched the same year. Captain Baker was a veteran who had already distinguished himself in the clipper ship Flying Dragon and was a worthy rival for any shipmaster. It was a great race between mighty opposites. After upwards of three months at sea, the two vessels finished only four days apart, Captain Richardson arriving in San Francisco 101 days out, Captain Baker, 105. Richardson had left Boston on May 3; on June 30, Cape Horn was in sight; on July 17, the crew began bending the old, fair-weather sails again; on July 25, she crossed the Equator headed north; and on August 13 the crew furled sails off Clark's Point, San Francisco. Here was glory enough for the Centerville captain, but more was in store for him when he went ashore and looked over the shipping news, which he no sooner read than he sat down and retailed them in an exultant letter to his wife:

FRISCO, *August* 13, 1852

Have just arrived after a passage of 101 days, the shortest of the season thus far. Shooting Star and Flying Cloud not yet arrived.... Howland in Sea Serpent beat the Stag Hound out several days. Do you not think he felt comfortable? Do you think McKay will tell Sampson of it? It's what he told Sampson when I left the ship.... Now I feel that it has been best that I took command of Staffordshire. She is a magnificent ship, and I can accommodate better than in any other ship that I ever commanded.

The reference to 'accommodating' is significant. The passengers who had come out with Captain Richardson had not only found their quarters luxurious, but had also been so charmed with the Captain's courtesy that they presented him with a silver pitcher 'as a slight token of respect for the many kind attentions received at your hands and the high considera-

Josiah Richardson

tion we entertain for the able manner in which you have conducted us through a long and perilous voyage and one which we shall ever remember as a bright spot in our lives.' 'So you see,' writes the Captain, 'your old gentleman has not disgraced himself much by quarreling this time.' In another letter, dated August 21, he says, 'The Flying Cloud has not yet arrived; is now 99 days out; there is a possibility the Staffordshire may triumph over her as well as [over] the Shooting Star.' The possibility became a fact, for much to his chagrin, the redoubtable Perk Cressy did not drop anchor inside the Golden Gate until September 6, after what was for him and the Flying Cloud a long passage of 113 days.

Captain Richardson was cock of the walk along the San Francisco water-front, a position shrewdly calculated to test the qualities of any gentleman. The shipmaster of fiction — and a good many shipmasters of history as well — would have seized the opportunity for a bit of relaxation, a bottle or two of champagne, perhaps, with less fortunate brethren, to lend eloquence to the tales of their exploits. If Richardson had thus indulged himself, nobody could blame him, but it would have been out of keeping with what has been shown of his character. What he did was to yield to the importunities of some of his passengers and the Superintendent of a Sunday School, to address a group of children in a religious meeting. At the conclusion of his talk, 'they insisted,' to use his own language, 'that I must visit all the Sabbath Schools in San Francisco, but I tell them I cannot go to but one on the Sabbath; my time is so much taken up with business, cannot study Sabbath School speeches, though I rejoice to see the efforts they are making here to build them up. I have had most of the Rev. Gentlemen on board the Staffordshire.' Here is an anomaly, indeed! A clipper-ship captain beats the fleet round the Horn to California and spends what time he can spare from the ship's business in port, bringing the Word of God to

Shipmasters *of* Cape Cod

Sunday School children! What, one wonders, has become of the mythical swashbuckler of the quarterdeck, whose every word was an oath, and whose pastime was caving in the skulls of sailors with iron belaying pins?

From San Francisco Captain Richardson took the Staffordshire across the Pacific to Singapore and thence to Calcutta, where she became, like the Stag Hound in Hong Kong, an object of the greatest interest. Here the Captain enjoyed himself thoroughly, making the acquaintance of business men, statesmen, consuls, and children. Two letters to his wife give a good idea of how he passed the time that was not taken up with business:

> The Staffordshire is the largest ship ever entered the Hoogly.... Next week the ship will be thrown open for Ladies as our painting is nearly done.

And again a week later:

> They [the children of a family with whom he went to church] know me as the commander of the large American black ship, for most of the people have been on board.... I have the cards of many of the noblemen; they have visited the ship with the American consul. I expect to dine with them at their club tomorrow evening.... Have purchased your shawl for $112.... Shall get George a monkey if it lives to get home to him — will delight him more than any other thing would do.... Have purchased two scarfs for my two oldest boys at twenty rupees — say about $10.50 each. If they do not want them, they will sell at home for $20 each.... Your shawl in Boston would cost me... $150.... You know I pay no duty, as it is for my family use. They look in the distance like the cheap ones of $10, but on examination you see the difference.... I have not spent in all $5 since leaving Boston for myself. That was for clothing. You see I hope to make some money this voyage.

About a month after this letter, Captain Richardson left Calcutta for Boston, taking his departure on January 25, 1853. The Staffordshire had already, on

114

the first leg of her voyage round the world, established what was then probably a record from Cape Horn to San Francisco — thirty days from 50° South to port. And now, on the home stretch, the Captain hung up what was an indubitable record of 83 days between Calcutta and Boston — a passage, indeed, that has been shortened only three or four times since. This performance is good enough without trying to shorten it further, but a contemporary newspaper item shows that the Captain, if he had been a reckless driver instead of a skillful shipmaster, could have clipped another day off his time. During the last few days of the voyage, the weather had been so thick that it was impossible to take an observation. Captain Richardson was as sure of his position as a man can be when he is sailing by dead reckoning, and was convinced that another twenty-four hours on the same course would bring him off Boston Harbor. However, strong as the temptation was to hold on and make an even more spectacular passage, he resisted it and stood offshore again, only to find the next day that his reckoning had been right and that he could have fetched port twenty-four hours sooner if he had been willing to risk piling his vessel up on Cohasset rocks.

The peak of the California boom being past, Train now decided to put the Staffordshire back on the Liverpool run, with a view to selling her to the British if he could get a good price. This suited Captain Richardson's book nicely. He had determined to give up long voyages and see more of his family; passenger-carrying across the Atlantic was an old story to him; so he remained in command of his ship, which became, as soon as she appeared once more in the Mersey, the queen packet of her day. No one could have guessed, when looking at her powerful hull, which showed strength and speed in every line, that she was doomed the same year to go down in one of the great shipwrecks of history. The precise truth about the disaster will probably never be known. No doubt the account given to the Boston papers by her mate, Joseph Alden, is as accurate as any. Lovers of the supernatural, pointing to Captain Richardson's last letters from Liverpool, will say that if he had followed the presentiments of evil that appear in them, he would never have taken the ship to sea. The letters are indeed striking, not only because they are the last which his wife ever received from him, but also because they show that an unaccountable distaste for this passage had come upon him. A few extracts follow:

LIVERPOOL, *November* 1, 1853

Train and Co. have sent me power of attorney to sell the ship, and as regards price leave me to decide. Shall do all I can to sell her.

LIVERPOOL, *November* 11*th*, 1853

Should much prefer selling the ship and returning home in steamer.... The Autumn has been very severe; many accidents have occurred to the best ships and most able commanders.... I notice the Staffordshire is up for California as one of Glidden & Williams line. Think she will go on her return to Boston. You may be assured your husband will not go in her at any price. I told Col. Train when at home last, should not go in ship on another long voyage.

LIVERPOOL, *November* 18*th*, 1853

Wish I was with you and did not have to make the western passage.... Captain Hallett of the Queen of the West is here. He made nearly half the passage to N.Y. Got dismasted and put back. Ship Jacob Westervelt, Captain Hoodless, has also put back disabled, all boarding at Mrs. Blodget's.... I expect to have enough of winter before seeing Boston or you.... At table when ships is introduced in conversation, all sing out 'ship.'

Then comes the last letter:

LIVERPOOL, *December* 5, 1853

On the other side you will see my account current with owners of ship Staffordshire. In case of any accident to

Josiah Richardson

me, this will show you how my account stands with him.
Then he must credit me with wages, $30 a month from
September 10th, and 5% primage on Freight from St.
John to Liverpool and 5% on Freight from Liverpool to
Boston. Freight to Boston £2874.16.7. Life is uncertain,
we both know, and all the property I possess I wish my
dear wife and children to have and enjoy.... We have the
greatest amount of freight on board ever taken from
Liverpool to Boston... about double the amount we had
when you was with me.

And two days later, on the same sheet:

Wednesday December 7th

My dear, expect to sail in the morning for Boston — all
well — have only 180 Passengers — no letters from you.
with affection
JOSIAH RICHARDSON

During the first part of the passage, the Staffordshire did well, having left the Grand Banks astern
twelve days out from Liverpool. Then the trouble began. The account which follows is that which Joseph
Alden, the first mate, gave to the *Boston Journal* for
January 17, 1854:

On the 23rd Dec. in a tremendous gale, the rudder-head
was twisted and we secured it with chains as well as we
could. We rigged a temporary tiller outside the ship and
with it managed to proceed pretty comfortably until
Wednesday four A.M., the 28th, when in a gale we lost the
bowsprit, foretopmast, fore yard and everything forward,
leaving the foremast only standing. The wreck of the
spars in floating astern carried away the temporary rudder with it. Captain Richardson went aloft after daylight
to examine the truss to see if it were practicable to rig
another fore yard, and in coming down his foot slipped
and he fell 35 feet and struck on his back, badly injuring
his ankle and receiving other serious injury. I immediately, with assistance, bore him to his stateroom where he
received attention from Dr. Maloney, the ship's surgeon.
I then cleared the wreck and made all snug as possible
and prepared to get a new fore yard aloft. The rudder

then was perfectly useless; the ship had no steerage way. We worked all Wednesday night and succeeded in rigging another tiller in the cabin. At 3 A.M., Thursday the 29th, wind from the East, heavy rain and blowing heavy. We run the ship all day Thursday on her course until 7 P.M. The barometer was very low — 28.46. We made all snug for the night. At 8 P.M. came on a hurricane from the N.W. At that time we judged ourselves 35–40 miles south of Seal Island. I consulted with Captain Richardson (who was confined to his berth) who ordered the ship to be kept to the northward until 12 o'clock, and then to wear ship. It was then the second mate's watch on deck, who was ordered to call me at 12 o'clock.

At ten minutes before 12, the second mate saw Seal Island Light and immediately called me. I at once informed Captain Richardson, who remarked that the current had set the ship in shore and immediately ordered her to be wore around. This was done without loss of time, and when coming up on the southern tack, the ship struck. It was then blowing a tremendous gale of wind with snow and very thick. The rigging and decks were covered with ice. The ship struck several times and then went off into deep water. I immediately sounded the pumps and found 14 inches. I informed Captain Richardson and set all hands at the pumps. Sounded pumps again in 10 minutes and found 4 feet of water in the hold. I got her head to the eastward, by the Captain's orders, and intended to beach her. In 20 minutes after, the wheel ropes parted and she came up into the wind. Then all chances of saving the ship were lost, and measures were taken to save the lives. The 4th mate, Stephenson, previous to this had left the ship, with nine sailors and one woman passenger in one of the quarter boats. The other quarter boat was swamped in launching and was immediately cut away to launch the other boats. We got the small life boat out. At that time the ship was settling fast and the sea coming in over both rails. I told them to launch this boat and save what they could, and nine or ten reached shore in her, after having two planks stove while alongside of the ship, before they could get clear. None of the mates were in this boat. The small boat was instantly put up on the starboard davits and was instantaneously filled with people; in lowering her to the water she stove a hole in her and was hoisted up again. The long boat was then launched to the side with very great difficulty, and thirteen men, including the 2nd mate, jumped into her.

While they were launching her, I went to the cabin for the third time to endeavor to save Captain Richardson and told him that all hopes of saving the ship were gone, her lower hold being full, and six inches of water in the cabin, and offered to carry him in my arms and put him in the boat. He refused, saying the ship was so near the shore she would strike before she could go down. I then said, 'It is impossible, for she will sink in a very few minutes.' The Captain answered, 'Then if I am to be lost, God's will be done,' which were the last words I heard. Finding it impossible to move him, I then left the cabin, and found the long boat was just leaving. I threw my big coat into her as she was leaving the ship. I went aft and the boat came to under the stern, when I jumped from the taffrail into the boat. We immediately got clear of the ship to prevent being drawn in when she should go down. We had only two small oars and no tholepins. The wind was blowing very heavy, as before, with snow. We saw the ship and lights for about twenty minutes, and then all was darkness.

We shipped a sea and filled the boat half full of water. We kept her off before the wind and sea till she was bailed out. Then we came up to the wind and remained till daylight, thinking to save lives if any were still above water. Not a stroke was pulled till daylight, when nothing was in sight. We laid still another hour, when we discovered land. We pulled for it and landed in about ten hours after leaving the ship, all exhausted and more or less frostbitten. The other two boats had landed about 4 hours previous. We were about 9 miles from Barrington on a small Island called Sable Island. We were very kindly treated by the fishermen and their wives, and next day I proceeded to Barrington. Before leaving Barrington for Halifax, I went back to where we landed to see that the crew were provided for and found that parts of the wreck had drifted ashore — the cabin-work, houses on the upper deck etc. I left the crew and five passengers who were saved as comfortable as circumstances would allow, and proceeded to Halifax, thence to St. John's, where I missed the steamer about 5 hours. I then came on to Waterville by stage and took the cars there for Boston.

So much for the mate's own version of the tragedy. It is no doubt substantially correct. But the final disaster seems to have been caused by Mr. Alden's inability to make the crew carry out orders which he had received from Captain Richardson. The Staffordshire in a North Atlantic gale was too big a command for the mate. Only men of the first magnitude, strong enough to control a panic-stricken crew and brave enough to turn disaster into victory, were fit to command the great clippers of the fifties. Such a man was Josiah Richardson. When he went down with his ship, the country lost a great captain and a courageous gentleman.

6

The Liverpool Packets

THE career of Captain Richardson presents a bird's-
eye view of the kinds of voyages on which the highest
type of American shipmaster was embarking between
1830 and 1850: general European trade; passenger-
carrying between Liverpool and the United States;
East India and China voyages; and driving clippers
round the world by way of California. There was
lively work in all these branches of trade, and Richardson was not the only man who tried more than one of
them. The general European traders, the East Indiamen, and the clippers will be dealt with later, each in
a section of its own; the present chapter will occupy
itself with the stormy routine of the Liverpool packets.

Enough has already been said to show the grueling
character of this business: stormy passages; hard driving, nicely balanced against safety; and unremitting
vigilance over the wildest crews that ever sailed under
the flag of a civilized nation. No sunny weeks in the
balmy trades relieved the tension of command for the
captain of a Liverpool packet ship; no thousand-mile
runs with all sail set and not a reef to be taken or a sail
furled. Summer and winter, storm and shine, schedules
must be followed and passengers kept happy. Such was
the life of the captains of these ships, a life of care and
anxiety that would have worn out any who were not
men of iron, and that called for such suavity as was

the heritage of only the most genteel. Not only must crossings be quick in order to please passengers, but in order to beat rivals as well, for between 1820 and 1845, ten or a dozen packet lines sprang into being in Boston and New York, each trying to outdo the others and as eager to publish its own triumphs as to gloat over the failures of its opponents.

In New York there were the Red and the Black Star Lines; the Swallow Tail, the Black Cross, the Red Cross, the famous Black Ballers, and, of particular interest to Cape men, the Dramatic and the Collins Lines. From Boston sailed the ships of the Jewel Line, operated by the Boston–Liverpool Packet Company, and the White Diamond liners of Enoch Train. All of these were on the lookout for captains who were the aristocrats of their profession — skillful, courteous, and brave; and a goodly proportion of those whom they selected came from Cape Cod. Captains Watson Chadwick and Rowland R. Crocker hailed from Falmouth. From Sandwich, never so prolific of sailors as the rest of the Cape, came Ezra Nye, one of the finest of them all. The Bursley brothers, Ira and Allen, were Barnstable men. Allen H. Knowles, Franklin Hallett, and the three Eldridge brothers — John, Asa and Oliver — all hailed from Yarmouth. Jabez Howes represented Dennis; and John Collins was born among the rolling hills of Truro.

Though all these men, and more whose names are forgotten, distinguished themselves as commanders in the packet trade, it is impossible at this late date to do justice to them all. Too much that is picturesque and important in their lives has been lost or forgotten. Captain Rowland Crocker, for example, a few years before his death, wrote an account of some of his experiences, entitled 'A statement of cases of distress wherein R. R. Crocker was the instrument of a kind Providence in saving thirty-two fellow beings from a watery grave.' But the manuscript was never printed, and what has become of it in the course of the last eighty years, nobody knows. Its loss is the more serious because Crocker was among the earlier packet captains, and his narrative must have presented, amongst other things, a good picture of trans-Atlantic travel about 1820. He gave up seafaring in 1833 to go into business and politics on shore; but neither business nor politics was new to him, for every shipmaster had to be a business man as a matter of course, and as for politics, the Captain had lived in France for a year or so in 1798, when relations between the two countries were at the breaking point and a state of war, though undeclared, actually existed at sea. The Captain's sojourn in France was not, as a matter of fact, an entirely voluntary one. He had commanded a letter-of-marque in which he had gone through an engagement with a Frenchman, in the course of which a musket ball had passed through his body, putting him out of the running for the moment. His mate surrendered, and the Captain's sojourn in France began. Though nominally a prisoner, he was granted almost complete liberty and he made the most of it, his great moment coming when he was presented to Napoleon and shook him by the hand.

When the trouble between the two countries was settled, Crocker for the first time went into the merchant service, and in 1807, while in command of the ship Otis, he saved his vessel and cargo by taking her, half-wrecked, through a gale into Dover Harbor. The maneuver was a particularly difficult one. The Otis had been lying at anchor in the Downs in the midst of a lot of shipping, and a gale had come up which blew her down on a frigate moored near-by. Before the two vessels could get clear of each other, serious damage had been done. The pilot of the Otis and most of the crew, believing that she was doomed, went ashore in the longboat; but the Captain, aided by the loyal members of the crew, got some sail on her, and brought her, crippled as she was, through the gale into Dover. For this exploit the underwriters presented him with a silver cup bearing the inscription, 'Forti et fideli nil difficile.' Quite as pleasing to Captain Crocker, it may be, was the sum of £500 which accompanied the Latin dictum: a generous tribute, to be sure, but not excessive if the report is true that the cargo of the Otis was worth half a million dollars.

This episode shows something of the mettle of Captain Crocker — a resourceful and determined commander, with a year or two of French polish on the side. Here were precisely the qualifications for the captain of a Liverpool packet; it was therefore entirely natural that his next move should be from the quarter-deck of a general merchantman to the quarter-decks of packet ships out of New York. 'In this difficult service,' says a contemporary newspaper, 'his urbane and gentlemanly manners, his interesting and varied conversation, his care for the comfort of those under his charge, and his humanity to all in suffering or want were as proverbial as was his skill as a mariner.' These encomiums, though gratifying, remain vague. It would be pleasant to know what ships he commanded and what luck he had in making fast passages; but, beyond the fact that he crossed the Atlantic 165 times without losing a vessel, no detailed information is available. After he retired, he went into the insurance business in New Bedford, and soon after was elected to the House of Representatives — two branches of activity which kept him comfortably occupied until his death in the winter of 1851–52.

Captain Ezra Nye, the next Cape man to distinguish himself in the Liverpool packet service, was not only the most celebrated shipmaster that Sandwich ever produced, but was a great figure even among the lordly aristocrats of the packet trade. He first made a name for himself in 1829 — four years before Captain Crocker retired — when he drove the Jewel liner Amethyst westward from Liverpool to Boston in twenty days. This passage, and his general reputation for carrying sail, placed Captain Nye so high in his

profession that four years later, when the new ship Independence was launched for the Swallow Tail Line in
New York, he was given command of her.

The Independence was one of the largest of the new
packets, 140 feet long, and under Captain Nye she became one of the most celebrated as well. For several
years he carried the President's messages in her to
England and in 1836 made the round trip from New
York to Liverpool and back in the record time of 34
sailing days. Both halves of this voyage were fast, but
the eastward passage — fourteen days and twelve
hours — was particularly remarkable in view of the
fact that the record for the course, made almost twenty
years later by Captain Asa Eldridge in the extreme
clipper Red Jacket, was only a day and a half better.
Some idea of Captain Nye's qualities as a carrier of
sail may be reached by a comparison of the two ships:
140 feet for the Independence, as compared with the
Red Jacket's 260, to say nothing of the latter's fine
clipper lines as against the full-bodied hull of Captain
Nye's packet. Obviously the statement made by a recent authority that he 'had a strong predilection for
carrying sail' is no exaggeration.

Captain Nye stayed in the Independence throughout the thirties, continuing to make fast passages.
Then, finding that his services were more and more
in demand, he left the big house that he had built in
Sandwich and moved with his wife to Baltimore to be
nearer his ships. His foresight was rewarded. In 1845
Brown and Bell launched for Grinnell and Minturn, of
New York, the Henry Clay, one of the biggest merchantmen of her day and a sensation in shipping circles. Nye was given command on her maiden voyage,
and during the next few years went through varied experiences in her. A memorable gale in December, 1846,
drove him on a New Jersey beach, but he got off again
with the loss of six men and finished his voyage to New
York. A pleasanter event was his entertaining Lord
William Lennox on board in Liverpool two years

later. 'Here,' writes Lennox, 'are some splendid American liners. I went on board the Henry Clay of New York, and received the greatest attention from her commander, Captain Ezra Nye. Nothing can excel the beauty of this ship; she is quite a model for a frigate. Her accommodations are superior to any sailing vessel I ever saw.'

The Henry Clay was the last sailing vessel that Captain Nye commanded. With the same progressive spirit that had brought him steadily up from the little Amethyst, twenty years before, to the command of the magnificent Henry Clay, the last word in sailing packets, the Captain now decided to have a go at steam. E. K. Collins had started his famous line of steam packets as a challenge to the British Cunarders, and had named them, with proper expansiveness, for the oceans of the world. The newest of them, the Pacific, he gave to Captain Nye, and the Captain, in May, 1851, as if to show that his record-breaking days were not over, took her across the Atlantic from New York to Liverpool in nine days, twenty hours, and sixteen minutes — the first time that a ship of any description had made the passage in less than ten days.

But Captain Nye was never in too great a hurry to help other ships in distress. A little more than a year after his great run in the Pacific, he fell in with the crippled British bark Jessie Stephens, that was going to pieces spar by spar in a high sea in mid-Atlantic. Captain Nye hove to until all the passengers and crew of the wrecked vessel had been transferred to safety on the Pacific, a performance for which Queen Victoria presented him with a medal and a gold chronometer. On another occasion, the great actress Rachel tried to get passage to New York with Captain Nye, but she applied too late; not a stateroom was left. When the Captain learned of it, he turned over his own cabin to her and received from her hands in gratitude 'an eagle pin studded with gems.'

In his middle fifties, Captain Nye decided that he

THE S.S. PACIFIC RESCUING THE CREW OF THE BRITISH BARK
JESSIE STEPHENS, 1852

had been at sea long enough. For a quarter of a century he had commanded Liverpool packets and had hung up records in both sail and steam. He retired from command a few years after his record in the Pacific and moved to Newark, where he was as busy for the rest of his life in owning and managing vessels as he had previously been in sailing them. But business did not drive from his mind thoughts of his less fortunate relatives in Sandwich. When he learned that a gale had blown down his brother Joseph's barn, he promptly mailed him a check to help pay for a new one, with the incisive comment, 'You must have a barn.' He also paid for the education of Joseph's children and followed their progress with deep interest. At his death, which occurred in 1866, flags in Newark were flown at half-mast while the cortège passed through the city. Among the pallbearers were Captain William C. Thompson, the Honorable Henry Grinnell, Captain Russell Sturgis, and A. A. Low — as distinguished a group of shipowners and captains as could have been found in the country.

Edward K. Collins, in whose steamer, Pacific, Captain Nye had set so high a standard for trans-Atlantic passenger-carriers, was a spectacular figure in New York shipping, the most picturesque, perhaps, of all the Yankee merchants who did so much for the prosperity of New York, and he is of particular interest to this history because he was born in Truro. When he was fifteen, he left the Cape for New York, worked as a clerk in a counting-house, and learned the shipping business by making voyages as supercargo. By 1825 he was managing a line of packets between New York and Vera Cruz, and five years later had control of some New Orleans packets as well. In 1836, deciding to join the crowd in the Liverpool passenger trade, he started the Dramatic Line, and named his vessels after eminent actors — Roscius, Siddons, Sheridan, and Garrick. A smaller ship, the Shakespeare, he already owned.

Newspapers of the fifties declared, perhaps with as much rhetoric as truth, that these ships 'were to the ordinary packets of the day what McKay's monster clippers are now to them.' They were, according to the same authority, 'the pride of New York and the marvel of Liverpool.' At any rate, they paid, and were such fine-looking ships that a Spanish naval officer who was sent to New York in 1841 to place a contract for two men-of-war for his Government, and who saw the Siddons, outward-bound, declared that his problem was solved: the man whose genius had conceived so handsome a ship was the man for him. Collins, in fact, was no shipbuilder; but he gladly agreed to direct the construction of the two warships for the visitor — a courtesy which was duly acknowledged by the Spanish Government when the vessels were completed.

As Cutler has pointed out in his *Greyhounds of the Sea*, an accident had brought about the change in design which distinguished the new Dramatic liners from their predecessors. Collins's trade with New Orleans demanded something approaching a flat-bottomed vessel, for the entrance to the Mississippi River had silted up until only shallow-draught ships could get in and out. One of Collins's captains, the celebrated Nat Palmer, in bringing the Huntsville, a flat-floored craft of this type, up from New Orleans, found to his surprise that the design of her underbody, instead of slowing her up, helped her to slip through the water faster than the usual V-bottomed ships. Collins wisely consulted Captain Palmer when he began to think of his new Liverpool line, and Palmer enthusiastically agreed to supervise the construction of the vessels. He gave all of them the flat floor of the New Orleans cotton-carriers, and all of them began to break records.

The first three Dramatic liners to be launched were the Garrick and the Sheridan in 1836, and the Siddons the next year. The even excellence of their perform-

The Liverpool Packets

ance encouraged Collins to go them one better in building his next ship, the Roscius, which, when she left the stocks in 1839, was the largest American merchantman afloat. Her mainmast was almost 160 feet tall and carried a main yard 75 feet long. She cost $100,000, but more than paid for herself by her fast runs and by the great amount of cargo that she could carry. She became, on her own merits, the flagship of the fleet.

Naturally enough, Collins wanted the best captains he could find to command these new ships, and, himself a Cape man, he looked to the Cape to produce them. They were forthcoming — his own uncle, John Collins, of Truro, among the first. It must not be supposed, of course, that a business man like Collins would entrust a new command to an uncle simply because he came from the Cape or because blood is thicker than water. Captain John had a long seafaring career behind him — much of it under the eye of his nephew. He had shipped before the mast as a lad of fifteen; had been a blockade-runner during the War of 1812; had been captured afterwards by the British while he was in command of a privateer, and had emerged from a British prison at the end of the war, wiser than before, but no less ambitious. After Captain John had spent ten years in the Mexican trade, Edward Collins gave him command of the Shakespeare, in which he did so well, both in carrying cotton and rice from New Orleans to New York and in carrying passengers from New York to Liverpool, that his nephew, about 1840, promoted him to the Roscius.

During the years that followed, the Captain was hard at work crossing and recrossing the Western Ocean, always eager for quick passages but, like Nye, always ready to heave to and assist vessels in distress. The Humane Societies of London and of Liverpool, the British Government, and his own countrymen, all, at one time or another, presented him with the traditional silver services or with gold medals for rescues at sea, notably those of the English bark Scotia and the Erin go Bragh. But more dramatic than either of these was his rescue of the crew of the wrecked Truro fishing schooner Garnet, Captain Joshua Knowles, off the Georges after the great gale of October, 1841. The Roscius, on her way to New York from Liverpool, was some two hundred miles off the Highlands of Neversink just before sunset on October 5; her lookout saw a schooner, almost awash, with a couple of patches of canvas set on the stump of her foremast, flying a distress signal. Captain Collins changed his course to bring him within hailing distance, and asked Captain Knowles what assistance he could give. Knowles replied that he had determined to abandon his vessel. A quarter boat from the Roscius came alongside, taking most of the crew and luggage on the first trip. While she was returning for the second load, Captain Knowles scuttled his schooner and stepped aboard the boat. His surprise on finding that his rescuer was John Collins, not only a fellow townsman and formerly his nearest neighbor in Truro, but also a connection by marriage, may be imagined. Inasmuch as one of the mates of the Roscius, Joshua Caleb Paine, was also a Truro man, the rescue must have developed into something very like a Truro old home week on salt water.

But just as he had outgrown his Vera Cruz and New Orleans packets and started the Dramatic Line, so now E. K. Collins, tired of his sailing ships and unable any longer to watch the Cunard steamers splash back and forth between Liverpool and New York unchallenged, decided to beat them at their own game by starting a line of steam packets that should eclipse them in speed, size, and comfort.

It was an ambitious and a patriotic undertaking. Cunarders had been running regularly and successfully for ten years, basking in the sunshine of generous subsidies from the Crown. But this was no deterrent to the sanguine ambition of Edward Collins. In 1846 he advertised the Dramatic Line for sale; in 1847 he signed a contract for carrying the mail in the steamers that he intended to build, though the terms of the Government were neither generous nor easy; and in 1850 the first of his new ships steamed out of New York. Congress agreed to pay him $385,000 a year for carrying the mail twice a month for eight months of the year, and once a month for the remaining four, and stipulated that the new ships should be of at least 2000 tons — 500 tons larger than the average Cunarder.

Though the mail subsidy was far less than the British were paying — smaller even than they had paid Cunard when he started ten years before — Collins was content. Instead of sticking to the letter of his contract, indeed, and producing 2000-ton vessels, he ordered from the finest steamship builders in the country four steamers such as no man had ever seen before, the smallest of them measuring 700 tons more than the terms of the Government demanded. The Arctic, 2856 tons, and the Atlantic, 2845 tons, were designed by the celebrated George Steers and built by William Brown; the Baltic and the Pacific, about 100 tons smaller, were launched from the yard of Brown and Bell. All four were about 280 feet long on the main deck, and like all good things, they cost much more than had been expected — $675,000 apiece; but they were worth it — the exuberant offspring of a young and lusty nation. Their frames were re-enforced with iron strapping; their planking was hard pine, copper-fastened below the water-line, and bolted above with galvanized iron. Throughout they were heavier and more strongly built than contemporary frigates; indeed, a few days' work would have transformed them into first-class men-of-war.

The luxuriousness of their accommodations matched the strength of their timbers. The dining-saloon of the Atlantic, for example, measured 60 feet by 12, and the lounge 67 feet by 20. She was steam-heated, her cabin decks were heavily carpeted, and she was finished in white holly, satinwood and rosewood, the effect being, in the language of a contemporary admirer, both 'chaste and beautiful.' But the beauty, it must be confessed, began and ended inside, for the Collins liners were ugly vessels to look at from without. The graceful clipper bow and bowsprit had gone, giving place to the straight wedge-shaped prow of the modern steamship. The smooth run aft, that made contemporary sailing vessels things of beauty, was broken by clumsy paddle-boxes; three stumpy masts, the first square-rigged, the after two schooner-rigged, made these steamships look like bastard barkentines. But beauty was not what Collins was looking for. He wanted speed and size and comfort, and he had achieved them all in these great vessels. All four made their first trips during the year 1850 and they averaged 10 days, 21 hours, for their eastward runs and 11 days, 3 hours, westward — about a day faster each way than the Cunarders.

Collins was content. So were the citizens of New York. In their opinion, Collins, thanks to his 'energy, talent, and enterprise,' had created a line of steamers which 'surpassed all competitors in speed, elegance, and comfort.' At a banquet held in his honor, a group of New York merchants presented him with a silver and gold tea service valued at $8000, inscribed as follows:

> This service of plate is presented by the citizens of New York to Edward K. Collins, in testimony of the public sense of the great honor and advantage which have been conferred upon the city and the whole country through his energy and perseverance in the successful establishment of an American Line of Trans-Atlantic Steamers. — August 1851.

Truro had a son to be proud of.

Captain John Collins, meanwhile, following his nephew's suggestion, had given up the sea in order to help in directing the shore end of the new enterprise, particularly the construction of the vessels themselves, and a large measure of their success was owing to his expert supervision. The two made a strong team: Edward, who, though he had never commanded a ship, was master of all the complexities of owning and managing them, and John, who after thirty-five years at sea in every capacity from foremast hand to captain, was an authority on the more technical side of the business.

But Captain John's retirement from command did not remove Cape men from the quarter-decks of Collins liners, for Captain Asa Eldridge, of Yarmouth, who had already commanded the old Roscius, now accepted an invitation to command the Pacific. For five years all went well. The Collins steamers in 1852 carried four passengers for every three that booked on the Cunarders. Shippers who were in a hurry sent their freight by a Collins liner, and the mail subsidy, which Congress had more than doubled after the success of the venture was demonstrated, helped through the lean months of winter.

Then came the three disastrous years from 1854 to 1857. First the Arctic, the largest ship of the fleet, was rammed in a fog by a Frenchman, sixty miles off Newfoundland, and went to the bottom with all hands in a desperate attempt to reach the shore. Edward Collins's wife and child were on board and were lost with the rest. The disaster plunged the whole eastern seaboard in gloom and brought the dangers of the packet service more poignantly than ever to the minds of all thoughtful people. Mrs. Ezra Nye, in writing to her sister about the tragedy, voices the anxiety that must have lain heavily on the hearts of hundreds of wives of shipmasters:

> I have learned to keep my anxious feelings to myself [she says] and hide an aching heart under a cheerful face, but I think I shall watch for my husband's arrival with more nervousness than I ever did. People say to me, 'You

have become so accustomed to parting you do not feel it so much.' But what good does it do to lay bare your troubles to the world? I say it to you, Lucy, if I had my life to live over again and my choice between the bare necessities of existence and such anxious hours and bitter partings, I would be content with one meal a day.

Collins, like all wise men, found solace in work. Six months after the Arctic went down, he launched a new ship, the Adriatic, to take her place — the largest and most expensive of them all — and four steamers still sailed under the flag of the Collins Line. But the end of his troubles had not yet arrived. In January, 1856, the Pacific met a mysterious fate somewhere in the North Atlantic. She, too, under the command of Captain Asa Eldridge, was west-bound from Liverpool, but never reached New York. What her end was no one can say. Some believed that she struck an iceberg; others that she burst a boiler; but speculation is idle; the truth will never be known. Captain Eldridge was as able a commander in both sail and steam as ever crossed the Western Ocean. His loss took from the country one of its finest shipmasters, and from Yarmouth one of the sons of whom the town was proudest.

The effect of this second disaster on Mr. Collins may be imagined. Half his original fleet was gone; his wife and child were dead; yet these misfortunes would not have conquered had not a more insidious blow followed. In 1856, a few months after the Pacific was lost, Congress, yielding to the oratory of the less intelligent Senators from the cotton and corn belts, withdrew more than half of the mail subsidy that the Line had been receiving. This move might or might not be a prelude to further hostile legislation; nobody knew, but to owners of steamships it looked like the writing on the wall. Collins had handled Congressmen before, however, and undoubtedly would have tried it again, had not the mainstay of his business and the sharer of his worries been taken from him the very next year by the death of Captain John. It was too much: his wife

CAPTAIN ASA ELDRIDGE

and son gone, half his ships sunk, his subsidy withdrawn, and his partner dead, Edward Collins, who with fairer fortunes would have kept the Stars and Stripes flying higher than the Union Jack in Atlantic steam, yielded to such a combination of misfortunes as few men have been called upon to face. The year after the death of Captain John, he sold his ships and retired to his home in Brooklyn, where he died in 1878, just twenty years after the death of his Line.

While Asa Eldridge was commanding Collins liners, his older brother John was in command of the Liverpool, of the Swallow Tail Line, and with him as mate was his brother Oliver, youngest of the three. John Eldridge was, in fact, a Herculean figure even among the hardy brotherhood of the Western Ocean. He weighed upwards of two hundred pounds, and had a voice that could be heard from the Yarmouth shore to the Sandy Neck Lighthouse. With the head and brow of a Gladstone and the physique of a professional wrestler, he presented a figure before whom the toughest crew of packet rats might well stand in awe. Even unregenerate Yankee foremast hands, in talking reminiscently of their livelier years, refer to John Eldridge as 'that old devil that lived over in Yarmouth.' Captain George Matthews, a fellow townsman, who sailed under him, said that he was very strict but very kind.

On one occasion, so the story goes, Captain Eldridge tilted an 1800-pound hogshead of tobacco to his thighs and lifted it clear of the deck, with no ropes or straps to help him; at another time he up-ended a hogshead of molasses with two fingers. A livelier example of his prowess occurred once while he and Oliver were taking in cargo at Mobile. A strike of some sort was on among the stevedores, and it was thought to be unsafe for ship's officers to venture ashore unarmed. But Captain Eldridge had business on shore and started off, with nothing more formidable than his hands in his pockets. Oliver, feeling uneasy, decided to follow him, and it was he who afterwards told what happened. Before Captain John had gone far, a gang of thugs began to form round him, one big fellow blocking the way in front, and the rest sneaking up behind. The Captain ordered the big chap out of the way; and when he refused to move, he grabbed the man by the scruff of his neck and the seat of his trousers before the others could close in from behind, slung him over his shoulder like a bag of meal, digging a thumb into his neck from time to time to keep him quiet, and carried him to the police station, unmolested by the rest of the gang and unaided by Oliver.

That Captain Eldridge handled his vessels as competently as he did gangs of thugs appeared while he was taking the Liverpool across the Atlantic in May, 1846. About halfway across he met the dismasted bark Espindola. He hailed the wreck and learned that the morning before, while under full sail with light northerly airs, she had been struck by a whirlwind and lost all three masts. She had four hundred steerage passengers bound for New York and she needed spars and provisions. Captain Eldridge braced up his yards and ran the Liverpool close-hauled for three miles while spare spars were being got out and lashed alongside and provisions packed for trans-shipping. He then ran back and lay to windward of the wreck, as close as he dared, for there was a high sea running. A picked crew under command of the mate manned a lifeboat and pulled toward the Espindola, the mate holding a light line which was made fast to a Manilla rope that held the spare spars. As soon as the boat was near enough to the wreck, the lashings of the spars were cut so as to let them drift down toward the Espindola. The mate backed his lifeboat close under the bows of the wreck, and, watching his chance, jumped into the chains and climbed aboard with his line. The rest was easy. The spars and provisions were hauled on board, the mate jumped back into the lifeboat, and, three hours after she had hailed the Espin-

The Liverpool Packets

dola, the Liverpool was back on her course. The mate who performed the ticklish maneuver so smartly was not Oliver, for Oliver was at the time commanding his own ships in the China trade. But whoever he was, he bore testimony to the excellence of his training in seamanship under the dominant eye of Captain Eldridge.

It is not to be expected, of course, that Cape men could continue to sail to and fro across the Atlantic in fair weather and foul without themselves coming to grief on occasion. The tragic fate of Captain Josiah Richardson in the Staffordshire and of Captain Asa Eldridge in the Pacific has already been cited, but they were not the first or the last men of Cape Cod to go to their graves in the Liverpool packet service. One of the early victims was Captain Allen Bursley, of Barnstable. In February, 1835, while master of the ship Lion, he was beating out of the North Channel in a sleet storm, homeward-bound from Liverpool for Boston. He had got as far as the granite cliffs that line the coast at Port Patrick in Scotland, where even on the calmest days a high surf pounds in from the Atlantic. On a winter's night like this, with a gale of wind flattening the sleet into planes of flying ice, the grimness of the spot may be imagined. Today a lighthouse marks the cliffs, but none was there in 1835, when Captain Bursley was beating his way past them. In the darkness he stood in too close; before he could claw off, the Lion was caught in the surf and struck at the foot of the cliff.

On the moors above lived a Scotch shepherd named Crawford. On the night of the wreck, some of his family were awakened by the barking of their sheepdog. Crawford and some others got up and followed the dog to the edge of the cliffs. Below they could just see a ship pounding to pieces against the rocks. Shipwrecks were nothing new on that coast. The men hurried back for ropes, leaving the women of the family to wave lanterns to cheer those on board, but in fifteen minutes, when the men returned, the Lion had

137

gone down in sixty fathoms. The next morning nothing but wreckage was left to tell the tale; but three days later one of Crawford's shepherds saw what he took to be the bodies of men caught on a rock at the foot of the cliff. Men were lowered over the edge on ropes and found eight bodies entangled in the remnants of a sail, one of them being identified by means of a ring as Captain Allen Bursley, master of the wrecked ship. The women of the neighborhood sewed shrouds for the corpses, and they were buried in a graveyard near-by, close to a little church that is to-day in ruins.

Captain Bursley came from a seafaring family, four of the six brothers being shipmasters: Samuel, Ira, Allen, and Isaac. Another brother, David, was a distinguished local figure, and for years Sheriff of Barnstable County. At least one of the brothers besides Allen commanded Liverpool packets; he was Captain Ira — second oldest of the family — and he kept at it for more than twenty years, beginning about 1827 as master of the Dover, and winding up in 1850 in the Hottinger, of the Swallow Tail Line, the same company for which Captain John Eldridge sailed the Liverpool.

But before he entered the packet trade at all, Captain Bursley was a full-fledged master mariner, having brought one of Daniel C. Bacon's ships from Calcutta to Boston when he was twenty years old. In the packet service, after leaving the Dover, he sailed chiefly for the Black Ball and Swallow Tail Lines, commanding the Silas Richards about 1830, then the Orpheus, and later the Cambridge, which he saved from loss in Liverpool during the great gale of January 7, 1839. The storm was of such violence that the English coast was strewn with wrecks, and three New York packets were driven ashore in the Mersey. The Cambridge, when the gale began, was anchored in the stream off her dock, but no anchors could hold in such a blow; the ship dragged nearer and nearer to the granite dock.

The Liverpool Packets

Captain Bursley hung bales of hay over her side as buffers and nailed a huge placard on her stern, bearing the announcement: '£1000 for anyone who will bring me a steamer to take my ship into the stream.' Nobody volunteered; but the Captain's exertions were rewarded. When the Cambridge was a few feet from destruction, her anchors held, and the vessel and her $300,000 cargo were saved. As soon as the gale was over, Bursley set sail for New York and was the first to bring news of the storm to this country.

The Captain ended his career eleven years later in the Hottinger under peculiarly tragic circumstances. Like his brother Allen, he was outward-bound from Liverpool. The Hottinger had cleared on January 10, 1850, with a full freight but only a handful of passengers, twenty-nine in all. Before daylight on the morning of the 12th, she struck on a ledge near Blackwater Bank, off the Irish Coast. The passengers, among whom was the Captain's son, Ira, Jr., were taken off by the coast guard, aided by a volunteer crew that put off from the shore in another boat. With them went about half the crew of the Hottinger. But Captain Bursley, believing that there was an off-chance of saving the ship, stayed on board with a dozen men, though the hold was nearly full of water and the seas were making a clean breach over her. He sent his son Ira ashore with the rest of the passengers, saying, 'Return to your mother that you may comfort her. I shall stick by the ship.'

The next morning the Hottinger floated off, but immediately struck again on the Arklow bank, where she went to pieces. Captain Bursley and all but one of his crew were lost. The cause of the wreck remains a mystery. None knew the Irish Channel better than the Captain, and he had often taken his ship through it in worse weather. Young Ira reached home *via* Halifax and stayed ashore for the rest of his life, but a nephew of the Captain's, Ira Bursley, 2d, also of Barnstable, following the family tradition, went to sea and distinguished himself in command of clipper ships.

These two disasters, with the loss of the Stafford-shire and the Pacific, give some notion of the rigors of the packet service. Other captains, though they were not wrecked, pulled through by the closest of margins. Josiah Richardson, while loading in Liverpool for his last voyage, speaks of Captain Franklin Hallett, of Yarmouth, whose ship, the Queen of the West, put back to Liverpool dismasted after having made nearly half her westward passage. Another Yarmouth man, Captain Allen H. Knowles, in McKay's great clipper-packet Chariot of Fame, made a crossing westward in January, 1854, that was a succession of lost spars and high head seas. With a cargo worth half a million dollars and about eighty passengers, she sailed out of Liverpool on January 11, less than a fortnight after the loss of the Staffordshire. The first night out Captain Knowles lost his jib-boom in a collision. In mid-Atlantic he ran into a westerly gale that blew his main topsail to ribbons and smashed the yard. The Captain had no sooner got the wreckage cleared than a sea came aboard that carried away four boats and a section of bulwarks and flooded the cabin. Before it blew itself out, the wind gained such velocity that it tore furled sails out of the gaskets and raised a sea that carried away the figurehead. In spite of a new main yard which was slung and new sails which were bent to replace those that had been lost, the ship made not a mile of progress westward for sixteen days. Captain Knowles finally beat his way almost to the entrance of Boston Harbor, only to be met with another north-wester that split the last of his spare sails. He put his ship before the wind and piloted her into Province-town Harbor through a blinding snowstorm. She was finally towed from there to Boston, where she arrived six weeks after her departure from Liverpool.

That Cape men were highly esteemed as captains in the packet trade is shown on the clear, hard judgment of owners and managers. Every few years these gentle-men, deciding to leave rival firms in their wake, came out with bigger and better vessels than had ever been seen, and about as often as one of these new record-breakers appeared, a Cape Cod captain appeared on her quarter-deck. When E. K. Collins, for example, decided to beat all comers with his Dramatic Line, and to that end built the Roscius, the largest packet ship or merchantman under our flag, John Collins and Asa Eldridge were her first commanders. Six years later, when the Roscius was eclipsed by the Henry Clay, Ezra Nye was given the command. Edward Collins then went into steam, built the four largest steamships that had ever been seen, and invited Ezra Nye and Asa Eldridge, one after the other, to take the Pacific. Josiah Richardson's Staffordshire was the largest sailing packet on the Atlantic until McKay built the Chariot of Fame, which was commanded by Allen Knowles. In short, these men of Cape Cod had reached what was then the pinnacle of a seaman's ambition, the command of crack Liverpool packets. They strode their quarter-decks the lords of creation, taking back-wash from no man alive. Some of them lost their lives in the service. Others lived on to achieve yet greater glory; and for them the packets were but a stride in the sweeping progress of their careers, for the dawn of the clipper-ship era was at hand. But before telling the tale of the clippers, it is necessary to say a word or two about another branch of trade in which Cape men were engaged on the Atlantic, while the packets were making history between Liverpool and New York.

7

Europe, China, and the East Indies
1830—1850

MISCELLANEOUS European trade, meantime, was going steadily on, irrespective of the more regular trips of the packets, with Yankee vessels calling at ports as far apart as Sligo and Smyrna. It was a type of seafaring admirably suited to young captains whose reputations were still unmade. The voyages were short; no telltale passengers were on hand to report mistakes or accidents; and, though crossing the Atlantic was hard work, it required only simple navigation; captains had no need to take lunars, nor were they forced, like their brethren in the East India trade, to pick their way through the treacherous currents of the Sunda Straits or to weather typhoons on the way to Canton. None who had in them the stuff of which great shipmasters are made remained in the business for long. Like Josiah Richardson, they graduated to the command of Liverpool packets, East Indiamen, or clippers, or became, like Osborn Howes, owners instead of captains.

Osborn Howes was born in Dennis, son of Captain Elisha Howes, who had distinguished himself during the War of 1812. As a matter of fact, young Osborn knew Boston and its environs better than he did Dennis, for his family had left the Cape for Dedham when he was twelve. But he took with him some vivid impressions of the impromptu schooling he had had there at the hands of mates and masters in the coasting trade who were at home during the winters: long on discipline they were, observed Howes, but short on grammar.

After they moved to Dedham, his father, Captain Elisha, continued going to sea, and about 1820 was in command of the brig Cipher, making two round trips a year to Königsberg in Prussia. In order to give his son Osborn every chance to learn both seafaring and the shipping business, he sent him at about the age of eighteen as a passenger on one voyage and as supercargo on another — both trips while the Cipher was in charge of the mate, for Captain Elisha himself was busy dickering in Europe for return cargoes. While he was supercargo, young Osborn spent a winter in Prussia, buying goods and learning German business methods, and in 1828, at the age of twenty-two, he got his first command, the brig Hebe. He took her from Boston to Brazil and then across to Marseilles. He was so well pleased with her that he bought a half interest and in 1831 went in her to Smyrna. Soon after passing the Straits of Gibraltar, headed east, he saw a volcano lift a new island into existence. The British, so he says, promptly took possession of it in the King's name, thus adding one more to His Majesty's insular possessions. But the island, after a brief sojourn above water, sank to the bottom again, carrying the British hopes with it.

At Smyrna, Howes loaded his vessel with figs, in spite of the plague that raged there, took them to Boston, improved his shore leave by getting engaged to Hannah Crowell, a young lady of Yarmouth, and was off to Genoa, still in the Hebe. After a few more voyages in her, he took command of the bark Flora, in which his father was a large owner, loaded her with flour and lumber in Boston, and set sail for Rio. From Rio he headed for Trieste, taking one hundred and four days to get there, and thence to Smyrna, where he ran into the plague again. But he got home with his health still sound, married Miss Crowell, and, figuring that he had earned a vacation, took four months off for a honeymoon. It is lucky that he did, for, after another voyage to Rio, Antwerp, and Cádiz in the Flora, he came home to find that his wife had been dead for three months. This virtually ended his going to sea. He afterwards married a sister of his first wife, and with his brother-in-law, Captain Isaiah Crowell, Jr., bought the bark Leda. But Captain Crowell died of yellow fever on board her in Havana; so Osborn formed a partnership with another brother-in-law, Nathan Crowell, and the firm, under the name of Howes and Crowell, became one of the leaders in Boston shipping circles.

None of Howes's voyages was remarkable for its speed. The young man's talents seem to have lain rather in business acumen than in record-breaking passages. Quite different was the round trip to Ireland and back which two Hyannis youngsters, Captain Rodney Baxter in the schooner American Belle and Captain Allen Crowell in the schooner Cabot, made in 1847 with corn and flour for the famine-sufferers. Captain Baxter has left a detailed account of this spectacular voyage:

> The shortest western passage across the Atlantic Ocean ever made by a fore-and-aft schooner [he writes], was made by the schooner American Belle the year of the famine in Ireland. This vessel was built in Connecticut and was bought by myself and others to run between this port [Boston] and New York in the Tremont Line. She tonnaged two-hundred-seventeen tons and was considered a large schooner. After making one trip, we chartered her for Sligo, Ireland, with a cargo of corn and flour. The rates of freight were eight shillings and six pence for flour and thirty pence for corn.
>
> The schooner Cabot, Captain Allen Crowell, loaded for the same port, and was consigned to the same house

in Sligo. There was only one ton difference in their register. As near as I can recollect, we sailed from New York
about the first of March, and when we laid in Coenties
slip, ready for sea, our scuppers were only thirteen inches
clear of the water.... We beat down the harbor of New
York together and left the Highlands of Neversink in the
distance.... The wind was blowing a gale from the west,
and the first night out we separated and saw each other
no more.... Nothing uncommon occurred until the 17th
of March. The old stevedore said to me, as I left the dock
in New York, 'Captain Baxter, look out for St. Patrick's
Day!' and sure enough, on that day we were scudding
under the bonnet of our square sail, hoisted part the way
aloft. The gale was blowing with great force from the
northwest, and the sea was running mountains high. The
darkness of night was approaching, the sea boarding us
occasionally, and I had made up my mind to heave to
that night for safety, but said to Mr. Petersen, my mate,
and to Mr. Bearse, my second mate (they are both dead),
'I think we had better not heave to, for if the Cabot
should keep on, she would beat us.' 'Oh!' said Mr. Petersen, 'the Cabot can't raise hell in this gale,' and advised
us to lay to.

We had already had one sea board us, and I was never
in such a perilous position at sea.... I ordered my men in
the forecastle to come aft, and had the forecastle doors
well secured. As the men were in the cabin at supper, a
sea boarded us. The man at the helm was lashed to keep
him from being washed overboard. I stood at the weather
side, also lashed, ready to assist him, while the men were
in the trunk cabin eating. One man was on deck, walking
the weather side of the trunk. As I saw this mountainous
sea coming with such force, I told the man on the trunk
to jump up the rigging to keep from being washed overboard. He just escaped the danger. The sea was occasionally running a little on our port quarter. I caught
hold of the wheel to assist the man at the helm to swing
the vessel off, so that the sea would strike us square in the
stern, and when it did so, it lifted her stern so that she
almost pitch-poled, with the end of the jibboom under
water some distance.... The stern frame received such a
shock, and the concussion made such a cracking, that I
expected the stern of the vessel was stove in. The man

at the wheel and myself would have been washed overboard if we had not been well lashed. We were not less than ten feet under water, and when we regained our places on our feet, the vessel's stern was down under water and we were up to our arms in it, with tons of water on the after part, and the weight caused her to present an angle of 45 degrees, bow out. The pressure of the water burst off the bulwarks and she recovered, after apparently struggling to live. We kept on all night, and the gale abated to a common one. We were all the passage under reefed sails. For seven days we had only a trysail on the main, with three-reefed foresail, and bonnet off the jib.

The twenty-second day from New York we approached the coast of Ireland, near the entrance of Donegal Bay.... As we were running under close-reefed sails with the wind blowing nearly directly on the lee shore with the rock-bound coast, most of it one or two hundred feet high, the receding waves, running down these cliffs, created a sensation not pleasant for the poor sailor.... As we came near the entrance of the harbor of Sligo, having all our sails set we could possibly carry, our only guide was our chart, which showed the lighthouse to be left on our port hand. There was a sunken reef extending from the shore on our right, which showed breakers. The sea was running high, and it was blowing a gale. I went aloft to see if I could see the entrance. I saw the lighthouse was on the end of the sunken ledge. Inside the breakers there was a small boat containing four men.... One stood up, swinging his hat for me to leave the lighthouse on the starboard side. We got into smooth water and took our pilot on board....

We got up to the dock just at dark.... The Cabot arrived four or five days after. She laid to in the gale we scud in.... Our consignee was the Mayor of the city of Sligo, by the name of Walker.... Captain Crowell and myself were invited to his house to a party made especially for us. I must say that I never received better treatment by any nation on the globe, and I have visited nearly all.

After we got our cargo all out and ballast ready for sea, the wind was blowing a gale from the west and we were detained until the Cabot was ready for sea. We sailed together, the Cabot for New York and we for

THE SCHOONER AMERICAN BELLE

Boston. I think we saw each other the third day out, and not after. After we had been out about seven days, we laid becalmed from 4 o'clock one morning until 10 A.M. — about six hours. We sent down our topmast when we left port and had rather a strange rig. When we were becalmed, our mainsail and foresail were lowered... to keep our gafts from swinging about and our sails from chafing. About 10 o'clock we saw a number of sail coming up to us, and before the breeze struck us, which was very moderate, a small brig came within hailing distance and asked if we wanted any assistance. We answered No. The breeze struck us, and at 4 P.M. the brig could not be seen from our deck astern.

On the seventeenth day from Sligo we shot into dock between T and Commercial wharf. Coming up the dock, we passed the schooner Lacon, Captain Robert Bearse. As he had just shot in ahead, he being deeply loaded from New York and we being in ballast, we went past him. He hailed, saying, 'How many days from Sligo?' I answered, 'Seventeen!' 'Just my passage from New York,' said he; 'I told them while on our passage that the wind would be easterly until you arrived.' This was Saturday afternoon. At 3 P.M. I hurried up to the Custom House but was too late. I started up to Mr. Bailey's house, who was Collector at that time, to enter my vessel, that I could go home on the 4 P.M. train to Cape Cod.... I found Collector Bailey at home and told him I wished to reach home that afternoon. 'Well,' said he, 'Captain, have you a cargo?' I said no. He took my manifest, just cast his eyes over it and said, 'Captain, you have made the quickest passage I ever heard of. Go home and see your family. When you come up next week, we will fix your papers.' His manner was always pleasing, and he was a Democrat.

So ended a voyage which has become a high spot in the annals of Atlantic crossings.

Captain Baxter says little about the suffering in Ireland, but another Cape shipmaster, Caleb Sprague, of Barnstable, is emphatic as to the desperateness of the situation. He was in Cork in command of the ship North Bend in 1847 and writes as follows under the date of November 28, 1847:

... This country is in very bad state. Murders are committed almost daily upon the landowners by the tenants, and the poor are suffering very badly for want of food and clothing, and no person can really imagine the amount of suffering until they have been here and seen for themselves. We Americans know but little about poverty.

Captain Sprague, however, did not confine his voyages to Ireland, nor did his correspondence from other European ports lack spice. He had begun his career as skipper of a Hingham fisherman, then had taken command of the brig Cummaquid in the merchant service, and in 1843 had been made master of the ship North Bend, owned by Matthew Cobb, of Barnstable. He was enjoying himself in her in Bordeaux in 1844 and writes pleasantly of the entertainment which he and his wife received:

... Dunkirk and Bordeaux are fine places... we have had more invitations to dine than we have wished, as the dinners in this country are very lengthy — say from three to four hours before you rise from the table — and then not dry.

The Captain, as a matter of fact, had a way of making friends wherever he went. Not only French merchants but South American bandits and Presidents were glad to shake him by the hand, as appears from a letter which he wrote from Malaga in 1852, while in command of the fine new bark, Rosario:

I have received letters from Guyaquil which give me great satisfaction to find that Flores and his band of robbers were completely defeated and mostly all killed, and it is a great pity he was not killed, as he is another Lopez or Rosas.... I was well acquainted with most of his officers, having been boarded by him four or five times, and I found that they were all bad fellows and expected to have a chance to sack the city of Guyaquil; but I always told them that they would all be killed if they made an attack on the city.

I felt greatly interested in the welfare of the Re-

Europe, China, and the East Indies

public of Ecuador and have many warm friends there — the principal men in Guyaquil — all of the Generals and Civil Officers and all of the first families — and when I return there, I shall be received with much happiness.... I offered my services to the acting President, that in case an attack was made whilst I was there, I would take charge of a 32 lbs brass gun and help defend the City in case there was more help needed; but thank God they ably defended their own City and there is no doubt would always do so against a pirate or any piratical expedition, which that was in every sense of the word.

An even higher tribute to Captain Sprague's gift for friendship was the way in which he got along on the Rosario with a Spanish crew and Spanish officers, even though he was not able at first to speak more than a word or two of their language. The Rosario, though a Yankee-built vessel, was owned by the Loring Brothers of Malaga. George Loring, founder of the firm, was a Hingham man who had moved to Malaga for business purposes, and so the Rosario flew the flag of Spain. Since the Lorings had an office in Valparaiso, a good part of the Captain's seafaring in his new bark was between that port and Malaga. He wrote from Valparaiso early in January, 1851:

I get along first rate with my officers and crew, altho' they are all Spanish except my carpenter.... I am learning the Spanish language fast and by the time I get to Malaga I shall be able to speak it correctly,...

And again in another letter:

I have never fallen in with a ship since leaving New York but what the bark Rosario passed her, and that easily.

One branch of European trade which held pretty steady at this time was cotton-carrying from our southern ports to Liverpool. Though some of the Boston packets went south to fill up before crossing, a big surplus of cotton was left, and New England shipowners sent vessels by the score to get it. Sometimes,

149

carrying tobacco as well as cotton, they called at Havre or Antwerp instead of Liverpool, and amongst them they formed an important item in our trade with Europe from 1830 on.

A well-known figure in this business was Captain Prince S. Crowell, of East Dennis. Like many ship-masters, he began his seafaring on coasters, being skipper of the schooners Soldam and Edwin in the middle thirties. In 1839 he took another schooner, the Deposit, to Palermo and brought back a cargo of lemons, macaroni, and bergamot; and the next year saw the beginning of his career as master of large vessels in the cotton and tobacco trade. He loaded the ship Aurelius at Richmond and Savannah with tobacco, sold it in Liverpool, was ordered thence to Havre, and returned to Hampton Roads. Another voyage, this time on the bark Autoleon, took him from Richmond and New Orleans to Antwerp with cotton; and still another, in the ship Ellen Brooks, starting from New Orleans, took in Havre, Hamburg, Bremerhaven, and New Orleans again. But such activity, prosperous as it may sound, was not making a rich man of Captain Crowell or of his owner, friend, and fellow townsman, Christopher Hall. A letter which Hall wrote to his young captain at this time shows that the shipping business was anything but booming, and that the philosophical Cape merchant, taking advantage of the lull, was enjoying himself on a vacation back in East Dennis:

EAST DENNIS, *Aug.* 6, 1840

... Everything as dull as possible here and at Boston. Willis was here a day or two ago and went with us seining, but I believe even that business is failing, as we have had but poor success lately. Consequently Uncle Joe and I have concluded to take up the gunning business, as we see this morning some flocks of birds in the meadows.

In spite of bad times, Captain Crowell was still carrying cotton in the Autoleon three years later, and was obviously getting homesick. In a letter to Christopher Hall from New Orleans, he gives a glimpse into the state of mind of a young New England captain, whose business took him away from home, and what is quite as interesting, an idea of the delightfully informal relations in which he stood with his genial owner:

> I should have written sooner [says Crowell], but have been waiting to hear from some of you, and I believe you think I am no great account anyhow, or at least not worth writing to. You and my family and friends are knocking about as usual, sick or dead or gone on a voyage of discovery to the Moon for aught I know or am likely to know; and I suppose Uncle Shiverick is grinding salt or making shingles or building ships, which would be all the same to me, providing he did not do it on my account.

Christopher Hall may well have smiled when he read this letter. He had himself commanded a ship at the age of twenty, and knew what it was to go without news from home. Now, retired and the local capitalist of Dennis, he bought and sold ships and put his neighbors in command of them, selling them as many shares as they chose to buy. A more genial, generous, or informal shipowner it would be hard to find. In 1840, for example, he bought the Ellen Brooks, gave the command of her to his neighbor, Levi Howes, and wrote to Captain Crowell, who was away on a voyage in the Aurelius, another of his vessels: 'How much interest do you want in the Ellen Brooks?... We have the whole of her in our neighborhood.... [She] carries 1900 bales of cotton and [is] a superb vessel.'

The freedom which Hall allowed his captains, indeed the almost Utopian democracy of his management, is amusingly shown by the offhand manner in which Levi Howes and Prince Crowell on one occasion arranged matters to their own liking in New Orleans, without consulting him. Howes had had the Ellen Brooks for two or three years, carrying cotton in her to Europe, and was tired of it. In 1843, Hall wrote to Crowell: 'The Ellen Brooks is loading in New Orleans ... for Havre.... I think of ordering [her] to James River from Havre. What do you think of it? I suppose Levi will think that he has made money enough to come home, but I think it best to keep the ship to *work*.' But she did not go to the James River; she headed instead for New Orleans again, and Levi did think he had made money enough to come home. In New Orleans he found Crowell and the Autoleon. Without more ado, the two men swapped vessels; Howes took the Autoleon north to Portsmouth with cotton, and Crowell blandly wrote to Hall: 'I suppose that you have been informed by L. Howes that he is coming to Portsmouth in the Autoleon at ½ cent per lb. for Cotton and that I am to take the E. Brooks.' Here was self-management with a vengeance — a state of affairs that would have scandalized the merchant princes of any large seaport in the country, but was cheerfully accepted as fitting and proper among the deep-water aristocracy of East Dennis.

As a matter of fact, Hall showed great good sense in giving those two captains and fellow citizens of his so free a hand in ordering their voyages, for Levi Howes was as canny and reliable a shipmaster as any owner could desire. His years as a cotton-carrier were few; his talents far surpassed the requirements of that trade, and he wound up in command of clippers. Prince Crowell, too, was a man of parts. Like Howes, he did not stay on Atlantic freighters, but ended his sea career with a voyage to China and afterwards became owner or manager of a whole fleet of vessels.

His China voyage was made in 1846 in the new ship Thomas W. Sears and is of particular interest, as he was sailing for our old friend, Daniel C. Bacon. Crowell had already taken the Sears on a trial spin to Savannah and reported that she had made nine miles an hour with the yards braced sharp up and had easily passed the Barnstable, another of Bacon's ships. Bacon himself regarded her as 'superior to most vessels in the China trade.' Loaded with flour, raisins, tobacco, fish, and $25,000 worth of American drills, the Sears sailed from Boston on February 22, 1846.

In his letter of instructions to Captain Crowell, Bacon, after mentioning the wages he was to receive (one hundred dollars a month and two tons free freight space home), concludes with the inspiriting remark: 'You will have two clipper ships to follow you from New York in a few days, and I hope you will use every exertion not to let them report you at Canton.' Captain Crowell did his best to reach Canton in less than one hundred days, but luck was against him. However, he did well enough, and taking out the time spent at Anjer, made the passage in 106 to Whampoa. What the clipper ships were that sailed after him and whether they beat the Sears, does not appear. He took on board a select lot of teas for Bacon, filled up with general freight, and wrote that he had two fast vessels, the Akbar and the Candace, to race home against. 'I expect to get beat,' he says, 'but shall use every effort not to do so.' Whether or not he got beat cannot be discovered, but he landed safely in New York late in October, 1846, after an entirely successful voyage.

Another shipmaster who was promoted from Atlantic voyages to the East India and China trade was Captain Eben H. Linnell, of Orleans, whose earlier years had been spent in the cotton trade, in a stout ship named the Cabinet. Later, while he was docked in the Thames, in command of the ship Norman in 1847, he received orders to proceed to Manilla and to be prepared to sail thence for Canton. His preparations consisted of purchasing a pair of light brass four-pounders in case he should fall in with pirates in the China Sea — a wise precaution, but, as it turned out, an unnecessary one. Three years later he was on his way from Boston to Calcutta with a cargo of ice in the Buena Vista, and returned with goatskins and linseed, glad to be rid of his outward cargo which, he complained, slowed the ship up greatly.

These voyages gave Captain Linnell small chance to show his ability as a sail-carrier, but the opportunity came in 1851, when he had the Buena Vista in San Francisco with orders to proceed to Calcutta. To his delight he found that Captain Levi Stevens, of Truro, commander of the clipper ship Southern Cross, was to sail the same day for the same port, and he decided to show what a full-bodied ship could do against a clipper. Both ships left San Francisco on October 24. The Southern Cross arrived in Calcutta in 56 sailing days, the Buena Vista in 60 — a fine performance, and a passage of which even a clipper captain might well have been proud. This was by no means the end of his East India trading, but his reputation was so much increased by his performance against the Southern Cross that his owners, Theodore Chase and Company, of Boston, put him in command of the clipper ship Eagle Wing and later of the Flying Mist. Of his voyages in these vessels there will be more to say anon.

But there were other East India voyagers from Cape Cod who, unlike Crowell and Linnell, had never done time on the Atlantic. One of them was Captain James B. Crocker, of Barnstable, who took the ship Eben Preble out to China in 1837. Half a dozen Cape men and boys were on board with him in one capacity or another. Joseph Crocker, of Barnstable, was his first mate; John C. Howes and Joshua Sears, of Dennis and East Dennis respectively, were able seamen; another Dennis lad, Allen Howes, was an ordinary seaman, and so was John Ainsworth, of Barnstable. They sailed from Boston on July 26, 1837, and soon discovered that their souls were to be cared for as well as their bodies, for Captain Crocker, who believed that Sunday was Sunday, on soundings or off, invited all hands aft to attend divine service every Sabbath throughout the voyage, weather permitting. Captain Crocker's method at these services was to read a chapter of the New Testament and then interpret it according to his own ideas, concluding with prayers from the *Seaman's Devotional Assistant.* Having thus attended to their spiritual welfare, the Captain ministered to their temporal needs by a thorough course in sail-making, as well as in making sennit and thumb line. The carpenter, meanwhile, put in his spare time manufacturing blocks. As the Eben Preble approached the pirate-infested waters of the Sunda Islands, Captain Crocker set his men at work making cartridges and improving their marksmanship.

The Preble passed the east end of Sandalwood Island and anchored in Boeroe Bay, where the Captain went ashore and arranged for a detail of soldiers to come on board and guard the ship while the crew were at work getting water and fresh provisions — a cautious commander, Captain Crocker, if not a maker of record passages. Two weeks later, they passed, at midnight, 'a burning mountain' on one of the Bashee Islands, and finally dropped anchor in Lintin Roads, 156 days out of Boston. Here they spent a week loading cotton and other merchandise before working up the river to Whampoa, where they lay for about two months; and on February 26, 1838, they dropped down the river with a cargo of tea and set sail from Lintin, homeward-bound. Again, before entering the Straits of Sunda, the watches were kept busy cleaning muskets. They arrived in New York one day too late to celebrate the Fourth of July, and after a ten-days sojourn there, rounded Cape Cod and anchored off Commercial Wharf in Boston on July 18, not quite five months from Lintin.

After a vacation of nineteen days, Captain Crocker again set sail in the Eben Preble for the other side of the world, this time headed for Calcutta. The crew had some fault to find because they had to saw wood for the cook, who, they asserted, 'was so much of a gentleman that he could not saw his own wood'; but their growls were soon forgotten in making preparations to exterminate the rats which infested the ship in thousands. However, 'the cunning rascals escaped and no blood shed.' The voyage was uneventful and pleasant, with occasional diversions such as occurred when two men slipped over the side for a swim, and the mate ordered them back on board before 'Mr. John Shark should happen along that way and make a yapper of them.' Captain Crocker, in fact, seems to have had a crew of aquatic enthusiasts on this voyage, for one of them lost his cap overboard and promptly dived in after it, emerging none the worse — probably the better indeed — for the bath.

These glimpses of life on board his ship show Captain Crocker as a pious, competent, and cautious shipmaster, neither a driver nor a weakling, but a commander who ordered his voyages and controlled his men on the basis of reason — a method made possible largely because he had so many smart young lads from the Cape among his crews. After leaving the Eben Preble, he commanded the ship Oxnard in 1840 and the Loo Choo in 1844, in both of which he continued to make voyages to the East Indies and China. Some time between 1840 and 1860 he moved from his birthplace in Barnstable to the neighboring town of Yarmouth, where, after retiring from the sea, he became a useful and highly respected citizen.

After Captain Crocker left the Eben Preble, her owners put Captain Franklin Hallett, of Yarmouth, who afterwards had the Queen of the West in the Liverpool packet trade, in command of her, and he took her out to Manilla from Boston, setting sail on June 26, 1840. From Manilla she went over to Canton and thence home, arriving in New York on August 22, 1841, 113 days from China, 83 days from Anjer, 45 days from the Cape of Good Hope, and 25 days from the Equator. These figures, though nothing to be ashamed of and regarded as worthy of summarizing in the log of the voyage, obviously failed to impress another veteran of the East Indies, Captain Joshua

Sears, of East Dennis, who was reading over the log years afterwards and added in pencil, 'I have beat that in the Orissa, deep loaded from Calcutta.' And so he had, being virtually a specialist in East India voyages from 1847, when he commanded what he describes as 'the old, square-bow'd Burmah,' until the beginning of the Civil War, when he resigned the command of the clipper ship Wild Hunter, and came ashore to stay. Long before he received his master's ticket, too, he had made voyages to the East on the Eben Preble, the Oxnard, and the Loo Choo under Captain Crocker, and in 1840 had served as mate of the Preble under Captain Hallett. Neither India nor China, therefore, held many surprises for him.

Captain Sears had a fondness for carrying sail which was in sharp contrast with the caution of Captain Crocker. In 1847, on his first voyage as Master, he took the Burmah from Boston to Calcutta with a cargo of ice and beat the American ship Geneva by sixteen days. The voyage out was uneventful except for a flurry with his first officer, an incident thus recorded in his log:

Oct. 11.... Had a quarrel with the mate, he finding fault with me for interfering with his work. Who ever heard of such a thing!

Having discharged his ice, he loaded with redwood, saltpetre, linseed, hides, ginger, and gunny cloth, and headed back for Boston on December 20. The first day out, he found that his chronometer was wrong and he concludes the day's entry in his log with the remark, 'Whether I shall ever find the way home or not I don't know.' A fortnight later he ran into trouble of another sort:

Feb. 6:... Violent gale.... At 1.00 o'clock it increased very suddenly.... Hove ship to under mizen staysail.... A very high turbulent sea, causing the ship to strain and make considerable water at the pumps. Sea making a highway over the ship.... At 5.00 P.M. it died away nearly calm. Ship fell off in the trough of half a dozen

different seas running half a dozen different ways, causing her to cut such figures as pen and ink cannot describe, constantly shipping water over both rails....
From 8.00 to 12.00 wind increased to a heavy gale....
Hove the ship to.... Now let her mull.

About ten days later he passed the bark Isabelle
Blythe (which had left Calcutta more than a week
ahead of him), in spite of the fact that his fore royal
mast was so rotten that before the end of the voyage
he reports that it is 'so weak it will not hold its own
weight.' The old Burmah certainly had had a shaking
up, for off Highland Light she was leaking two hundred
strokes an hour. However, he got her safely into Boston, where, after a sojourn in the shipyards, she was
declared once more fit for sea.

But she was not fit for such a driver as Captain
Sears. He took her out to Madras, leaving Boston on
June 27, 1848, and covered the 14,000 miles in 108
days. In a letter home, written the day after he arrived, Sears says: 'The old Burmah has beat the clipper ship Tonquin two days from Boston to Madras....
Business is very dull here and no chance of us going to
China.' He went up to Calcutta instead and thence to
Boston. On the homeward voyage he was surprised
one calm night as he lay in his bunk to hear water
running in on both sides of the ship. He called the
carpenter, ripped up the ceiling, and found a large
stream flowing in freely under the fashion piece. He
promptly hove to, caulked the leak, and proceeded.
Here was the result of some more sail-carrying; clearly
the tender old Burmah was no longer the ship for
him. Realizing this before it was too late, his owners
gave him a newer vessel, the Orissa, in which he made
five voyages to Calcutta between 1849 and 1854,
sometimes stopping at Mauritius on the way and sometimes varying the monotony by dropping in at a
China port.

His wife bore him company pretty regularly during
these years, and was as delighted with the gorgeous

sunsets in the Bay of Bengal as she was horrified by the big snakes that she saw swimming there. The Captain, on one of these voyages, demonstrated his mechanical skill by making a windmill which the sailors used with success in twisting up rope yarn for seizings; and all went merrily until 1853, when the Orissa was on her way out to Hong Kong. In the China Sea she ran into a typhoon which, in the Captain's phrase, 'struck us like a clap of thunder.' It lasted from nine in the morning until three in the afternoon and blew every sail to ribbons except two, carried away fifteen feet of bulwarks, fifty feet of the monkey rail, six water casks, stove in the galley, and carried away the topgallant forecastle lockers and everything in them. In writing to his charterers, Sampson and Tappan, in regard to the damage, Captain Sears remarks:

> I never saw a ship in such a state as she was in about decks before in my life. She also started the fore and main mast coats, and I fear let down some water.... I passed the ship Tsar ashore on the mud bank in the Straits of Banca. She got off shortly after.

This was destined to be a slow voyage for Captain Sears. It took a long time for the Hong Kong shipwrights to get the Orissa ready for sea again, and from Hong Kong he went to Shanghai and Woo Sing, where he received orders for Calcutta, which he reached after a tedious passage of seventy-seven days, perhaps because the Orissa, like the Burmah before her, was beginning to show signs of the hard driving she had been put through. When she anchored off Calcutta, the Captain condemned her fore yard, which was badly sprung; her copper was old and ragged; her seams so soft that in some places a knife blade could be pushed into them four inches. Truly Captain Sears must have been tired of taking derelicts round the world. However, there was nothing for it; he patched her up enough so that she would hold together for the voyage home, loaded her with the usual Indian products —

Shipmasters *of* Cape Cod

saltpetre, linseed, ginger, gunny cloth, hides, hemp, indigo, shellac, and bags of cutch — and brought her back to Boston. He made only one more voyage in her, leaving Boston for Bombay in the summer of 1854. It took him 112 days to get there, and he lost one of his crew on the way — young William Wright, a West Barnstable boy, who was killed by a fall from the main royal yard. In Bombay he loaded with salt for Calcutta, and once more drove her back across two oceans to Boston, where he bade her good-bye without a tear.

Captain Sears's remaining years at sea were spent in a command worthy of his talents — the lovely little clipper, Wild Hunter; but the story of his experiences in her must be deferred.

Two other Cape men who were contemporaries of Captain Sears in the Calcutta trade were Captains Bangs Hallett, of Yarmouth, and William H. Burgess, of Brewster. Captain Hallett had the ship Herbert in the East India trade in the late forties, and in 1850 took young Burgess along as mate. Nine other Cape boys were before the mast. In 1851 he turned the command over to Burgess for a voyage, while he took a vacation. Burgess, who like Levi Howes, Joshua Sears, Eben Linnell, and Caleb Sprague had the qualities that were soon to put him on the quarter-deck of a clipper, set sail from Boston on September 17, 1851, carried away his flying jib boom and split the sail-ends a week later in what he calls 'brisk breezes from the S.S.E.'; found that his three compasses all pointed in different directions; corrected the one in the binnacle for the proper variation for his position, and arrived at the Sand Heads off Calcutta in 119 days, 14 hours. After loading the Herbert with the East India staples, he set sail for Boston on February 5, 1852, and arrived on July 17, taking leave of his ship with the following flourish in the log:

So ends the voyage of the ship Herbert, W. H. Burgess, Master, from Boston to Calcutta and back again, per-

160

forming the same in 10 months to a day. Having been mate of said ship 18 months and Master 10, I now resign her to her former and able Commander, Bangs Hallett, Esq., wishing her pleasant and successful voyages.

We, too, shall take leave of him, and of the rest of the stalwart captains who drove their apple-cheeked commands out and back round the Cape of Good Hope, trading ice for goatskins and linseed and saltpetre. Some of them had grown old in the business and by 1850 were ready to retire; others were at the very peak of their powers and, tired of their clumsy, barrel-bottomed vessels that shipbuilders were still turning out, were looking round for something better. They did not look in vain, for the dawn of the clipper-ship era was breaking along the Atlantic Coast, heralding the arrival of a maritime epoch unequaled in the annals of sail.

8

The Clippers

THOUGH the clipper ships did not spring, like Cytherea, in full-blown beauty from the sea, they did something very like it. Builders began to grow restless as early as 1841, influenced, it may be, by the teachings of John Griffeths, a marine architect of New York, in whose brain the idea of ships with clipper lines had taken root; and throughout the forties, vessels appeared which, though not really clippers, were much sharper than the old models and have sometimes been listed in the clipper class. One of the best known of these was the bark Coquette, built by Samuel Hall at East Boston in 1844, and commanded by Captain Oliver Eldridge, of Yarmouth, who had learned his seafaring in Liverpool packets. On her maiden voyage Captain Eldridge took her out to Canton from Boston in 99 days — fast time, beyond a doubt; but Prince Crowell, it will be remembered, took the ship Thomas W. Sears, which nobody has ever called a clipper, over the same course in 106 days and had hoped to do it in less.

The Coquette's name for speed, however, did not depend on her first voyage, but on the consistently fast passages that she made between ports in the East. Captain Eldridge had the satisfaction, while dining in Liverpool on one occasion, of overhearing a reluctant British tribute to his prowess as a driver and to the

162

The Clippers

sailing qualities of his celebrated bark. A group of English shipmasters sat at a table close to his, discussing maritime affairs. 'I've beaten everything in the China Seas,' said one of them, 'except that damned Yankee, Coquette.'

Just as the dawn, once it has appeared after a long night of darkness, lights the whole landscape in an instant, so the art of the shipbuilder, once it had broken away from the traditional models, was quick to abandon such hybrids as the Coquette and produce genuine clippers in their full splendor. No sailing vessels ever launched have equaled in beauty or in speed the matchless creations of the late forties and the fifties. Long, lean, and rakish, with hollow cheeks instead of the old bluff bows, and a stem sweeping forward from the water-line in a graceful concave arc that blended sweetly with the slant of the bowsprit, the clippers, in their entrance lines, ran counter to every previous principle of marine architecture. Their widest point, instead of being up in the eyes, as formerly, was brought about as far aft as the fore rigging, and from there the rest of the way aft they tapered gradually, ending in a nicely modeled elliptical stern, happily at variance with the square-tailed old-timers.

Not only did the clippers have finer lines than had ever been seen, but they were far more heavily sparred as well. To have spread so much canvas as they carried, above a hull shaped like that of the Orissa or the Eben Preble, would have meant sleepless nights for her captain. To spread it above a hull that had been pulled out fore and aft until it was shaped like a codfish instead of a sperm whale was, in the opinion of the Jeremiahs, flirting with eternity. Even the optimists among shipowners realized that a new technique was called for in handling these sensitive new vessels; taking them round the world was a very different matter from barging from sea to sea in the leisurely bottoms of the old school. Merchants wanted the best sailors afloat for the quarter-decks of their clippers, and they got them, which meant that the captain of a clipper ship had reached a new pinnacle in his profession — an eminence from which he might look down with condescension even on the lordly commanders of Liverpool packets; and his salary jumped from a hundred dollars a month to two hundred dollars.

Of the many who rightly believed that they should be called, few were chosen, for as yet confidence in clipper ships was so rare that only the most progressive firms placed orders for them; the bulk of our carrying trade was still handled by stout old vessels that bobbed along contentedly and got there in the end. But the discovery of gold in California in 1848 put an end to all hesitation; when it came to staking out claims in the gold fields, it was first come, first served; speed was everything, safety nothing. Clipper freights to San Francisco went sailing skyward to such figures that even the most cautious merchants blew the cobwebs from the principles of a lifetime and ordered clippers. By 1850 the mallets of every shipyard on the Atlantic Coast were pounding trunnels into the planking of clipper ships, and as fast as the lovely hulls slid off the ways, more captains were called from their old commands to share the glory and profit of the new day.

The grueling fifteen thousand miles round the Horn to San Francisco made usually only the first leg of a clipper ship's voyage, for from California it was more profitable and almost as easy to come home round the world, stopping at Hong Kong and Calcutta on the way. This gave the smaller vessels, which were too light to bang their way westward in the teeth of gales off Cape Horn and frequently had to wait for something like a favorable slant, a chance to redeem themselves later in racing their bigger sisters across the Pacific or in skimming jauntily home from China round the Cape of Good Hope. But even the little ones, if they were properly handled, sometimes worked

THE CLIPPER SHIP STAGHOUND

wonders against the wild Cape Horn seas, as was shown by Captain Judah P. Baker, of Brewster, when he raced his lovely little Shooting Star against Captain Josiah Richardson in the huge Staffordshire, and reached San Francisco only four days behind him. This race has been described in an earlier chapter, and it was by no means the only fine run that Captain Baker made in his short career. He had already taken the Shooting Star round the world on her maiden voyage in 1851, in the course of which he had, in common with many of the captains of early and lightly rigged clippers, lost his main topgallant mast and been obliged, much to his disgust, to put into Rio for a new one. But he had redeemed himself on the last leg of the voyage when he came roaring home from Macao to Boston in eighty-six days — splendid time for any ship and the best work that anyone ever did in the little Shooting Star.

The next year, after his race with Richardson, Captain Baker took the new clipper Flying Dragon on her maiden voyage, starting for San Francisco from Boston in the summer of 1853. His grim battle off Cape Horn and the relentless style in which he struggled week after week to drive her westward against the great sweeping seas, is briefly told: he was over a month off the Cape and in the course of it sprung his bowsprit and fore yard and carried away his jib boom. The strain was too much for him; after finally getting his ship round the Horn and safely past the Equator, headed north, he died before reaching San Francisco. What further fame he might have achieved is a matter of conjecture; but as he was only forty-six when he started his last voyage, it is a safe guess that some good years would have lain ahead of him.

Racing round Cape Horn became, as the demand for clippers increased, the national maritime sport, and few were the shipmasters who at one time or another during the boom years of the early fifties did not test their mettle against some mighty opposite or other over this great course. Captain Justus Doane, of Chatham, got into such a race in 1852–53 — one of the most thrilling contests in the annals of the sea. Doane had already made a place for himself in the front rank of clipper captains by his performance in the R. B. Forbes, which he had taken on her maiden voyage round the world the year before. On the first lap he had hung up a new record for merchantmen by reaching Honolulu from Boston in 96 days, 12 hours — land to land. He followed this by a run of 21 days, 13 hours, to Hong Kong for the second leg of the voyage — remarkable time and close to the record; and he wound up by beating the Sea Witch home from Whampoa by six days. Any one of the three sections of this voyage would have done him credit; taken in combination, they placed Captain Doane close to the top of his profession. He got home in July, 1852, took the summer off, and in October was ready to go to sea again, this time in command of Samuel Hall's new medium clipper, the John Gilpin.

He left New York in her on her maiden voyage, bound for California; two days behind him came Captain Nickels in Donald McKay's new extreme clipper, Flying Fish, one third larger than the Gilpin and much sharper. The question was whether Doane could hold his lead against such a competitor and reach San Francisco before him. Two days was not much of a margin over a course where anything under 110 days was called unusual, and where the record — made only three times in the history of sail — was 89 days. But Captain Doane didn't intend to be overtaken if he could help it. At the Equator, Nickels had caught up, but because he thought that he was wiser than the sailing directions and tried to cut corners, he found himself too far to the westward and wasted precious time in clearing Cape St. Roque. While Nickels was thus trying to beat the doldrums, Doane was flying south as fast as driving could carry him, and off the Horn he was a day ahead.

The Clippers

But here the Flying Fish showed her quality. Her great size and weight and her enormously heavy spars carried her to the westward even in the teeth of the head gales, and she came up with and passed the little Gilpin, which in spite of everything that Doane could crowd on her, was no match for the terrific head seas that swept her from stem to stern. Nickels, so the story goes, invited Doane to dine with him on board as he roared past. Doane's reply — fortunately, perhaps — is not recorded. Until they reached the Equator, Nickels held his one-day lead; then Doane and his vessel hit their stride: the Gilpin came up with the Flying Fish, passed her, and sailed into San Francisco one day ahead, after a passage of 93 days, 20 hours. Nickels, who came in the next day, had, to be sure, made it in 92 days, 4 hours, but Doane was content. And well he may have been, for on the merits of sheer seamanship he had easily surpassed his rival, having outwitted him at the Equator, having taken only two days longer to get by Cape Horn, and having passed him on the Equator headed north — all in a smaller and fuller-modeled ship.

After this great race, Captain Doane retired and went home to Chatham, where he intended to pass the rest of his life in peace. But not many men like him were to be had, and owners kept after him until he finally consented — albeit reluctantly — to make one more voyage. With his wife, he went to Calcutta; both came down with cholera, and both were buried there in 1853, one day apart, beside the foul waters of the Ganges.

On the same day that Captain Doane had left New York on the start of his race against Nickels, another Cape captain, Freeman Hatch, of Eastham, had set sail from Boston, bound for the same port, in the fine clipper Northern Light. But luck was against him all the way out, so that instead of arriving with the first flight, as he had hoped, he took 118 days to reach his destination. Though this was respectable time, and though in making it he had tied two other clipper ships — the Wild Pigeon and the Dauntless, which had sailed about two weeks ahead of him — Captain Hatch was disgusted. He was particularly angry at having been badly beaten by a couple of New York clippers, the Trade Wind and the Contest, which had made the passage in 103 and 100 days respectively — remarkably fine time, though a week slower than that of Doane and Nickels, the first two of the fleet to finish. What, therefore, was his delight to learn, on arriving at San Francisco, that the two New-Yorkers, like himself, had orders to bring their ships home direct, instead of continuing round the world. Here was his chance for revenge. A Boston merchant who was in San Francisco at the time, and was a stalwart backer of Bay State ships, offered Captain Hatch a new suit of clothes if he beat the Trade Wind on the return trip. The Contest, being considered a faster ship than either the Trade Wind or the Northern Light, was tacitly conceded the victory, but it looked like a good race between the other two.

On March 10, 1853, the Trade Wind got away, homeward-bound. Two days later the Contest set sail, and on the 13th the Northern Light weighed anchor and was after them. Captain Hatch's mate, young Seth Doane, of Orleans, must have heaved a sigh of relief when the Golden Gate finally faded from sight astern; for though there was plenty of work ahead if the Northern Light was to overtake the Trade Wind, it was better than the feverish and incessant toil of getting cargo on board and champing at the bit when stevedores were slow. Now that they were on blue water, let the New-Yorkers beware!

Early in the game Hatch virtually won his suit of clothes, for he passed the Trade Wind easily, and she never figured in the race thereafter. 'That's that!' thought Hatch, and took after the Contest. In the swinging seas south of the Horn he came up with her, and, so the story goes, shouted to Captain Brewster,

The Clippers

'Sorry not to stop, but I can't hold my horse.' But fiction, for all its picturesqueness, must yield to fact; though Hatch did catch his rival at the Horn, as even the log of the Contest admits, he did not pass her. The two ships were in company for a day or two; then the Northern Light dropped behind while the Contest vanished ahead. But Hatch was not out of the running. At the Equator, by dint of terrific driving, he was some forty miles ahead — not much of a lead, to be sure, in such a race, but something at least. Far more important, as it turned out, was his windward position, 140 miles to the eastward of the Contest, for it enabled him to bring his ship into Boston two and a half days before the Contest reached New York, and in the amazing time of 76 days, 8 hours, a record never equaled by a sailing vessel before or since.

Captain Hatch got ashore early in the morning, before the counting-houses were open, and, jumping into a hack, ordered the driver to take him to Roxbury, where his owner, James Huckins — a Barnstable man, by the way — had his residence. According to the Captain's story, he woke Huckins from a sound sleep, shouting, 'Here I am with the Northern Light, but I've strained her dreadfully getting here.'

'Did you beat the Contest?' asked Huckins. When Hatch replied that he had, Huckins rejoined, 'Then I don't care a damn how much you've strained her!' There were a few sportsmen, it seems, even in the hard-headed breed of shipowners!

But, strained though she undoubtedly was, the Northern Light's racing days were not over. On her very next voyage, a little more than two months after his conversation with Huckins, Captain Hatch was off again for San Francisco in another remarkable race, this time between seven clippers, all of which started during the twelve days from August 4 to August 16, 1853. One of the other entries was Hatch's old friend, the Trade Wind; another was the Raven, commanded by Captain Josiah Crocker, of Barnstable. The other contestants were the Witch of the Wave, the Hurricane, the Comet, and the Mandarin. Here, then, among seven clipper-ship captains, were two Cape-Codders, eying each other askance, with Hatch keeping a weather eye on the Trade Wind as well, for between them honors were even.

The outcome of the race is an extraordinary tribute to the seamanship of American shipmasters. After sailing a course of some 15,000 miles, all seven reached San Francisco between December 10 and December 16. The winner was the Witch of the Wave, 117 days; second came Josiah Crocker in the Raven, 119 days; the third was Hatch in the strained Northern Light, 122 days. Though his Barnstable rival had beaten him, he had beaten his old antagonist the Trade Wind (to say nothing of the rest of the fleet) by three days, a victory made all the more decisive because the Trade Wind had sailed from Philadelphia and the Northern Light from Boston. If this race is a tribute to American seamanship, it is a yet higher tribute to the seamanship of the men of Cape Cod. Barnstable and Eastham might hold their heads higher than ever when the news reached home.

Captain Hatch's next command was the Bonita, another of James Huckins's clippers, whose lines had been drawn by the Barnstable merchant himself. Hatch took her on a two-years cruise, leaving Boston in June, 1855. His first port of call was Batavia, which he sighted 77 days out; thence he headed for Havre and arrived in 83 days. He then dropped over to Cardiff for a cargo of coal, which he took out to Shanghai in 78 days, receiving orders there for London, which he reached in March, 1857. There he loaded with railroad iron and headed for Calcutta in April, but two months later, on June 18, he found her leaking so badly that he had to put into Algoa Bay, where she was condemned.

Meanwhile Seth Doane, of Orleans, Hatch's mate on his seventy-six-day record run from San Francisco, had bought the Northern Light from James Huckins in 1854 and taken command of her on voyages to the East Indies. Her first voyage under her new captain but old officer, showed that she had not lost her turn for speed, for she raced the clipper North Wind home from Calcutta even. Doane, pleased but not satisfied, determined to do better, and on his next voyage he succeeded. He left Boston for Manilla, and arrived in 89 days, a record for the course, and evidence enough that this fine ship was still a flyer and that her captain had learned something from Freeman Hatch about driving.

Proof that the Northern Light was staunch as well as swift was forthcoming on her next voyage, when she left Boston for Manilla again, sailing in December, 1856. South of the Pelew Islands she ran into a typhoon that beat anything Captain Doane had ever seen. For seven days, virtually under bare poles and never with more than a weather cloth in the mizzen rigging, she rolled her yardarms almost under and took so much water on deck with every roll that there was danger of her swamping or breaking up. But the old ship did neither. The worst she did was to roll the main topgallant mast out of her. Then, when the blow eased up a little, Captain Doane got some sail on her and brought her into Manilla. In the course of the next two years he made one more East India voyage in her and another round to San Francisco and Shanghai and then back to San Francisco and home *via* the Horn, arriving in Boston in the fall of 1860. This was Captain Doane's last voyage in the Northern Light. Under another commander, she went down the following year in a collision with a Frenchman, and Doane took command of the clipper Black Hawk, which he kept from 1862 or so until about 1867, running between New York and San Francisco and Liverpool and San Francisco. He wound up his sea career by having a go at steam in the S. S. America, which he took from New York to Hong Kong.

Shipmasters *of* Cape Cod

The next clipper captain about whom something must be said is young William H. Burgess, of Brewster, who, while still in his early twenties, had commanded the slow old Herbert in the East India trade. But his restless and impulsive nature demanded something livelier than East Indiamen, and at the age of twenty-two he was given command of the new clipper ship Whirlwind, then on the stocks at Medford. Captain Burgess had just married a young lady from Sandwich and was spending his honeymoon in Boston, sometimes driving her out to Medford to see how their new ship was progressing, sometimes offering her green turtle soup in Brigham's Saloon, which, because she thought it looked like muddy water, she politely declined in favor of a piece of pie. Mrs. Burgess was, in fact, a wise woman for a girl of her years and a shrewd observer of her husband's character. 'I am happy in the love of my husband,' she writes, 'yet one thing grieves me; he does not carry out those principles he once professed to sustain. In his letters written to me at sea, he appeared to enjoy sweet communion with his God. O that he might again experience this happy feeling!'

After one voyage out to San Francisco and back in 1852–53, Captain Burgess sailed there again with his wife in February, 1854. Her sea journal, kept during this second voyage of the Whirlwind, is, unlike most of the journals of captains' wives, full of shrewdness and interest: 'William,' she remarks, 'is very fond of planning out work for others to do.' Pious at all times, Mrs. Burgess set herself the task during this long voyage of curing the Captain of his unfortunate habit of swearing, and with such marked success that after being at sea for some three months, she was able to record, 'When you have head winds and calms, it is "awful papers," William says.' The voyage was, for a clipper, a long and tedious one, well calculated to try the patience of so fiery a youth as the Captain. 'But,' writes Mrs. Burgess in true wifely style, 'I think he stands it very well, considering his disposition.'

On May 17, 1854, having rounded the Horn and crossed the Equator on the northward half of their voyage, Mrs. Burgess writes: 'Crossed Equator 102 days at sea.... We have had a long passage, but I hope may not be beat by all the ships.' While the crew were busy painting the Whirlwind in preparation for entering port, the Captain himself — like Cæsar on another occasion — seized a brush and acquitted himself so creditably that his wife remarks, 'He makes an excellent painter.' From time to time the Captain himself wrote an entry in his wife's journal; 'Bad luck attends us well,' he says on June 8 — '124 days at sea.' But five days later they were in San Francisco, where they learned to their satisfaction that Mrs. Burgess's hope that the Whirlwind would not be beat by all the ships was realized, and that she had beaten the Queen of the Seas by a week. Both ships, in fact, reached port the same day, but the Queen had left Boston a week ahead of the Whirlwind.

From San Francisco the young couple took their ship to Callao and thence back to New York, where Captain Burgess turned her over to a new commander while he and his bride stepped to the quarter-deck of another clipper ship, the Challenger, in which they headed once more round the Horn over the old route. Leaving San Francisco, Captain Burgess had orders to pick up a cargo of guano at the Chincha Islands and proceed with it to Havre. But at the Islands he was taken ill and could not leave his berth. The nearest reliable doctor was in Valparaiso — twenty-two days away. The mate, Mr. Henry Winsor, though able to shoot the sun, could not work out the ship's position from his observations. Mrs. Burgess, nothing daunted, made all the calculations, and together she and Mr. Winsor navigated the Challenger to Valparaiso. The Captain died forty-eight hours before they reached port, but even in this crisis Mrs. Burgess was mistress of the situation. She arranged for her husband's body to be brought home in the ship Harriet Irving, and returned with it herself; it lies buried in West Sandwich — now Sagamore — where his widow spent the rest of her long life serenely and usefully.

During Captain Burgess's illness, both his wife and his mulatto steward, David Graves, had been in constant attendance beside his berth. When Mrs. Burgess left the Challenger, she gave Graves her Bible, with an appropriate inscription, as an expression of gratitude for his devotion. Graves kept the present with him constantly for the next six years — until 1862, when he was serving as steward on the Ringleader, another clipper ship, commanded by Captain Otis White, of Yarmouth, and bound from Hong Kong to San Francisco. In the course of the voyage she was wrecked, in May, 1862, on Formosa and was looted clean by Chinese mooncussers, who seem to have been as expert in the business as their western brethren.

A day or so later, a certain Mr. Dennison, while idly visiting the scene of the wreck, happened to see a Bible among other unprized objects abandoned by the Chinamen. He picked it up, identified it by the inscription as having belonged to Mrs. Burgess, and, thanks to the good offices of Richard Henry Dana, succeeded finally in having it forwarded to her in West Sandwich, where it reposes today in the rooms of the Sandwich Historical Society. Captain White, of the Ringleader, who had previously commanded the clippers Competitor and Renown, spent two months on Formosa arranging affairs in regard to the wreck. His health, which had been poor throughout the voyage, was not improved by his sojourn on the Island or by the anxiety connected with the disaster. His business completed, he returned to Yarmouth, where he died soon after at the age of thirty-seven, and another fine shipmaster was lost to the nation.

The Ringleader, as a matter of fact, throughout her whole career had been commanded by Yarmouth men.

The Clippers

Captain Richard Matthews took her new in 1853 and stayed in her until 1861, indulging in some pretty lively races to San Francisco during that time. The closest of them was in 1853–54, when five clippers and one full-bodied ship set sail over the long course within six days of each other, all leaving between October 19 and 25, 1853. They were, besides the Ringleader, the Samuel Lawrence, the Matchless, the Golden City, the Spitfire, and the San Francisco. The Golden City won the race in 108 days; two days later, Captain Matthews came boiling in, in 110 days, tying the Matchless for second place, both having left Boston the same day and arrived at San Francisco the same day. The Spitfire was next, in 120 days; then came the Samuel Lawrence in 127, but as she, unlike the rest, was not classed as a clipper, her run must be regarded as a very fine one. The luckless San Francisco would have made the best time of all, but she was piled up at the entrance to the harbor 106 days out, and became a total loss.

Captain Matthews left the Ringleader in the fall of 1861, and in the late sixties took command of the school ship George M. Barnard. Captain John White, of Yarmouth, a brother of Captain Otis White, took the Ringleader for a short time, and then turned her over to his brother, who lost her. Captains John and Otis, by the way, were nephews of the Eldridge brothers — Captains John, Asa, and Oliver; so their choice of a career was virtually a foregone conclusion.

In January, 1853, a voyage round Cape Horn was made that reads like fiction, pure and simple. Nothing except mutiny is lacking of all the trials that have made this grim promontory a byword among sailors. Captain Alvin S. Hallett, of Hyannis, in the clipper ship Phantom, left Boston January 6 with three New York clippers, the Eagle, the Celestial, and the Rattler, one day and two days behind him, the Celestial with the redoubtable Nat Palmer on her quarter-deck. But the Phantom was a fine ship, brand-new and very heavily sparred for her size. Captain Hallett saw no reason why he should not beat his rivals handsomely. He drove his ship mercilessly, was off Rio twenty-three days out — a record that still stands — and boiled along south into the teeth of a furious Cape Horn westerly. But the Captain held her to it, with every stitch of canvas she could struggle under, though part of her stem was swept away, her stern mouldings gone, and some of her channels started by the seas, which more than once made a clean breach across her. Fifteen men took to their bunks from overwork or from injuries received by being banged about her decks. But still the Captain drove her westward, mile by mile, until the new-fangled steering-gear broke, leaving the rudder swinging useless under her counter. Nothing daunted, Captain Hallett got tackles round the rudder-post to hold it steady while the carpenter cut a hole through it and shoved in a huge tiller. What was left of the crew rigged tackles to handle it with, and the Phantom was put on her course again. Almost immediately the tiller broke. The Captain, who could feel the hot breath of the New-Yorkers on the back of his neck even through the icy blasts of Cape Horn, devised a new steering apparatus that worked, banged his way round into the Pacific, and came booming into San Francisco in a passage of 104 days. The Eagle, the first of the New York clippers to reach port, arrived ten days later, with the Celestial and the Rattler a week or so behind her.

In San Francisco, Captain Hallett received orders to proceed to the Chincha Islands, load with guano, and return to New York. In carrying out these orders he stepped into one of the most picturesque international complications of the period. The guano islands had become a gold mine for the Peruvian Government. For centuries the unmolested haunts of millions of sea birds, they had accumulated literally mountains of fertile guano which brought a good price, particularly in the European market. So great was the demand that scores of vessels might be seen there at any time, lying at anchor, awaiting their turn to go under the chutes. Such a monopoly and such a demand gave rise, of course, to abuses. The guano had to be shoveled into wheelbarrows under an equatorial sun and rolled to the chutes — work that no sailors and few Peruvians could be made to perform. Consequently the villainous practice of importing Chinese coolies as laborers had been resorted to — nominally under a five-year contract, but as often as not for life — and these poor devils, who had been decoyed across the Pacific by glamorous tales of the California gold fields, were virtually kidnaped on the China Coast and brought into what amounted to slavery at the Chinchas — sometimes, it must be confessed, by Yankee shipmasters. So much for the first and most serious abuse. In the second place, in order that the interests of the Peruvian Government might be safeguarded, an official Commandant and a guard-ship were detailed to the Islands with a company or two of marines. South American petty officials have not a name for either wisdom or integrity, and the Peruvian Commandant who was in charge when Alvin Hallett brought the Phantom to her anchorage at the Chinchas was no exception to the rule. The trouble which followed is well described in a letter which the Captain wrote to the local Barnstable newspaper:

*Inhuman Outrage upon American Shipmasters
at Chincha Islands*

CHINCHA ISLANDS, *August* 19, 1853
S. B. PHINNEY, ESQR., *Collector of the Port of Barnstable:*
DEAR SIR:
Allow me to describe to you one of the most gross outrages on the American flag that ever occurred. On the 16th inst. Captain McCerran, of the ship Defiance, of New York, sent his boat with four men seining, which he had done daily. They being absent to a late hour, Captain McCerren sent his first officer in search of his

boat. At 9 P.M. the mate found them on board the guardship in irons and chained to the deck. He inquired the cause of this arrest and was answered that they had killed a pelican with their oar. He asked them what was the penalty. They answered the fine was one dollar, and he tendered it to them, saying that he wanted his men on board, as the ship was to be hauled from her berth the next morning. The Lieutenant saying that they should not be given up to the mate, he returned on board and reported to the Captain.

Captain McCerren, now went on board the guardship and demanded his men, saying he was waiting and ready to pay all lawful demands against those men in irons. They now surrounded him and thrust him into their boat and took him on board the guardship under guard of their marines. On the following day the American shipmasters assembled on board ship Defiance, and it was mutually agreed by all to call on board the guardship and to ask the privilege of an interview with the Commandant. Accordingly we all proceeded to go on board the guardship, totally unarmed, peaceably and quietly. When we came alongside the guardship, we asked permission to call on board. The Lieutenant invited us to go up. We then asked our interview with the Commandant, to which he replied that he was not on board, but on the Island. We dispatched a boat with four men in her requesting an interview with him on board his ship. He, twenty minutes after, came on board his ship, refusing to have anything to say with us on any business and immediately ordered his troops and marines to load their muskets and charge muskets upon us and to kill us and drive us, some thirty in number, from his deck; and they did, wounding several of us severely.

I was knocked off the gangway with a musket into the water and came near drowning, as I was stunned by the blow. I also received a bad wound by a bayonet-thrust in my leg. Captain McCerren, of the ship Defiance, was badly wounded; Captain O. B. Bearse [Orren B. Bearse, of Hyannis], of the ship Berlin, was wounded in his thigh by a bayonet; Captain Ellery, of ship Toronto, was also wounded by a bayonet; Captain Penhallow, of ship George Rogers, was badly wounded in his head — I think dangerously, and several others. We all then retreated on board ship Defiance and with the assistance of a doctor dressed the wounds of those wounded, after which we organized, drew up a petition, and chose a committee to proceed to Lima and report this outrage committed on American shipmasters, to the American minister at Lima, and have likewise sent copies of the same to the President of the United States and several editors of newspapers in New York, New Orleans, Boston, Baltimore and likewise to Valparaiso.

My object in writing you is, knowing your great attachment to the American flag, that you will not let this matter rest until the offenders in this most disgraceful outrage are fairly and fully punished. I flatter myself that the President of the United States will see the matter adjusted to our entire satisfaction. I suggest, Mr. Editor, that the great amount of shipping always at these Islands requires a man-of-war to be stationed here to make things go smoothly and quietly, especially as the Commandant says he is head over all; and in fact he is *absolute*. There are some sixty American ships at these Islands, and the gross outrage of yesterday might have been the cause of great sacrifice to American property. I doubt very much if it does not for the future, unless there is someone here to protect the American flag. I flatter myself you will take a lively interest in the above affair, as I am well aware of your great influence in political affairs. Leaving the whole matter to be disposed of as you may think proper, I remain yours very respectfully,

A. S. HALLETT
of ship Phantom of Boston

The matter was amicably settled between the two governments, and Captain Hallett, after retiring from the sea, served as Collector of the Port of Hyannis, a position of some consequence in the days when that village was a thriving coasting port.

For rivalry pure and simple, nothing in the history of sail was ever keener than the feeling between captains who came from neighboring towns on the Cape. To the citizens of 'High Barnstable' the rest of the Cape was unworthy of serious consideration; Brewster, even today, takes backwash from no one on earth; Provincetown has, from the days before the Mayflower, always been a law — and sometimes no law at all — unto itself; Dennis, realizing complacently that her list of deep-water captains was a proud one, looked upon other Cape shipmasters as little more than fishermen; Yarmouth defied any town in the country to show finer captains than the Eldridges, while Eastham and Orleans, secure in the records established by Hatch and Linnell, were content to let Sandwich boast its Ezra Nye, and Truro point proudly to the Collins boys.

In such a state of affairs, it may easily be imagined that when the captains of two racing clippers both hailed from Cape towns, their crews had a hard time of it. An interesting and heart-breakingly close contest of just this sort took place in 1853 between Captain Frederick Howes, of Yarmouth, in the Climax, and Captain Moses Howes, of North Dennis, in the Competitor. Both ships were clippers and both were making their maiden voyages. Captain Moses and the Competitor got away from Boston on March 27; Captain Frederick and the Climax got away the next day, both headed for San Francisco. But there the resemblance ends: two shipmasters more different in temperament, technique, or motive, it would be hard to find. Moses, who has been called 'the star captain of North Dennis,' was a ruthless and often reckless driver both of vessels and of men. He went to sea, in the opinion of his friend Captain Joshua Sears, 'for the glory and honor of the thing,' a motive far different from that of most Yankee captains. As he took the Competitor out of Boston, he was keenly aware of the dramatic nature of the race with the Climax and felt more interest, perhaps, in getting to San Francisco first than in bringing his ship there safely with his cargo in good order. Throughout the voyage he crowded on every stitch of canvas that his spars could carry and drove his crew accordingly.

The Clippers

One day behind him came Captain Frederick in the Climax — methodical, skillful, prudent, a master of his craft, a student of the ways of the sea and of ships. Seldom, if ever, in his career did he spring a spar or allow a sail to stand until it was blown from the bolt-ropes. Earlier in life he had been a cabinet-maker, and something of the nicety required by that work found its way into his handling of vessels. He was a man whom owners fought for, because, though he seldom made records, he could be relied on for consistently fast passages, and his ships reached port in good order, with cargoes undamaged. So, while he was just as anxious as Captain Moses to reach San Francisco first, he had no intention of trying to beat him there at any price.

Such were the men who, on March 27 and March 28, 1853, started their long race. Which, one may ask, was the better captain? The result of the race is the answer to the question. After 115 days, they finished as they had begun, Moses still a day ahead, Frederick still a day behind. But here is a significant thing, and one that will throw some light on Moses as a driver. Both had taken fifty-three days to the Horn, but there Moses, in a desperate attempt to get round into the Pacific, had crowded sail on the Competitor until, new though she was, he split her stem, starting a serious leak. There was nothing for it; he had to heave to for five days and chain-strap it, allowing Frederick in the Climax to jockey his way round into the Pacific with a four-day lead, which only further remorseless driving was able to overcome. Two fine shipmasters, temperamentally as far removed from each other as the East from the West and both significant figures in our merchant marine.

This race must have been of special interest to Captain Frederick, for he had equipped the Climax, whose building he had supervised throughout, with the new Howes double topsails, an invention of his own and one that had never before been tried on any ship. The purpose of it was to divide and conquer the huge, unmanageable single topsails which were then in use. The scheme worked so well that it was adopted by most new vessels and was patented by the Captain the next year.

A good picture of Captain Frederick and his wife in their later years has been left by Julian Hawthorne, who, while his father, Nathaniel, was serving as American consul in Liverpool, boarded at Mrs. Blodget's, a house which was patronized largely by Yankee shipmasters and their wives during their sojourns in port.

> The lady paramount of these, in my estimation [writes young Hawthorne], was the wife of old Captain Howes, the inventor of Howes patent rig, which he was at that time perfecting. He would sometimes invite me up to his room to see the exquisitely finished model which he had made with his own hands. He was commodore of the Captains — the oldest, wisest and most impressive of them; a handsome, massive, jovelike old gentleman, with the gentlest and most indulgent manners, and a straightforward, simple mariner withal. He had ceased to make voyages and was settled for the time being in Liverpool. Mrs. Howes seemed, to my boyish apprehension, to be a sort of princess of exquisite and gracious refinement. I could imagine nothing in feminine shape more delicate, of more languid grace, of finer patrician elegance.... Beside the heroic figure of the Captain she looked like a lily mated with an oak, but they were as happy a pair and as well mated as one could hope to see.

Captain Moses Howes, true to type, while Captain Frederick was perfecting the model of his patent rig, continued to make smashing passages to San Francisco even after the full glory of the clipper-ship era had departed; and he usually arrived well up among the leaders of the fleet. A veteran San Francisco stevedore, Henry Ames, in a letter to Captain Joshua Sears, shows the sort of thing that Captain Moses was up to:

The Clippers

SAN FRANCISCO, *May* 10, 1861

... the Andrew Jackson has arrived again in 102 days.... but Moses Howes in the Reporter was after him with a sharp stick. He arrived the next day in 103 days, which I think is the passage of the two, as the Reporter has the most cargo according to the tonnage of the different ships. The Romance of the Seas and Spitfire were 106 days, the Talisman 112 days, the Mary L. Sutton 110.

If then, as Joshua Sears believed, Captain Moses went to sea for the glory and honor of the thing, he did not go in vain.

The town of Dennis was, in fact, full of Captain Howeses. At least twelve of that name hailed from East Dennis alone, all of them deep-water shipmasters, and one particularly distinguished Howes family had three brothers, Levi, William F., and Allison, all of whom commanded clippers. Captain William had one of the loveliest ships ever built on the Cape — or anywhere else, for that matter. She was the clipper Belle of the West, built by the Shivericks in East Dennis, a firm which, thanks largely to the backing of Christopher Hall, did much to promote the prosperity of the Cape throughout the fifties. The Belle was not a very big ship — 178 feet over all, some 60 feet shorter than the famous Flying Cloud — but she was very heavily sparred for her size and in every respect the perfect model of a clipper. Thomas F. Hall, son of Christopher Hall, went in her for four years or more as mate under Captain William Howes, and declares that she was the handsomest ship he ever saw.

Captain William had the Belle from 1853, when she was launched, until 1859, sailing her wisely and well, but never driving her and never making any sensational passages. His two voyages to San Francisco, made in 1853 and 1859, are typical of his even and moderate sailing — 132 and 133 days respectively. For the rest of her career under him, she was in the East India trade, operating with the reliability of a steamer, but never with the speed that we have learned

183

to associate with clippers. In 1859, Captain William turned her over to his brother Allison, who continued making voyages in her to the East Indies, and on one occasion had a fine chance to race the third brother of this seagoing family, our friend Captain Levi Howes, of the cotton trade.

Captain Levi had given up the sea about 1850 and gone back to East Dennis to join forces with Christopher Hall and Prince S. Crowell as owner and manager of ships. His investments, though not large, he believed adequate, and all went well for the next seven or eight years. Then things began to flatten out. The California boom was a thing of the past; China and the East Indies, though still good, were not what they had been; the stablest firms in Boston and New York were beginning to shorten sail and to place fewer orders for new clippers. By the end of 1855, the thought of taking to the quarter-deck once more had begun to cross Captain Levi's mind as an unpleasant possibility. 'I tell you what, Joshua,' he said to Captain Sears, 'it would come mighty hard for me to go to sea again.' But the panic of 1857 settled the matter, and what was misfortune for him was good news to Boston owners. He took command of the clipper Starlight and sailed her four times round the world.

It was while he had her in 1863 that he fell in with his brother, Captain Allison Howes, of the Belle of the West, in Calcutta. By a happy accident the two ships sailed for Boston only twelve hours apart, Captain Levi ahead; they sighted each other three times during the passage and finished in exactly the same relative positions, Levi reaching Boston twelve hours ahead of Allison, a remarkable performance, for the Starlight was by no means so sharp a ship as the Belle, and only twelve feet longer. Before he gave up the sea for good, Captain Levi had two other fine commands, the Orpheus and the Asa Eldridge, both clippers and the latter named for the celebrated Yarmouth captain who had been lost in the Collins steamer Pacific. When

The Clippers

Levi Howes retired this time, he had money enough to see him through. His declining years were spent in East Dennis, where he took great interest in the schools and served as Superintendent of them until his death in 1874.

There is a certain monotony, it is to be feared, in mentioning so constantly the maiden voyage of this ship or that as being made by a Cape captain. But maiden voyages, always important, were of particular significance in the case of clippers, for learning the tricks of these wild new flyers took nerves of steel and wisdom which was intuition mixed with the gift of prophecy. So it is no mere chattiness that prompts the mention of maiden voyages; and here is another man, coming from Brewster, who took two clipper ships to sea for their first trips, and in one of them covered himself, his ship, and the town of Brewster with glory. He was Tully Crosby, younger brother of Captain Joshua Crosby, who in 1822 gave Tully his first taste of the sea by signing him on as cabin boy in the brig Telemachus for a voyage to Surinam. After ten years under his brother, Tully, at the age of twenty-three, got his first command, the Plymouth-built brig Old Colony. From such modest beginnings Captain Crosby rose, *via* the bark Arab and the ships Charlotte and Monterey, to the command of the new clipper ship Antelope in 1851. He took her round the world from Boston by way of San Francisco, Shanghai, and back to New York with such success that two years later William Lincoln and Company, of Boston, put him in command of the fine big clipper Kingfisher.

Here was a command worthy of Captain Crosby's talents, and to add to his satisfaction he had a mighty rival to race against on his first voyage to San Francisco — Captain Caldwell in Donald McKay's great clipper, Bald Eagle. The ships were virtually of a size, the Bald Eagle being 225 feet long over all, against the Kingfisher's 217. On October 1, 1853, Caldwell weighed anchor in Boston Harbor and was off; two days later, Crosby was after him, straining every nerve in the long stern chase. By the time they reached San Francisco, Crosby had caught him, and the two great ships swept in through the Golden Gate almost within hail of each other, and that in spite of the fact that Crosby had been hopelessly becalmed in a fog for five days off the very entrance to San Francisco Harbor. This victory was a fitting climax to a long career at sea. Crosby brought his ship back to New York *via* Callao and Hampton Roads, and retired, turning the command of the Kingfisher over to a fellow townsman, Captain Zenas Crosby. He spent the rest of his life at home, serving his town as Representative to the General Court at various times between 1856 and 1865. He died in 1891 at the age of eighty-two.

Other Brewster men, too, distinguished themselves in clippers — as indeed Brewster men have always done in every branch of the merchant service. It would be interesting to go into details of the experiences of such men as Captain Benjamin Freeman, who in 1854 took the Witchcraft from New York to San Francisco in ninety-eight days and then took command of the Climax; or of another Brewster captain, William B. Cobb, who commanded McKay's great clipper, Empress of the Seas, and who afterwards went into steam on the Pacific. Captain Allen Crowell, of Hyannis, who back in 1847 had taken the schooner Cabot to Ireland, had by the later fifties risen to the command of the clipper ship Archer, and kept on at sea until he had completed forty-six years as master, retiring in 1887. But details of the careers of these men are not at hand, and perhaps it is just as well, for if they were, they would fill a volume. The same is true of the three Bearse brothers of Hyannis. One of them, Captain Frank, in 1854 made the amazing run of thirty-four days in the Winged Arrow from Cape Horn to right off the Golden Gate, and then lay becalmed for a week, champing at the bit and shortening his life;

186

the next brother, Captain Richard, in 1853 ran the Abby Pratt on Old South Shoal, Nantucket, in a December snowstorm; but as if to show that the accident was no fault of his, he was put in command of the new clipper ship Robin Hood on her maiden voyage to San Francisco the next year and brought her back from Shanghai to New York in ninety-five days.

The third brother, Captain Warren Bearse, was perhaps the most celebrated of the three. On September 28, 1854, he left New York for Melbourne in command of the Flying Scud. When two days out, he ran into a terrific thunderstorm in the Gulf Stream, during which his ship, a target for the lightning because of a cargo of iron, was struck twice, luckily with no damage beyond knocking down the crew and deranging the compasses so that for some time they had to be put on the end of a plank lashed pirate-fashion out over the ship's side. The lightning — or something — had further galvanized the Flying Scud into such fabulous activity that shortly after the storm she is said to have made a run of 449 miles in twenty-four hours. But though reputable authorities are inclined to believe this extraordinary record — which, if true, would eclipse the 436 miles made by the ship Lightning earlier in the same year — it must be relegated to the realm of fiction, where it belongs. However, Captain Bearse got the Flying Scud to Melbourne in eighty days, and brought her home by way of Calcutta and Marseilles. On her return he left her for the John Wade. His friend Captain Rodney Baxter, also of Hyannis, took command of the Flying Scud and began to put her through her paces in notable fashion.

That he was a driver had already been shown by his record Sligo–Boston voyage in the schooner American Belle; and he was as good a man in a clipper ship as he was in a fore-and-aft schooner. In December, 1855, he took the Flying Scud from New York to Marseilles in the record time of nineteen days, twenty hours, deep loaded with grain and drawing twenty-two feet of water. Another remarkable passage — a record at the time and beaten on only two or three occasions since — was his eighty-one days from New York to Bombay, made in the spring and early summer of 1856. (The Captain himself called his time eighty-two days.) This was an eventful passage in more ways than one. The crew twice mutinied, once in New York Harbor and once in the Indian Ocean. The Flying Scud lay off the Battery ready to sail. Captain Baxter was ashore, attending to some final details with the owners. When at last he was ready, he took a tugboat and started for his ship. Here is the way he tells the story of what followed:

> On my arrival in the tugboat alongside, stepping on deck, I saw a lot of blood.... I immediately inquired of my first officer, Mr. Campbell, 'What was the matter on board?' Said he, 'Fifteen of the men came aft to take charge of the ship. Mr. Faunce, second mate, gave them a good pounding, and the leader, I fear, will not be able to do duty for some time. Mr. Faunce stood right here between the rail and the water tank so that they could not get behind him and he only struck them a blow apiece, and they crawled forward like so many lame ducks. I was ready to assist him, but he did not need my help....'
> ... we stopped at Mauritius twelve hours. After leaving that port we experienced a hurricane... and were caught in the vortex. It commenced with a moderate gale and increased so that we were under three lower topsails... It struck the ship, laying her on her beam ends with the lower yards in the water. The topsails blew from the yards like so much light cotton cloth, and nearly all the sails that were furled were stripped to atoms. The men were crawling to windward, holding on to the weather side, catching hold of any piece of rope or belaying pin that was at hand. The ship lay in that position about five minutes....
> I don't think it was forty-five minutes from the time the cyclone struck until it was perfectly calm and smooth water, as the wind blew the top of the sea off. After dinner all hands were ordered to turn to, as we gave our men

watch and watch all the voyage. The afternoon watch below refused... There was our ship, unmanageable — no sails that could be used.... The fragments hanging to the yards had to be stripped off and new ones bent. Said I, 'Mr. Campbell, send one watch aloft to strip off the old sails and order the men who have refused duty to come aft,' which he did. 'Now,' said I, 'men, I consider you in a state of mutiny. No excuse will answer for refusing to do work you are ordered to do. You know well we cannot manage the ship as she is.' (My officers were prepared for any emergency, as we are commanded to watch as well as pray.) Said I, 'Now you must either do the work I ask of you or go in irons.'

The Captain then put them in irons and triced them up to a line by the wrists, their arms over their heads, and stripped to the waist to be flogged. But they consented to go back to work before any stripes were laid on.

On their arrival at Bombay, Lord Elphinstone, Commissioner-General of India, visited the Flying Scud, to congratulate Captain Baxter on his quick passage, which he said was a record, and invited him to take a sail in his yacht in order to criticize her rig, for he was dissatisfied with her behavior. The Captain consented, and gladly gave his advice as to rerigging her. She had a lovely hull, the Captain says; but her spars and top hamper were too heavy in proportion and the lower masts too short. As the Captain put it to Lord Elphinstone, 'Silk stockings and rope-yarn garters do not compare well together.'

Here is the Captain's account of another brilliant piece of work in racing against the Boston Light, commanded by Captain Elkanah Crowell, Jr., of West Yarmouth:

I was in Calcutta in command of the Flying Scud. The clipper ship Boston Light, Captain Elkanah Crowell, arrived there about the time I was ready to sail for Bombay. On our arrival at Bombay, we discharged our cargo and took another and sailed for London. Having rounded the Cape of Good Hope on our homeward bound passage, we saw, one morning, about six sail in the distance ahead. We were in the trade winds, had our studding-sails and sky-sails set, with the wind on our quarter. At four P.M. we had passed all the fleet excepting one; at nine o'clock that night, we passed the last one, which sailed faster than the rest. We hailed her, and they answered, 'Ship Boston Light, from Calcutta for Cowes.' As we passed her, we saw the letter H painted in black on her fore-topsail.

In the later fifties Captain Baxter went into steam in the employ of George Low, of New York, running packets between New York, Aspinwall, and New Orleans, and Captain David Swinerton, of Barnstable, took over the Flying Scud. 'I regard him,' writes George Low of Captain Baxter, 'as one of the best merchant captains I had in the employment of the line, and I know of no man in the merchant service that I would select before him to command a steamship or a sailing ship.'

After he retired, Captain Baxter amused himself with religious controversy, taking particular delight in attacking the Trinitarians and in expressing his views emphatically on such matters as the Virgin Birth. 'There are a great many Trinitarians that would, no doubt, like to pay their debts by giving one dollar for three,' he writes. 'One of them owed me $1000, and I got three cents on a dollar. The third in the Trinity, the Ghost, paid me.'

The conclusion of another article—this time against the belief in the Immaculate Conception — is equally amusing: 'There are no less than six Bibles or sacred books of different nations which claim a prophet of immaculate conception; therefore the birth of Christ could not be a very uncommon occurrence, especially as they were all before him and none since, except one on Cape Cod; but they could not make anyone believe it outside the family. This is a fact, and I can give the names of the parties.'

But we have wandered far from the clippers and their voyages. It is time to return to them, and incidentally to begin a new chapter.

9

More Clippers

CAPTAIN ASA ELDRIDGE, of whom mention has already
been made, lived to see the era of clipper ships well
under way and was himself anything but idle during
the early years of it. After leaving the packets of the
old Dramatic Line, and before taking command of the
clipper ship Red Jacket, he accepted an invitation
from Cornelius Vanderbilt to take his new 260-foot
steam yacht North Star on a cruise in European waters,
sailing from New York in May, 1853. Mr. Vanderbilt
expressed the hope that Mrs. Eldridge would accom-
pany the Captain, and she did so.

Today the position of captain of a yacht is an
anomalous one. Though not quite a servant, the captain is by no means master. Socially, he is nowhere, at
least while on board, and the fault, if fault there be, is
neither his nor the owner's, but the result of inevitable
lost caste among officers of our merchant marine con-
sequent upon the lost caste of our merchant marine itself. With the virtual disappearance of our flag from
the sea, the pride of command that once attended it
has vanished as well. But in the forties and fifties, a
man who had commanded Liverpool packets was the
equal — afloat or ashore — of any man alive; and Captain Eldridge and his wife, throughout the voyage of
the North Star, were on terms of entire equality with
all the ship's company. When the yacht put in at

191

Southampton, and the Mayor invited Mr. Vanderbilt and his friends to a gala luncheon, he included, as a matter of course, the Captain and Mrs. Eldridge; and when, after lunch, the speeches began, the Captain was called upon with the rest, and he justified the toast-master's confidence by a series of remarks so pertinent and pithy, and above all so brief, that they quite out-shone the efforts of earlier speakers.

The lunch was, in fact, a tremendous affair; most of the distinguished men of Southampton were on hand, and, in the words of one of the guests, 'the presence of nearly one hundred ladies gave a charm to the occasion.' But it took more than a hundred ladies to bother a Cape Cod shipmaster. Alderman Andrews, in intro-ducing Captain Eldridge at the end of a lengthy ad-dress, proposed as a toast, 'Success to the North Star, her commander, officers, and crew.' The toast (not the first in the course of the proceedings) was drunk amid prolonged cheers, and Captain Eldridge rose to his feet. He was much obliged to them, he said, for the honor which they had done to the toast; it went down as though it was good! (Laughter and cheers.) It was always gratifying to a man, especially on such an occasion, to have his health drunk so unanimously and with such kind feeling. He was glad to say he felt quite at home. The reception they had met with was a source of gratitude to himself, his officers, and his crew, most of whom, he was proud to say, were the sons of gentlemen. (Cheers.) This was the first time he had visited Southampton, and he was much pleased with the port, the entrance of the docks, the excellent accommodation afforded (Loud cheers) — with the courtesy they had experienced, and with the police and all other regulations appertaining to the docks. (Hear!) The visit of the North Star, he continued, had created some interest, and he thought it was justly due. It was a noble and glorious enterprise, and he felt proud of the ship and of the position he held in her. The Commodore had conferred an honor upon him by giving him the command, and he thanked him for it. He was proud of him as a man and also of his sons and daughters — he loved them all. Every captain was proud of his own ship, and he had no wish to be particular in this respect. (Laughter and cheers.)... The North Star, he reminded them, had been open to the public the week before, and he had then hoisted the English flag by the side of the American, and so he hoped the two flags would long continue. (Loud cheers.) England and America, if separated, might get into difficulties; but united, they would whip the world. (Loud cheers.)

That Captain Eldridge's seamanship was as good as his oratory appeared not long after this festive occasion. The North Star, in the course of her cruise, visited a number of Mediterranean ports, in many of which the regulations required that a pilot should be employed. While one of these local experts was taking the yacht through a ticklish piece of channel, Captain Eldridge and Mr. Vanderbilt stood together on the bridge, watching the maneuver.

'If that chap doesn't look out, he'll have us aground in a minute,' remarked the Captain.

At that moment the steamer grounded on a mud-flat, and had to be hauled off by tugs. Thereafter Mr. Vanderbilt made a practice of consulting the Captain when entering harbors — and wisely, if the opinion of the ship's company is to be believed. 'Everyone on board the yacht,' writes one of them, 'felt the amount of indebtedness under which he labored to Captain Eldridge, whose nautical skill is only equaled by his cheerful-hearted, everyday kindness. I do not exaggerate when I say that those who have seen him navigate the Mediterranean, where he had never been, and enter ports without a pilot, are quite satisfied that an abler seaman never trod a quarter-deck.'

After a four-months' cruise, during which she sailed some fifteen thousand miles, the North Star returned to New York, where Captain Eldridge was presented with a silver service as an expression of the gratitude of Mr. Vanderbilt and his guests. By this time, as a matter of fact, Cape houses all the way from Sandwich to Truro must have been pretty well cluttered up with similar massive tokens, not always ornamental and never used. But then — a silver service was a silver service.

While the Captain was abroad, George Thomas, the fine old shipbuilder of Rockland, Maine, had been at work on a new clipper, the Red Jacket, designed by Samuel Pook. She would not be ready until about four months after the return of the North Star, but her owners, Seacomb and Taylor, of Boston, invited Captain Eldridge to take command of her. This suited the Captain nicely; it gave him a good vacation, with a fine ship in prospect at the end of it. He enjoyed them both, and on January 11, 1854, he put to sea in his new clipper from New York, bound for Liverpool, on a voyage that was to become unique in the annals of our merchant marine.

Through snow, sleet, and hail on every day of the crossing, Captain Eldridge drove the Red Jacket to a record passage of 13 days, 1 hour, from dock to dock, a performance never equaled by a sailing ship before or since. And what was more, on the ninth day of the run, he logged 413 miles, a distance that has been beaten by only three other sailing vessels in maritime history. But perhaps the most spectacular part of the voyage was the beautiful piece of seamanship that Captain Eldridge provided for the throngs of watchers that lined the banks as the Red Jacket came sweeping into the Mersey under her own sail and with every stitch drawing. At exactly the right moment he gave the order; her upper sails crumpled, the wind was spilled from her courses, and the Captain shot his great ship into the wind and backed her alongside the dock without so much as a pull from any of the puffing tugs that surrounded her: a maneuver so delicate that not one shipmaster in a hundred would have dared to try it.

More Clippers

If anything was needed to add to the fame of Captain
Eldridge, this flourish did it. The world was at his feet,
and he might choose what command he would. The
Red Jacket was sold to the English almost immediately on her arrival at Liverpool, and the Captain,
whose reputation had been made on the Atlantic,
ended his days on the same gray ocean, almost exactly
two years later, in the Collins liner Pacific.

Meanwhile, Captain John Eldridge, the oldest brother of the family, had left the Atlantic packets, where
his robust talents had found appropriate expression for
years, to take command of the Young Brander, built in
1853 by Jotham Stetson of Chelsea. She may or may
not have been a clipper — authorities differ on this
point — but at any rate she was a fine ship, one that
any captain might have been proud to command.
She was very soon sold to New Orleans owners, however, and afterwards to the British. Later Captain
Eldridge took command of a troop ship in the Civil
War, appropriately enough the old Collins liner Baltic,
which the Government had taken over at the beginning of hostilities.

A story that shows something of his character is
told of him while he was thus engaged. The Baltic
lay in a southern tidewater harbor where she was to
pick up General Terry. Captain Eldridge notified the
General that the latest moment for sailing was nine
o'clock the following morning; it would be impossible
to get out of the harbor after that. Nine o'clock came,
and the General had not appeared. Eldridge ordered
the gangplank in and was in the act of casting off when
Terry came riding pompously down the wharf. 'Too
late to take your horse!' shouted the Captain. 'You'll
have to jump if you're coming yourself.' But Terry
was not used to taking orders, nor did he believe that
any man would dare to sail away without him. So he
took his time, confident that Captain Eldridge would
hold on. What was his fury to see the Baltic swing
clear of the dock and head out of the harbor. He had

to commandeer a tug to catch her and then climb up over the side like any bum-boat man.

Some months later Captain Eldridge was dining in a New York hotel. At a table near-by sat General Terry, surrounded by members of his staff. Catching sight of the Captain, he jumped to his feet, crying, 'There's the ruffian that sailed without me!' Walking over to the Captain's table, he continued, 'I wish I'd taken this sword and slashed you with it!' 'Another word out of you,' replied Eldridge, 'and I'll take the sword away from you and smash it over your head.' Verily, the Army and the Navy do not always see eye to eye.

After the war, Captain Eldridge left the sea for good to spend the last years of his life in Yarmouth, where he died in 1874 at the age of seventy-five, the only one of the three brothers to end his days in his native town.

The youngest of them, Captain Oliver Eldridge, whose work in China waters in the Coquette had aroused British envy in 1844, and who in 1848 had taken Warren Delano's early clipper Memnon out to China on her maiden voyage, was given command of Daniel C. Bacon's big new clipper ship Titan on her maiden voyage to Liverpool in 1855. The Titan was described as late as 1857 as 'the largest and finest clipper in the world'; but the launching of each new Yankee flyer lent itself so readily to similar hyperbole that the description need not be taken literally. Be that as it may, she looked good to the French Government, which promptly chartered her to carry troops and munitions from Marseilles to the Crimea. Captain Eldridge left her and came home; and for the next few years his activities are not recorded. Then, in spite of his wife's wish that he should leave the sea, he took command of the old Collins liner Atlantic, which he ran as a transport in the Civil War. Later the Pacific Mail Company offered him a salary of twenty thousand dollars a year in gold to take charge of their business in San Francisco, and he accepted. His new position did not take all his time or energy, however, for in addition to it, he became president of the California Dry Dock Company, president of the Capital Gas Company and of the Stockton Gas Company, president of the Sunset Telephone Company, vice-president and founder of the Title Insurance and Trust Company, director of the Wells, Fargo Company, and organizer and director of the Spring Valley Water Works.

An illuminating anecdote is told of him during these years in San Francisco. By the time he got out there, the days when an officer might knock a man down and hear no more of it were about over. A good deal of rhetoric was being expended, chiefly by humanitarian landsmen, in defense of 'Sailor's Rights,' and thus encouraged, sea lawyers began to appear in the forecastles of many ships. Keeping abreast of the times, nominally at least, the Pacific Mail Company made a rule that no officer on any of its vessels should strike a member of the crew. Young Cyrus Bassett, of Yarmouth, while mate of one of their ships, was in charge of a crew of Chinamen that he had ordered to get out some cargo. They refused to work; so Bassett jumped into the hold and knocked down six or eight of them. He was immediately taken to task and sent before Oliver Eldridge.

'Cyrus,' said the Captain, 'was it you that knocked those men down?'

'Yes, Captain, it was,' replied Bassett.

'What for?'

'They refused to get out the cargo.'

'Go aboard your ship,' ordered Eldridge. 'If I'd been there, I'd have done just as you did.'

When the Captain had left the Titan in Liverpool and she was chartered by the French, another Cape man was on hand to take command of her — Captain J. Henry Sears, of Brewster, a youngster of twenty-six, but a veteran shipmaster. At twenty-two he had commanded the Faneuil Hall in the European trade, and at twenty-four had taken the clipper ship Wild Ranger to San Francisco on the first two voyages of her career. For the next two years, he was busy carrying troops and munitions between French ports and the Crimea in the Titan. Then came the year 1857, the most exciting of Captain Sears's career. The Crimean War was over, and the Titan was ordered to New Orleans to load cotton for Liverpool. Sears took on 6900 bales — the largest cotton cargo that had ever been shipped — and headed across the Atlantic. But the Titan, owing perhaps to a collision with the iron steamer Marley Hill during her service as a transport, had become leaky; the rough weather which she now encountered increased the leak, and off Liverpool she ran into a full gale. Captain Sears picked up a pilot and was in hopes of getting into the river before the leak became dangerous. Luck was against him, however; the wind heeled the big hull way over on her bilge, and the water, all running to leeward, listed her until she was almost on her beam ends and would not steer. To put her on an even keel the main and mizzen masts had to be cut away. Thus eased, the hull righted and was towed into the Mersey.

After she had been rerigged and caulked, Captain Sears took her out to Melbourne with about a thousand passengers and a lot of cargo. There he received orders to proceed to the Chinchas and load with guano for Queenstown. With his cargo safely on board, he left the Islands late in the year only to run into a Cape Horn snorter that opened up the old leak or started a new one. After fighting it for four days, during which the water in the hold rose steadily, Captain Sears abandoned the Titan in the South Atlantic, 1100 miles off Brazil, and all hands took to the boats. A week later they were picked up by a Frenchman and landed at Pernambuco.

After a year or two more at sea, making voyages to California and Australia in the Franklin Haven,

More Clippers

Captain Sears came ashore at the beginning of the Civil War to go into the shipping business in Boston. There he remained until 1898, when he retired and moved to Brewster, occupying himself during his later years by collecting data about the master mariners of the town and handing the results down to posterity in the form of *Brewster Ship Masters,* one of the most valuable books of the sort extant.

In the fall of 1853, James Curtis launched the lean and lovely clipper ship Eagle Wing at his yard in Medford. Captain Eben H. Linnell, of Orleans, who had distinguished himself in the cotton trade in the blunt old Cabinet and had afterwards, in the Buena Vista, given Captain Levi Stevens and the Southern Cross a run for their money from San Francisco to Calcutta, was now promoted to the command of this fine new ship. By midwinter she was ready for sea, and Captain Linnell took her out of Boston on December 20, 1853, headed, like all clippers of the early fifties, for San Francisco, but destined to complete a cruise of more than two years before she came home again.

Linnell soon had a chance to test the seaworthiness of his command. Four days out he ran into a gale of such violence as even the North Atlantic in mid-winter seldom provides.

> First part threatening weather [says his log]. Shortened sail; at 4 P.M. close-reefed topsails and furled courses; hove ship to under close-reefed main topsail and spencer, ship lying with lee rail under water, nearly on beam ends; at 1.30 A.M. the fore and main topgallant masts went over the side, it blowing a perfect hurricane; at 8 A.M. moderating; a sea took away the jibboom and cap of bowsprit; in 31 years at sea have never seen a typhoon or hurricane so severe. Had two men washed overboard, saved one.

In spite of this strenuous start, Linnell reached San Francisco in 105 days, convinced that he had not only a remarkable sea-boat but a flyer as well. He took her across to China, arriving in the spring of 1854. By this

199

time the California boom had flattened out to such an extent that tea-carrying between China and London offered better profits for Yankee vessels, particularly since the British had not as yet learned the art of building clippers of their own, and Londoners, for all that blood is thicker than water, did not enjoy waiting for their fresh consignments of tea. Theodore and George Chase, therefore, owners of the Eagle Wing, ordered Linnell to load with tea for London. He accordingly sailed from Foo Chow on the last day of July, 1854, on a voyage that took 113 days and taught the Captain some new tricks in the ways of the China Sea. Ten days out he was nearly wrecked by a typhoon, and had to finish the voyage virtually without a mizzen mast; that he limped into the Thames in 113 days is a high tribute to his seamanship. His bill for repairs in London amounted to £1470, but as he carried 1308 tons of tea at a freight rate of £8 a ton, the voyage was not entirely disastrous.

After a tedious sojourn in London, while the leisurely British riggers were putting his vessel in commission, the Captain headed for Hong Kong, taking his departure from the Downs on April 17, 1855, and arriving in Hong Kong on July 10, after a passage of 83½ days — a record for the course, and a mark at which all the British clippers of later days were to shoot in vain. As if to prove that this record run was no lucky fluke, Captain Linnell, after four months in China, sailed from Woosung for New York on November 22, and arrived in 86 days, a remarkable passage, in the course of which he overhauled in the Straits of Sunda McKay's early pre-clipper, Joshua Bates, which had sailed three weeks ahead of him, and later spoke McKay's famous flyer, Romance of the Seas, which had left Shanghai with a fortnight's lead.

Two years and two months away from home had earned a vacation for Captain Linnell, and he took it. For the next nine months he stayed in Orleans and amused himself by inventing an improvement on Captain Frederick Howes's double topsail rig. Sixty-four vessels — including a number of Shiverick-built ships — adopted this rig soon after it was patented.

The Chases, meantime, had been building a new clipper, named the Flying Mist, and they invited Linnell to take command of her. He felt that he had been idle long enough; so in November, 1856, he set sail for California with his new command. Arriving there after a good, though not remarkable passage, he wrote to his owners: 'The Port Warden, in making his report, states that the Flying Mist is the only ship that ever came to this port entirely free of sweat or dampness, also the least broken packages.' From San Francisco he set sail for Valparaiso and thence took a short jog north to Caldera, also on the coast of Chile. On this leg of the voyage, he sighted a yacht in distress. Bringing the Flying Mist alongside, the Captain rescued all hands, including two South American gentlemen, Martin Manterola and Peter Uncondo, one of whom tendered the Captain his undying — and at times, it must be confessed, embarrassing — gratitude. 'I desire above all things to be rich,' wrote Manterola to Linnell, some months later, 'so as to make a handsome present to your wife, and thus manifest, to some small extent, the gratitude I owe the Saviour of my life.'

Nothing very exciting occurred on the way home from Caldera. The Flying Mist reached the Chesapeake August 23, 1857, in the very fast time of fifty-one days from Caldera, but Linnell was used to carrying sail, and fast passages were expected of him. He then took her out to Singapore and Hong Kong and back to New York by way of Manilla, reaching home in time to spend Christmas of 1858 in Orleans with his family. Next he went to Hong Kong, where, finding business very dull and cargoes scarce, he decided to cheer things up a bit by giving a ball on board ship. The date set for the event was November 25, 1859 — Thanksgiving Day in New England — and Captain Linnell, who was never one to do things by halves, spread himself to make it a gala occasion. The Hong Kong *Daily Press* for November 26, 1859, gave a florid account of the ball, in which the reporter expressed pity for those 'pouting beauties who stayed on shore.' Captain Joshua Sears, who was in port with the Wild Hunter, was among those present, and gives a more detailed description of the festivities in a letter to his wife back in East Dennis:

> Captain Linnell of the Flying Mist, gave a great Ball on board his ship last Thursday evening. Invitations were sent to all, from the Governor down to the shipmaster. It was really a grand affair. I should like to have had you and Lulu there, for crinoline was very much in demand, as there is only about fifteen ladies in port, and some of them have got such d——d jealous husbands that they cannot let them dance with anyone else out of their sight. What a happy life they must live. One poor Devil of a Captain here has got a wife eighteen years old, and he can't bear for anybody else to look at her. Another poor fellow six feet, four inches tall weighing two hundred and fifty pounds, has got a wife four feet, two inches tall, weighing eighty-three pounds. He, too, cannot let his wife out of his sight. Poor Devil, he is even jealous at sea, with nobody but his officers on board. Happy man he, don't you think so?

From Hong Kong, Captain Linnell crossed to San Francisco again, put in at Baker's Islands for guano, and sailing from there in midsummer of 1860, finally returned to New York. At this point he took a year off, which he undoubtedly spent in Orleans, probably building a big new house, for he did, at some time or other, erect such a mansion on the Bay Side of the town, patterned after one that had taken his fancy somewhere in the south of France. In February, 1862, he picked up the Flying Mist again in London, took her to Glasgow, loaded 1760 sheep for New Zealand, hired eighteen shepherds to look after them, and set sail in May — 'all in fine trim,' as he says. He made the voyage in eighty-one days, picked up a pilot off Bluff

Harbor, and, with his ship riding to two anchors, believed that his troubles were over. Instead, they were just beginning, for, by one of those inexplicable accidents that sometimes occur at sea, the ship dragged both anchors in a flat calm, went on a rock and became a total loss. Here is Linnell's letter to his owners:

BLUFF HARBOR, *August* 26, 1862

GEO. B. CHASE, ESQR.,

DEAR SIR:

I am sorry to have to inform you of the loss of the Flying Mist in the Harbor of the Bluff on the morning of the 27th instant. I arrived off the Port on the 26th at 1 P.M. took a Pilot, the wind being scant to run up to the upper anchorage. The Pilot brought the ship to anchor at the lower or old anchorage with one anchor. We furled the sails, then gave the ship a broad shear and let go the second anchor, and when the pilot left the ship, he said to me, 'the Ship is perfectly secure' and he would be on board in the morning and drop the ship up to the inner harbor.

The ship lay all one ebb, blowing fresh, and the next flood, when it fell calm; and the following ebb until within an hour of low water. It being fifteen minutes to six in the morning, when I was wakened by a rumbling noise of the chains. I ran on deck and found the ship dragging and shearing over to the east side of the channel, and the next minute she struck on a rock about three cables' length from where we lay the night before. After swinging her head down the channel, she slid off and swung to her anchors and in ten minutes she had five feet of water in her hold and filling fast. I sounded; had seven fathoms, the ship settling fast. I slipped one of the chains and sheared her over on the west side where it was sandy bottom and grounded in about three and a half fathoms, it being about low water; and in a half an hour the lower hold was full of water, the water flowing in the ship as fast as the tide came. The S. S. Aldinga was lying in the upper harbor; she came alongside and took all the sheep that could be got out before the water came to the upper deck, and at high water the lee rail was level with the water. It getting rough, the steamer left. We saved a part of our luggage, a few stores that was under the poop, and in the confusion the most of them was stolen before they reached the shore. About everything was in the lower hold. They are all lost.

The next day I called a survey, as one of the marine surveyors was to leave for Australia. We went to the ship and disposed of the wreck and what can be saved for the benefit of the underwriters and all concerned. Therefore I write this to notify the abandonment. At present nothing has been saved. The gale is still raging so that no one can get to the ship. When it moderates, I shall try to save all I can; then advertise and sell, as if the wind comes to the east, she will break to pieces. I find there will be a difficulty of getting men to dismantle her, for every one that can work has left the place for the gold mines. However, I shall try my best to save what I can from the wreck before sailing. I shall write you more fully in a few days as I have much to do at present.

Your humble servant
EBEN H. LINNELL

Another letter, dated from Bluff Harbor, September 8, 1862, gives further details:

I never before saw such wholesale robbery in my life. I put a part of my papers in a valise and it was missing. I have been told that one of the Steamer's passengers was seen with it that was going to Melbourne. I have the man's name and place of business. If I have to go there to get home, I may get it.... This disaster I cannot reconcile myself to: after a splendid passage of eighty-one days, and the ship safely moored in Port, as everyone thought, and to become a total loss. Even now I cannot see any reason for the ship's starting her anchors or how she possibly got to the bank where she struck. I had an investigation before the magistrate to see if I could ascertain the cause of the loss, but no light could be brought on the subject. Both of the Pilots testified that the ship was safely moored.

The Captain finally got £75 for the hulk as she lay and £281 for what he had taken ashore from her; but as

it had cost him £67 for labor, she came pretty near
being a total loss. He went back to the Eagle Wing
after this disaster, but his luck had turned. On a voyage to San Francisco in 1864, he was caught in a bight
of the spanker-boom vang, while the sail was jibing in
a squall, and dashed against the spokes of the wheel.
He lived only a few days. For native ability, energy,
and shrewdness, few American shipmasters were his
equal; his record from London to China remains a
thorn in the side of the historians of British sail.

Meanwhile, a neighbor of Captain Linnell's, Captain Luther Hurd, of Eastham, was bringing the clipper
ship Charger from Calcutta to Boston, leaving the
Sand Heads on Christmas Day, 1858, on his second
trip round the world in her, and arriving in Boston on
March 19, 1859 — a passage of eighty-four days and
one of the five best ever made between the two ports.
Captain Francis Gorham, of Barnstable, had the
lovely Winged Racer on the China Coast and was
ready to sail from Swatow with a cargo of coolies to
shovel guano in the Chinchas. But disquieting rumors
reached the owners, Sampson and Tappan, in Boston,
to the effect that the coolies, dimly realizing, perhaps,
the sort of slavery they were being sold into, had resisted, with the result that sixty of them had been
flogged in one morning — a grim business, if the report is true. After an investigation of some sort, the
Winged Racer sailed, and Gorham landed the coolies at
the Chinchas early in 1856, to inhale mustard-colored
guano dust until they died.

Shipping had fallen upon evil days, indeed, when
Yankee shipmasters and Yankee owners had to resort
to such traffic to fill their holds. Our nation has ever
been given to extremes, and our shipbuilders, like true
sons, had turned out an enormous number of clippers
during the past eight years. While the California
boom lasted, there had been enough work for them all.
But now that the gold rush was over, many of them
were forced to jaunt about from port to port like

peddlers, glad of a chance for rice-droghing in the East or the gleanings of their former freights out of Hong Kong. So much Boston and New York capital was invested in ships that the meager returns which they were now bringing in caused consternation in the high places. Old Ezra Nye, the Sandwich lad who had become dean of Liverpool packet captains and was now in the shipping business in New York, writes to his brother from New York under the date of October 10, 1857:

> Such a state of things financially has never been seen in New York. Everything and everybody is bursting up. When it is to end, I know not. There is no confidence and no money to be got, no matter what amount of property you may possess.... I hope this state of things will not last forever.

No better picture of the work of a fine ship and a fine captain in these lean years can be had than is provided by the letters and log books of Captain Joshua Sears, of East Dennis, a veteran of the East India trade, who in 1857 took the Shiverick clipper Wild Hunter out of Boston on a voyage that lasted three years and a half. With him, before the mast, sailed young Thomas F. Hall, fifteen-year-old son of Christopher Hall, the fellow townsman and financial backer of the Shivericks. It was the lad's first voyage, and he bears picturesque testimony to the qualities of his captain. Writing reminiscently years afterward, he says: 'Joshua Sears was as accomplished a sailor... as sailed the seas in those days. The Wild Hunter in every port was a show, so complete in every respect was she kept — her decks always bright, her paintwork and rigging in immaculate condition. Even a capstan bar could only be laid on deck pointing fore and aft.' He adds that the Captain was also a driver; that he would come on deck when the ship was in the doldrums, turn his cheek to a stray zephyr, and order all yards braced up to catch the faintest breath.

CAPTAIN JOSHUA SEARS

More Clippers

The Wild Hunter sailed from Boston on March 7, 1857, and arrived in San Francisco after a passage of 129 days. Here young Hall and another lad ran away, not greatly to the concern of Captain Sears, for in his opinion the boys were only following the fashion. In writing to his friend, Prince S. Crowell, he says: 'Thomas F. Hall and Heman S. Kelly have run away from the ship.... It is the custom here for everybody to leave their ships, and they don't want to be behind the times.' After two months in port, the Wild Hunter left San Francisco for Singapore in ballast, with a crew of 'two half-way sailors, white; eight boys; one shoemaker; four Manila men; three Malays and three Kanakas.' The first night out, Captain Sears was up to his old tricks of driving, as his log shows:

> *Thursday, April 6th....* at 8 P.M. took in Top Gall sails and outer jib. Midnight split the upper main Topsail, unbent it and bent another.... Ship going like a mad horse.

A month later, after a week of light airs, came this:

> *Saturday, September* 5. That heavy swell keeps running from the West. Patience, Patience, — Put your trust in God. Distance run 66 miles.
> *Sunday, Sept.* 6.... Slow getting along — Thy ways, O Lord, are inscrutible.
> *Wednesday, Sept.* 9.... The Lord is my Shepherd; He'll guide me safe through.

Then he got some wind and made the most of it, for he carried sail until he split his fore topgallant sail, and remarks:

> I wish there was someone else to share this weather with me; Misery loves company.
> *Sunday, Sept.* 13.... O for a Cot in some Wilderness.

A week later, after a night of thunder and lightning and squalls:

> This is certainly very tedious, but I trust it is all for the best — J. Sears. Thy ways, O Lord, are past finding out.

> *Friday, Sept.* 25. Dead calm all this day; Current set the ship 20 miles due East. I never had such hard luck before. I feel almost discouraged. Think some of going down the China Sea if I ever get out of this calm place.
>
> *Saturday 26 Sept.* Commences calm, dead calm... latter part moderate and ends dead calm. Oh how disconsolate I do feel. Next voyage I will go down the China Sea and face all the Typhoons that blows.

Two days later he got a fresh breeze dead ahead, and his decision was made:

> At 1 P.M. kept her off North to go around Luconia and down the China Sea.... It is a hard case either way... but the best miss it sometimes.
>
> *Tuesday Sept.* 29. I am trying to wear away some of the tedious hours making a little sailing vessel for my nephew, Ezra F. Sears. I am going to name her Louisa Maria, after my little girl.
>
> *Friday October 2.* Barometer falling — heavy swell from West — Typhoon brewing to the North of us — Got the ship all ready.

But the typhoon missed them, and Captain Sears brought the Wild Hunter into Singapore on October 24, after a passage of seventy-seven days. Six hours later the clipper ship Mameluke arrived, which had left San Francisco four days before him; so there was some balm for the Captain's feelings after all.

He found little business for the ship in Singapore. 'There is nothing for ships to do in China,' he writes to his owners, 'and the only thing that can be done here is to go to the rice ports and load for Europe.' One other possibility that he mentions was to load lumber for Shanghai, but the Wild Hunter was ill-adapted for a lumber-carrier, and he abandoned the idea. He stayed in Singapore only long enough to have his copper attended to. 'It corrodes and crumbles away around the nail-heads,' he explains, 'and the whole sheet comes off without starting a nail.' Then, in December, 1857, he took his departure for Akyab in company with the

More Clippers

clipper ship Antelope. The two vessels stayed together
for five days before losing each other. Two weeks later
they came together again; the Wild Hunter then
passed the Antelope and arrived at Akyab on January
5, 1858.

Here Captain Sears enjoyed himself fully with what
he described as 'the steadiest set of Captains that I
have met with since my going Master.' Boat-sailing
was the great sport, with impromptu races and genial
times throughout. But cargoes were still scarce, and
after a little over a month he set sail on February 18,
1858, for Falmouth for orders.

Calms surrounded him on the first leg of this voyage.
The entry in his log for March 9, 1858, is characteristic: 'The whole Ocean as far as the eye can see is one
complete Mirror; not one breath of air the blue waves
do curl — nor make the ship go either.' And the next
day: 'Oh for a home in some vast wilderness, where
the waves of the Ocean will trouble me no more.'
Even after he picked up the trades, he was not satisfied, for the Wild Hunter had sprouted a crop of
barnacles that slowed her up. 'Ship going 8 knots,' he
writes on March 16; 'the fullest ship that ever was
built will go as fast as that.' In a letter to his wife,
written on board a few days later, he is even more
emphatic: 'We got the trades in Latitude 10' South,'
he says, 'and had them strong, but the dam'd old ship
won't go over 260 miles a day. I think she is rather
too much by the stern.... Another thing, she is very
crank. For two or three days, running with strong
trades, with royals and studsails set, her lee plankshear would be under half the time. Once in a while
her upper channels would go under.' Again, on April 4,
he continues, 'We have got a staggering breeze from
the North East. The old ship is going twelve knots and
tearing the water up some, I tell you.' Certainly Captain Sears was driving her to the limit. 'The ship is so
crank,' he says, 'that I never think of taking in sky-
sails until the lee plankshear goes under water.'

His mechanical turn of mind proved a great resource during this long voyage, as it had on his passage across the Pacific. On April 25 he continued his long letter to his wife:

> Last Tuesday I commenced, with the assistance of one of the sailors that is a bit of Jack Knife Carpenter, to make a turning lathe, and finished it complete Friday afternoon, and it is a capital one. I can turn anything four feet long and eleven inches in diameter. One of the boys turns the crank, and it goes like lightning. Yesterday I turned some belaying pins and a lot of door knobs ... I expect I could turn a little baby all but the legs and some other little fixings that it would want to make it perfect.... Next week I am going to turn out a set of belaying pins for the poop rail from a piece of hard red wood that I got in Singapore.

He was as good as his word, for the mate, who wrote the entry in the log for May 15, records: 'Captain so busy turning pins with his turning lathe that he cannot get the trajectory.'

But his troubles began again when the new belaying pins were finished. On May 23 he writes — still to his wife:

> We have painted the ship all over, outside and in... and she shines now like a nigger's eye.... We had four or five vessels in company last week, and they all sail as fast as we do, and some of them outsail us. I don't know what is the matter with the old ship. One ugly looking Portuguese brig kept company three days, the darndest looking dugout that I ever saw. I have been almost angry enough to sink the old ship sometimes.
>
> *May* 30: I am lonely, lonesome, disconsolate and low-spirited and have got the blues the worst kind — Oh for a cot in some vast wilderness, but on Cape Cod will do.... When you get this letter, I shall be forty-one years old — time to hang up my harp.

The Wild Hunter arrived off Falmouth June 6, 1858, after a passage of 108 days. Here Captain Sears received orders to proceed to Bremerhaven, where he anchored June 20. His opinion of Germany is amusing:

More Clippers

The living at the hotels is miserable [he writes]. They only have one meal a day and that is a very poor dinner, consisting of an enormous quantity of potatoes, some raw ham, a piece of roast beef cut out of the hind quarter of a bullock, hard and dry, and cooked to death.... Their coffee is excellent.... They are a happy and nice people that enjoy themselves more than any other nation that ever I fell in with.

His orders were next to proceed to Cardiff and load coal for Ceylon. On the way to Cardiff he started another letter to his wife, which shows him in a fit of righteous wrath:

This morning I was informed that one of my young men in the forecastle had lost all his clothes. I immediately roused everybody and everything out of the Forecastle, overhauled every chest and bag, but of course could find nothing, for the thief would have been a fool to put them in his chest; however I was in hopes to find some little thing, just enough to condemn the man or men. If I had, I will bet a goose they would have remembered the Captain of the Wild Hunter all their lives. I would have given them marks that they could show their friends the day before they died. After searching in the Forecastle, we overhauled the rest part of the Ship. Under the Top Gallant Forecastle we found the greater part of them stowed away under the blocks and old rigging, the thieves intending to take it on shore the first night in and raise some money on them. There yet remains three woolen shirts, two woolen drawers, two Flannels, socks, handkerchiefs etc. The owner is a young German, fitted out with clothes by his Father and Mother, most of them made by his Mother. He felt very bad I tell you. There is three that I suspect; if I could only get any, proof is all I want. I have offered $10 reward, and if I could find out the right ones before I get in, I would give 20 doll's.

The Wild Hunter sailed from Cardiff on September 5, 1858, with fifteen thousand tons of coal and ran into dirty weather, with head winds all the way down the Channel, and two severe southwest gales between there and the Western Islands. Captain Sears did the hardest driving of the whole cruise on this leg of the voyage.

> We have run up our Easting, and a pretty time we had of it for four days [he writes].... I had the cabin shut up as tight as I could get it, and then it took two boys about all the time to bail the water out. My room sometimes was three or four inches deep with water. Her main deck was from one to three feet deep all the time, and when the sea did not break in over the weather quarter, she would dip the lee quarter all under so she was completely flooded with water all the time, stem to stern, but tight in her bottom. All this time she was running with the wind two points abaft the beam, part of the time with royals and all the time with topgallant sails on her. She ran for four days 268, 265, 280, 272 miles, which I call pretty good going, drawing twenty-one feet, three inches of water. Ask Levi Howes if he has got a ship that will beat that and carry 15,000 tons of coal, too. Oh for a cot down by the sea-side where we could dig clams.

On the whole, gales and hard driving agreed with the Captain. Here is how he described another stretch of rough going on the same voyage:

> For about eight days her decks were anywhere from the main rail to knee deep with water, and I have only seen them dry once since we left Cardiff.... We have been running now for three or four days with a fair wind, studsails out alow and aloft and all three skysails set and the sea rolling in right over the top of the monkey rail amidships, and she does not hesitate to take it on the poop in large quantities, too... but she keeps tight and she sails faster than ever she did before, since she was launched. She goes eleven knots on the wind with skysails set, and twelve or thirteen with the wind a little free.... She is as stiff as a church, and I can carry sail on her just as long as the spars will stand, *and they will stand some, I can tell you*.... I am now on my nineteenth voyage to India and I suppose I shall have to go one more some time or other to make up twenty.... I have been acting the captain this voyage thus far and I find that I get along much better than ever I did before.... I give

my orders to Mr. Scott and I need not tell you he sees them executed.... I stay below, loll on the sofa, read novels, smoke cigars, sleep all I can and take lots of comfort.

But the good winds flattened out finally, leaving the Captain disconsolate enough during the latter part of the voyage. It was a weary mariner who on December 19, 1858, raised the land of Point de Galle, thirty-five miles away.

This is the longest passage for the distance that I have made since I have been master [he writes]. My luck has turned and it is time that I left the sea.... I hope and pray night and day that I shall have orders in Galle to go to Calcutta and load for home. If I have to go to China, I really believe that I shall lay right down in the furrow and let them plough me under.

There is but one step between this place and prison [he continues]. I am the only American in the place and I have got to spend six or eight weeks of my life in this miserable way. It is ten times worse than Akyab. There is neither company nor wind for sailing, so I mull about the decks all day.... Everything in the shipping line is as dull as it can possibly be. There is now about three hundred and seventy vessels in the China waters, and not one tenth of them employed.... My owners [Bush and Wildes, of Boston] don't write me one word of instructions but throw everything on my shoulders.... One thing, I don't keep my spirits up by pouring spirits down for I have been a teetotaler ever since I arrived, and think I shall remain so the few short years that I have to live.... Mind and wear good thick shoes cruising about evenings and don't keep too hot a fire in the stove.

To add to his troubles, the crew that he had shipped in Cardiff all ran away — no more than the Captain expected, to be sure, for all crews had the same slippery habits in port, but here in de Galle, where few American ships ever put in, it was next to impossible to find sailors to take their places. 'I have shipped eighteen miserable-looking natives,' he writes, but a week later adds: 'Twelve of my crew jumped overboard and swam ashore — all but one poor Devil that was drowned. I have caught six of them and got them in jail, and today, after very hard work, I have succeeded in shipping twelve more. Oh, what a life to lead!'

As a matter of fact it was only a high sense of duty, and the pride inherent in Yankee shipmasters of Captain Sears's type, that kept him from shaping his course for Boston as soon as he had discharged his coal at de Galle. Bush and Wildes had indeed left him flat — probably because they had no idea what instructions to send him — and playing the tramp from port to port with a clipper ship was a business unworthy of the Captain's talents. Yet that is what he did. With his wretched crew of frightened natives, he headed for Singapore in ballast, hoping against hope to find some sort of cargo there. Another year had swung round while he lay in de Galle; the date of his sailing for Singapore was February 16, 1859, making it just under two years since he had left Boston. He looked in at Rangoon on the way, on the chance of picking up a cargo of rice for Hong Kong or Canton, but was disappointed, and proceeded to Singapore, where he arrived in April, 1859.

He found no freights here for any part of the world, and being still further convinced that his owners had 'abandoned the ship altogether,' and that she was now 'all on his shoulders,' he decided to act henceforth according to his own views. After lying in Singapore for a time in hopes that freights would improve, he circulated the Wild Hunter for Hong Kong on the chance of thus picking up some miscellaneous cargo and getting away from Singapore by the end of June. 'Sometimes I feel as if I wanted to jump overboard,' he writes, 'but now I have got a great desire to live and see my home again.'

He arrived in Hong Kong at the end of July, 1859, having weathered a typhoon on the way that must have taken his mind off his troubles for a little while,

More Clippers

at least. In a letter to his owners, describing it, he says: 'The fore mast has crushed the step and settled about five inches. I am going to lift it and put a new step under it. My crew that I shipped in Singapore are by yet, and I am going to do the work myself.'

This job — exactly the sort of mechanical work that Captain Sears excelled in — kept him busy and happy in Hong Kong for a while. On August 23, 1859, he writes: 'I have lifted the fore mast and put a new step under it. The old one was entirely rotten, but the keelson was sound.... There is now about twelve ships in port doing nothing, and there is certainly no prospect of employment of any kind for large ships.' Two weeks later the situation was worse, for the number of ships had increased about a third, with no change in the freight situation. A month later still, in another letter to his owners, he reports that 'there is nothing offering for tea now, and ships are flocking in daily from all parts of the world.'

Some of these vessels were very welcome to Captain Sears, for before he left Hong Kong, a goodly number of Cape men had blown into port on one or another of them. On Christmas Day, he writes: 'Captain B. P. Howes [Benjamin Perkins Howes, of Dennis, master of the clipper ship Southern Cross] came to see me, and we had a good time talking about home.... He says that he saw you to the auction in North Dennis, introduced himself and had quite a talk with you.' Another man from home was Calvin Clark Howes, second mate of the ship Eliza and Ella, who called on the Captain and told him that he had left his family all well — good news indeed, as it was almost a year since Captain Sears had had any letters. Captain Bailey Foster, of Brewster, master of the clipper ship Santa Claus, was there, too, with his wife; so was Captain George Wood, of South Yarmouth; Captain Eben Linnell and his ball on the Flying Mist have already been mentioned. Besides these, there was Captain Elkanah Crowell, Jr., of West Yarmouth, in the clipper

215

ship Boston Light. Crowell was seriously ill, had been away from home for almost three years, and was mentally and physically in a critical condition. Captain Sears's own troubles were temporarily forgotten in his concern for his sick friend. He visited him every day on board the Boston Light, arranged for a consultation of physicians and finally had him sent home on another ship. Happily Captain Crowell pulled through and, as will presently appear, was able to go to sea again.

But Captain Sears's own health was beginning to show signs of the work and worry he had been through. A melancholy picture of his condition is given in a letter dated December 16, 1859:

> I have been very unwell the last month. Four weeks ago tomorrow night I was taken with a sort of cholera so bad that I thought I should hardly live through the night and I have not seen a well day since. I have had a constant belly ache ever since.... I begin to think that I have got on the other side of the Hill and am sliding down, and when a person gets going, they are apt to go pretty fast. ... I have never seen the need of a wife before so much as I have this voyage. But it will certainly take six months to get me tame enough to live with one. I have lived alone and in solitude so much lately that I have become as cross and crabbed as a bear.... I tie myself up on board my ship like a hermit. It seems as if I have no desire to go anywhere or see anybody here.... I think sometimes that I am getting hypochondriacal and I rather think that it grows on me, for I have dreadful melancholy spells at times. Sometimes I get very homesick and think I cannot hardly stand it; and at other times it seems as if I did not care whether I ever see home again or not; and so I am wearing away my life day after day, week after week, and month after month, and first thing we know there is another year gone, and every year is bringing us nearer the end, which is not far off.

A few days later, he adds: 'My flesh is falling away pretty fast, and I am growing rather weak. I don't feel as if I could knock a sailor down now without hitting him twice.' Through all this adversity, the Captain never ceased trying for a cargo. He decided to lay the ship on for California, and to take any kind of freight that offered. If he made any mistake, it was in believing that his Chinese broker, Wohung, was as good as his word. One hundred and twenty tons of granite, which he had promised Sears, shrank by the time it reached the Wild Hunter's hold, to a little over twenty tons. The slippery merchant also assured Sears that he had a large number of coolies to be carried to San Francisco, and agreed to send them on the Wild Hunter at $28 each. Thus encouraged, the Captain fitted up a section of his between-decks with bunks, only to find that Wohung had shipped most of the coolies already on two other vessels. There was nothing for it but rip out the bunks and try to get freight instead.

Finally on January 1, 1860, with 1070 tons of granite and rice, 80 cases of opium, which exactly filled one stateroom, and 58 coolies, Sears set sail for San Francisco. His freight and passenger money amounted to $13,000; his disbursements in Hong Kong were $3500. Two weeks out — on January 16, to be exact — he ran into bad weather which is thus recorded in the log:

> Comes in with a strong gale from N.N.E.... very high turbulent sea running... at 4.00 P.M. came suddenly into a short sharp sea, causing the ship to pitch dreadfully. Took in jib. While furling it, pitched away jib boom and sprung the bowsprit badly. Washed four men overboard. Lowered the boat and picked up one only; the other three were drowned. Five life buoys were hove right among them, and only one caught them.... All hands busily employed clearing away the wreck and securing the bowsprit.

On February 4 he lost a lot of new sails, and on the 7th in a high sea, with the ship rolling heavily, the footrope to the upper maintopsail parted, and the sail split up to the reef band. On February 26, 1860, he

anchored in San Francisco with the remark: 'So ends
this passage. All well.'

Still he had no word from his owners, although he
had written them regularly, giving precise accounts of
his proceedings. The ship needed a new bowsprit and
bitts and a number of new sails. Captain Sears sent
another letter to his owners under the date of March
4, 1860: 'I am certain that I shall not have one cent of
money to remit home, and I am afraid I shall not have
enough to meet expenses here, but I assure you that I
am working as economically as I can.' A fortnight
later he says: 'Things look very dark everywhere and
I don't know what to do.... There is nothing to be
had here except the wood charter, and I don't think
that pays enough to leave the ship in Europe the first
of next winter.' For want of something better, he finally decided, on the strength of a report from Callao
that guano charters were improving, to try his luck
there. With a farewell letter to his owners, stating his
determination and concluding with the remark, 'My
disbursements here exceed the freight money by
$675.06 for which I have drawn on you,' he set sail for
Callao on March 25, 1860, and arrived after a sixty-
days' passage. The good news in regard to guano charters turned out to be a myth. He waited, still hoping
that prospects would improve, but they did not, and
on June 2 he writes to his wife:

> I think that I had better come home and start new, for
> it seems now that every move I make, I get deeper in the
> mire.... Today when the mail arrived and no freights, I
> felt as if I should settle right down and be nothing left
> but a grease spot, and I shall have the blues for a week
> to come.

As a matter of fact, he had more than the blues to
contend with. On the voyage from San Francisco he
had received a blow on the head, and this wound became troublesome.

> I have passed a very unpleasant night [he writes]; I

More Clippers

awoke about 12 o'clock with a violent pain in my head, and the wound was swelled to the size of a hen's egg. Then I got nervous and fancied that my brain was affected and that I should go crazy and have to be sent home; but finally about 3 o'clock I got to sleep, and now the headache is all gone, but the swelling remains and the cords are sore way down my neck. It seems as if I would give a small fortune to be at home and go to church with you today.

With two farewell blasts to his owners — 'At present there is nothing to be obtained to any part of the world except a small ship to Mauritius' and 'There is now seven ships in port without charters.... I think it best for the Wild Hunter to go direct to New York' — he set sail June 10, with nothing but ballast in his hold, on the last leg of his voyage, round the Horn and home. In his log for July 8 is the following entry: 'Shipped a sea over the starboard quarter and broke off six stanchions of the hand rail — washed away the binnacle — stove in two windows of the cabin and filled it with water, wetting charts, books and nautical instruments. Latter part more pleasant — Round Cape Horn.' His private journal reveals more of his emotions. Under the date of July 19, he writes: 'Oh for a cot in some vast wilderness where I shall never see a ship again. If ever one poor fellow was tired of anything, it is I, Josh Sears, that is sick and tired of going to sea.' But he was master still, both of himself and of his ship, as appears in the dry entry in his log for Tuesday, August 21: 'Scraping, painting, holy-stoning, and the Devil knows what not. Sandy Hook N.N.W. 454 miles.'

So ended a voyage that had lasted three years and a half. Throughout, Captain Sears's salary had been two hundred dollars a month and board; but he regarded it — as any shipmaster worthy of the name would have done — as a complete failure. Those who have followed his fortunes from port to port will be convinced, however, that the failure was not his

219

fault. No man ever tried harder or more consistently to make money for his owners, and incidentally dividends for himself, for he owned one sixteenth of the ship. It is pleasant to record that in New York his spirits revived. He put up at the United States Hotel, where so many shipmasters resorted, and wrote to his wife on September 16, 1860, 'I like the Hotel first rate. One thing, we get capital fodder. Don't have to carry the kid aft and grumble any.' He shipped most of his dunnage home by schooner and followed as soon as his business was concluded, to enjoy a long rest in East Dennis. He never went to sea again, though his owners kept making him offers of new commands — notably in 1862, when he received a telegram from them saying, 'Will you go immediately to Europe and join ship Rival?' But he refused them all, and spent the rest of his life at home with his wife and daughter.

10

The Last of the Clippers

WHEN Joshua Sears took charge of Captain Elkanah
Crowell in Hong Kong, he probably saved his life; and
Captain Crowell was a man well worth saving. In 1853
he became mate of the clipper Spitfire. His account of
the appointment is amusing:

> Captain John Baker [he says], of J. Baker & Co., ship
> chandlers of Commercial St., Boston, sent for me. When
> I went into his office, he said to me, 'The new clipper ship
> Spitfire is loading for San Francisco, and Captain John
> Arey is a driver. He wants a mate that can jump over
> the fore yard every morning before breakfast.' I said I
> was the man for him, if it laid on deck. I made the voy-
> age with him, and a hard one it was — 102 days to San
> Francisco.

In the course of it, the Spitfire sprung her bowsprit
and two of her topmasts and put into Rio for new ones;
here Crowell discharged eight of the crew for incom-
petence, and had the satisfaction afterwards of passing
the Cyclone off Cape Horn and beating her into San
Francisco by four days.

In 1856, Crowell was promoted to the command of
the clipper Boston Light, in which he made a tremendous voyage, that lasted from June, 1856, to April,
1859, and terminated at Hong Kong. In the course of
it he had visited most of the foreign ports in both
hemispheres — some of them twice — before arriving

sick on the China Coast. Here, as has been said, Joshua Sears arranged to have him sent home, on the doctor's orders, and the voyage, with no responsibility and plenty of rest, restored him so completely that by the summer of 1860 he was ready to go to sea again, this time in the Fair Wind, which had sometimes been listed as a clipper, but which Captain Crowell did not so regard. His wife was unwilling to let him set sail without her, after his close call in China; so they embarked in company, with orders for San Francisco. On arriving there, the Captain wrote to Sears, giving his opinion of the ship: 'The Fair Wind is a fine ship — 1300 tons; not a clipper; a comfortable ship in every respect, only very slow at the heels, but I like her for all that.... [She is] as solid as a pump bolt.' To this letter Mrs. Crowell added a postscript to Mrs. Sears: 'Give my kind regards to Captain Sears and tell him his kindness towards Elkanah in China will never be forgot by me.'

From San Francisco Captain Crowell took the Fair Wind to Honolulu in eight days, eighteen hours, the fastest time ever made by a sailing vessel between the two ports. To show that he was a navigator as well as a sail-carrier, it may be added that he laid the straightest course over the route ever made by a ship under sail — 2104 miles — only twenty miles longer than the shortest steamer route today. There can be no doubt that the Captain had fully recovered his health. Perhaps, too, he had changed his mind about the sailing qualities of his new command. From Honolulu he went to Baker's Island for guano, and thence headed for Hampton Roads for orders; but at the very end of the voyage he ran the Fair Wind aground at Hog Island. A tug pulled her off and towed her to New York, leaking twenty inches an hour. The damage turned out to be slight, however, for after a brief sojourn in the shipyards she was ready for another voyage. Captain Crowell stayed in her until 1864, sailing to such ports as the Chinchas, Cork, Hong Kong, and

The Last of the Clippers

San Francisco. Then he left her and took command at
one time or another of the ships Galatea and Carrie
Read, the bark Gerard C. Tobey and the auxiliary
steamer George S. Homer. He finally retired after
twenty-nine years as master, and went back to the
Cape.

His brother, Captain Sturgis Crowell, had been
having troubles of his own with Elkanah's old command, the Boston Light. He set sail in her for San
Francisco on May 23, 1861, with the memory of a 192-
day voyage which he had made in 1849 as mate of the
old Angelique under Captain Phineas Windsor in the
back of his mind. Far fresher in his thoughts was his
letter of instructions from the owners, Hallett and
Carman, of New York. Owners' letters have a quality
to be found nowhere else in literature, unless it be in
the utterances of the Delphic Oracle, and the letter
which Hallett and Carman handed Captain Crowell is
a good sample of this sort of composition:

> We hope you will make a short passage [they wrote],
> but trust you will run no unusual risk or crowd your
> ship too hard in order to do so.... We trust you will make
> the shortest cut to the Line and not have too much fear
> of falling to leeward, but at the same time to remember
> that a *few* miles *too* far to the westward may cost you
> many days.... We trust you will be as provident as pos-
> sible on the passage of your provisions and water as well
> as wood and coal.... There may possibly be some of Jeff
> Davis's people out, altho' we think the chances small.
> Should you fall in with any such, however, you will re-
> member that your heels are good, and you had better let
> them crack at you some time before giving up the ship,
> trusting to a breeze springing up and night coming on.

The best thing for a shipmaster to do with such instructions would be to throw them over the side and
use his own judgment; and this is probably what, in
effect, Captain Crowell did. He had at least two other
Cape men with him on the voyage, his mate, J. G.
Baker, of Dennis, and a younger brother, Oris Crowell,

before the mast. The presence of these men may have been some comfort, and he needed all the comfort he could get. It was his first important command; the ship was loaded too deep; the Civil War was on; Cape Horn lay ahead. The business end of the voyage, too, was complicated by a power of attorney which his owners had given him to sell the ship if he could get the equivalent of $32,000 for her.

Off Cape Horn the Captain had one of the toughest times on record. He was hove to for weeks under a close-reefed maintopsail — all he could carry with the ship so deep, but not enough to keep him from being blown back by a succession of westerlies. The decks were swept clean of everything; the rudderhead was sprung and finally carried away; the figurehead went by the board; the ship, unmanageable because of the loss of her steering-gear, and swept by every sea because she lay so low in the water, drove helplessly south with a change of wind. Captain Crowell, if he had fished out his letter of instructions again to see what his owners recommended in this emergency, would perhaps have found this sentence useful, 'You will please remember that your ship is deep... and when off the Horn had better hug the land and let her go along as easily as possible.'

Crowell decided that, if he was ever to reach San Francisco, he must get his ship on top of the water instead of underneath. He threw overboard a lot of cargo, which not only lightened the ship but enabled him to get at the smashed steering-gear and repair it. Then the mate, Mr. Baker, was stabbed by one of the crew and died. That, however, was the end of the Captain's troubles for the moment. He brought the battered Boston Light in to San Francisco, on November 2, 1861, after a passage of 163 days. After a month in port, he went to Honolulu, McKean's Island, Ripolo, Mauritius, and Calcutta, where he arrived on July 27, 1862, and found some more correspondence from Hallett and Carman, whose policy seems to have been just the opposite of the methods of Bush and Wildes, who had written Joshua Sears nothing.

> Our idea is, if you cannot sell the ship for about $40,000 or more, you had better keep her out there in some local business until you can get a good freight... home, but as soon as you can get that, to take it, unless business to remain out should be very good.... You might remain out for three years from the time you left here, provided you can make it pay.... You might get a good freight up to China, and it would be about the right time of the monsoon, but we should not advise your going to China with the hope of getting a high freight there.... Should you go to Sidney, which is a very cheap port, we should advise your buying about 1000 tons of coal there and taking it to Hong Kong, Bombay or Calcutta, wherever there is the best look.... Should you sell your ship, we would advise your coming home in some ship, as the overland route is very expensive.

It is to be doubted whether these instructions helped Captain Crowell much. Because he was a conscientious captain, he read them through; then, let us hope, he consulted them no more. What he did was to carry a cargo of rice to Hong Kong, sail thence to Bombay, arriving on January 30, 1863, sell the ship there for £5000 and write in his log, 'So ends the ship Boston Light.' He showed by this transaction that he knew his owners and was able to read between the lines of their orders, for though the price he received was $15,000 less than the last figure mentioned in his instructions, Mr. Hallett wrote him that he was much pleased with his proceedings, both in regard to the voyage to Hong Kong and in the sale of the ship. This business concluded, Captain Crowell came home by steamer and took a rest until the following December.

His next command was the Volunteer, which does not seem to have been a clipper. In December, 1863, he took her out to the Pacific Coast and back, stopping at some Mexican ports on the way home, and reached New York after an absence of almost exactly a year.

In the spring of 1865 he took the clipper ship Orpheus, which he kept for five years, making voyages to San Francisco, China, and the East Indies.

The cargo list of one of these voyages (1865) shows the sort of miscellanies that shipmasters were picking up in San Francisco for China. Among other items appear flour, wheat, shrimps, shrimp-skins, fish-fins, treasure, shells, Mexican dollars, old bones, hay, gold bars, silver bars, abalones, and axes. How Captain Crowell satisfied his new owners it is hard to see. They told him, for example, that they expected him to bring the Orpheus back from her first voyage round the world — San Francisco, Hong Kong, Batavia, and New York — looking five years younger than when she set sail. They showed less concern as to whether the Captain himself might look ten years older as a result. But there was a lot of fake of one kind or another mixed up with the shore end of the shipping business. Somebody, perhaps her owners, had printed as a heading to the ship's articles of the Orpheus, 'No Sheath Knives or Profane Language Allowed on Board,' a regulation about as sensible as requiring Captain Crowell to turn the flight of time backward in regard to the appearance of his ship.

The Captain left the Orpheus in 1870 to take command of the Belvedere, and for the next two years, except for one East India voyage, he was at work in the old cotton-carrying trade between our southern ports and Liverpool. One cargo consisted of 19,000 bales, which makes Captain J. Henry Sears's previous record of 6900 in the Titan look small, and shows in striking fashion the change that had taken place in the design of ships during the last ten or a dozen years. Full-bodied cargo-carriers had taken the place of the lean lines of the clippers of the fifties. The American merchant marine was on the down grade, and the best that captains could hope for now was one of the old flyers that had not been strained into uselessness, or a new vessel which bore the honorary title of medium clipper but was built on lines that considered capacity first and speed afterwards. Such a vessel was the Belvedere. In May, 1872, Captain Crowell left the sea for good and went back to the Cape, where he spent the last thirty years of his life with his wife and daughter in South Yarmouth. He died in 1911 at the age of eighty-nine.

Old Captain Winslow Lewis Knowles, of Eastham — himself a fine example of a shipmaster of the pre-clipper school — endowed his sons with a good share of the salt that was in his blood. One of them, Captain Allen H. Knowles, has already been mentioned in connection with the Liverpool packets; another, Captain Thomas, died at the age of twenty-nine on a voyage to San Francisco; a third, Captain Winslow, Jr., after learning seamanship under his father on the Albatross in 1849, became master of a number of East Indiamen and died in Calcutta in 1863; and the fourth brother Captain Josiah N. Knowles, became one of the most brilliant of the commanders of the late clippers, conspicuous first for a dramatic disaster and afterwards for a record passage.

The disaster came in 1858, after Captain Knowles had been in command of the medium clipper Wild Wave for four years, engaged in miscellaneous trade between ports as far apart as Genoa and San Francisco. In 1856, sailing between Callao and Havre, he was off Plymouth in seventy days — a record which is believed never to have been broken. Two years later came his great disaster. On the voyage in question, the Wild Wave sailed on February 9, 1858, from San Francisco for Valparaiso. At one o'clock in the morning of March 5, when the ship was going through the water at the rate of thirteen knots, the lookout cried, 'Breakers,' and at the same moment the Wild Wave was on top of a coral reef. A terrific surf broke over both reef and ship; all three masts went over the side, and sheets of copper, torn from the bottom of the vessel by the coral, were picked up by the breakers and hurled across the deck. What with falling masts and spars, tangled rigging, swinging blocks and dead-eyes, flying sheets of copper and waves breaking clear across the deck, it is a miracle that everyone on board was not killed.

At daybreak Captain Knowles discovered that what he had struck was a circular reef that lay about two miles off the uninhabited island of Oeno and completely surrounded it. The island, as figured in the chart, was twenty miles out of its true position — a mistake which was responsible for the wreck. The island itself is a low strip of sand, half a mile in circumference and covered with meager shrubs. All day long the crew boated provisions ashore through the surf, wondering with every trip whether the ship would hold together for another one. They pitched two big tents on the beach, one for the officers and passengers, one for the crew. Luckily there was plenty of water on the island, as well as sea-birds' eggs — for what they might be worth — and there were prospects of good fishing. The steward cooked supper, and all hands turned in, though with little prospect of sleep because of thousands of land crabs that lay hidden in conch shells and coconut husks and bit deep with claws like a lobster's. There were rats on the island, too, from an earlier wreck, the remains of which were still visible.

In the morning Captain Knowles called his mate, Mr. J. H. Bartlett, for a consultation, the upshot of which was that the two should sail in one of their boats to Pitcairn Island, twenty miles south, on the chance of getting some sort of craft there from the descendants of the mutineers of the Bounty. A boat was made ready for the trip, but for the next four or five days it blew a gale, kicking up a surf that completely buried the hull of the Wild Wave and of course made it impossible either to start for Pitcairn or to get any more supplies from the ship. Finally, after a week of waiting, the surf flattened out, and the Captain started. 'I cannot divert my mind,' he writes in

The Last of the Clippers

his diary, 'from the one subject — home and friends.' Bartlett and five men went with him; they left the second mate in charge at Oeno with orders to proceed to Pitcairn with the rest of the ship's company if the Captain was not back in a month. He also took several sea-birds from their nests, on the chance that they could be used as carrier pigeons to take messages between the two parties. As the little boat pushed off, the rest of the company gave three cheers. Before finally laying his course for Pitcairn, however, the Captain stopped at the wreck to pick up $18,000 in gold, an item that had been worrying him ever since the ship struck.

On the first night came a return of the bad weather, with thunder, lightning, and a high sea that made the boat dance about so wildly that it was impossible to read the compass. They shortened sail and the next morning found that, as nearly as they could figure, they were ten miles farther from Pitcairn than when they had started, and it was blowing so hard that for most of that day they could not carry any sail. However, what with rowing until they were ready to drop, and long after Captain Knowles's hands were raw from the unaccustomed labor, and now and then setting a patch of sail, they raised Pitcairn at dusk. But they were on the wrong side of the island, where the surf ran so high that no boat could land. They lay on their oars all night and in the morning found a spot where it was possible to run through the surf. Once on the beach, they found that a thickly wooded mountain separated them from the settlement. They made their way over it only to discover, when they reached the other side, that all the inhabitants had left, having migrated in a body to Norfolk Island. The houses stood empty, with live stock and chickens running freely in and out. Knowles and his party returned over the mountain to the boat and there, after letting the birds go with messages to Oeno, had their first sleep for fifty-six hours, Captain Knowles and

Bartlett each with half the gold buried in the sand under his head.

The next morning the surf was too high for them to sail round the island to Bounty Bay, where the houses were; they therefore took the tedious overland route again. Once arrived, however, they made themselves comfortable enough, clearing out a house, broiling chicken, catching a goat, and in every way taking a new lease of life. But their boat, left on the far side of the island, was smashed to pieces by an unusually high surf which reached it even in what they had supposed its safe position well up on the beach. The Captain and Bartlett brought the gold to 'town' and buried it under a flat rock on the shore. With it they brought a compass and a chronometer, still undamaged, and they began to consider what their next move should be. Whatever they did could not be done in a hurry. Tahiti, which they had had some idea of trying to reach in their boat, lay fifteen hundred miles northwest, and all that remained of the boat was a mast and sail. The rain began and continued. Captain Knowles passed the time reading *Jane Eyre*, which he picked up in one of the houses, hunting goats, and worrying about his young wife in Brewster. They kept, of course, a constant lookout for ships the while. 'Nineteen goat meals this week,' he reports on March 24; and on March 28, still in the midst of rain, he writes, 'Read, walked and thought of home.'

Before the month was up after which the second mate was to join them at Pitcairn, Captain Knowles had reached his decision: he would build a vessel and sail to Tahiti. A miscellaneous assortment of old tools had been left in the settlement; trees for timbers and planking were at hand. On April 5, one month after the wreck, the party began to cut them down and hew out a keel and a stem, using rusty axes from the abandoned houses. For the first two weeks the Captain suffered severely from blistered hands; after that, they hardened up nicely. The chief trouble was the rain.

The Last of the Clippers

'What a host of troubles that blunder of *somebody's* had made for me,' writes Knowles, thinking of the hydrographer who had drawn the chart. April 20 came and went, with no sign of the second mate. Work on the vessel progressed between showers; but a constant cloud over the Captain's spirits was the thought how his wife would worry when no word of the arrival of the Wild Wave at Valparaiso reached home.

On April 28 they killed a wild hog and salted the pork with sea salt. On the 29th they finished hewing planks for the vessel and stood them up against the church to dry. They made sails from such pieces of canvas and stray rags as they could find, and began picking oakum from old rope. 'I didn't think I should ever get down to that again,' writes the Captain, 'but so it was.' They burned houses for nails and collected scraps of metal for fastenings — the scarcity of which was their chief concern. On May 26 the Captain writes: 'My 28th birthday.... My friends think I'm lost.' They made a charcoal pit and burned charcoal for fuel for the voyage, began work on a rope walk, and always, when it rained, picked oakum in the church, living the while on goat's meat, coconut milk, and chickens.

By June 3 the hull was finished, a schooner thirty feet long, eight feet wide, and four feet deep. The next job was caulking her, and by the time this was finished, it was found that the green wood had shrunk so much that she had to be caulked all over again. While some were busy at this, others were shaping spars, using the flagpole for one of the masts; then they painted her, with paint left in the houses, salted a quantity of goat's meat for the voyage, made some old barrels into water casks, wrote letters to leave behind them, and on July 23 launched the vessel. They provisioned her, in addition to their salted pork and goat's meat, with twelve hundred oranges, made an ensign of such rags as had not gone into the sails, and christened her the John Adams, after one of the former inhabitants of the island. The Captain and Bartlett dug up their gold from under the flat rock, and, bidding farewell to three of their company, who preferred to take their chances on the island, hoisted sail for the Marquesas, as the wind was dead ahead for Tahiti.

The John Adams developed a peculiar and uneasy motion at sea, which promptly made all hands sick; but she was staunch and able, and in time the sickness wore off. On July 25 she was bobbing along nicely through a heavy sea; on the 26th it was calm enough to bring the stove on deck. During the next week the schooner logged anywhere from 100 to 124 miles a day, and on August 3 looked in at Resolution Bay in the island of Ohitahoo, one of the Marquesas, but the natives appeared so hostile that the Captain decided to try Ohevahoa instead. A flat calm prevented them, however, and they headed for Nukahiva, which they sighted the next day, August 4. They had decided, if there was no prospect of a vessel there, to continue their voyage to the Hawaiian Islands, but as they rounded the headland into the harbor of Nukahiva, they sighted the American sloop-of-war Vandalia lying at anchor, the only vessel in port. Captain Knowles headed for her and hoisted his ensign.

Their tale was soon told. The Vandalia promptly headed for Oeno to pick up those of the company of the Wild Wave that had stayed there, and Mr. Bartlett went with her, subsequently joining her as an officer. Captain Knowles, after selling the John Adams to a missionary for $250, went along too as far as Tahiti, whence he took passage for Honolulu on the French sloop-of-war Euridice and made the rest of the voyage to San Francisco on the bark Yankee, arriving on September 29 — seven months after he had left there in the Wild Wave. He met many friends in port, who had thought him dead, and was interested to hear that he had become the father of a girl already seven months old. On October 6 he left for New York on the

The Last of the Clippers

S.S. Golden Gate and in due time joined his family in Brewster.

This experience, hard though it was, by no means ended Captain Knowles's career at sea. His next voyages were, indeed, of an extremely ticklish nature, running the gauntlet of Confederate cruisers between Boston and San Francisco in the medium clipper Charger from 1863 to 1865. His hardest trip during this period was on the way out in March, 1865. The Charger, scudding under bare poles in the North Atlantic, shipped a tremendous sea which stove the after hatch and carried three men overboard. She was ten days rounding Cape Horn and 133 days in reaching San Francisco. But the Captain had better luck on the return voyage, arriving in Boston in the excellent time of 96 days.

This was Captain Knowles's last voyage in the Charger, or in any other ship for a few years. Times were growing worse and worse, with fewer freights and smaller profits. Not until 1871 did he go to sea again, and then he went in a ship that would have tempted any man away from home, the famous Glory of the Seas, a medium clipper and the last of McKay's great fleet. When Knowles took her, she was two years old, and her owner, J. Henry Sears, had put her to work in the grain trade between San Francisco and Liverpool, a comparatively new business. For the next five years, Captain Knowles kept her steadily at it, with only one interruption when, in 1873, instead of returning from Liverpool to San Francisco, she went to New York instead. This was a lucky order for the Captain, for in taking the Glory out to San Francisco again from New York, he made the best time over the course in her career, 96 days from anchor to anchor. This passage has not been beaten since, and only eight times previously had a ship covered the distance in less time.

During Captain Knowles's years in the grain trade, he had a number of races with other vessels, but in none of them was the time remarkable. In 1874, for example, he beat the British ship Langdale from Liverpool to San Francisco by a meager margin of one day. Captain Jenkinson, of the Langdale, took it hard, however, and expressed his displeasure in print, objecting to some items in Knowles's published account of the voyage. Knowles's reply in the columns of a San Francisco paper shows urbanity and poise:

> If it will satisfy the Captain of the Langdale [he writes], I will say that whenever I raised his ship, she was astern of the Glory, but came up and passed her. When I got to San Francisco, there was no Langdale, but as the passages of the ships were 131 and 132 days respectively, I think that is sufficiently long to prevent any discussion as to the great speed of either.

But the next year Captain Knowles and the Glory hung up an absolute record for the first and last time in her career, making the run between San Francisco and Sydney in 35 days, 11 hours, from anchor to anchor — an average of a little over eight knots an hour throughout the 7026 miles sailed. It was one of those rare lucky passages that gladden a captain's heart. On the same day that he lost the northeast trades, he picked up the southeast; he was never completely becalmed and he never encountered heavy weather. This was fortunate, for the ship was lightly ballasted, and Captain Knowles writes, 'Ship very crank, so cannot carry as much sail as otherwise would.' The Captain stayed in the Glory until 1880, and then left the sea to go into the shipping business in San Francisco. The fine old ship was laid up for a while; then in 1885, Captain Joshua S. Freeman, another Brewster man, took her and for eighteen years carried coal in her from port to port on the Pacific Coast.

Captain Knowles's brother, Captain Allen H. Knowles, was meantime making the best of the bad business conditions in another of McKay's medium clippers, the Chariot of Fame, which had started life as a Liverpool packet but was now engaged in general

THE CLIPPER SHIP CHARIOT OF FAME

The Last of the Clippers

trade. He set sail from New York in the spring of 1856, bound for Acapulco on the west coast of Mexico with a cargo of coal. Extracts from the log give a good picture of the voyage and of the Captain's emotions:

Monday, August 18, 1856. Have had violent gales and a high dangerous sea the last three days. Saturday morning, the fourth mate in irons for threatening desperate vengeance on me for reprimanding him for neglect of duty.

Sunday, 24th August, 1856.... All hands employed securing the coal. Ship has got a 4 streak list. What hard luck I do have.

Monday, August 25.... Very thick snow storm; a heavy sea from the west.

Wednesday, August 27, 1856. This is the longest and hardest passage I ever had round Cape Horn; in fact it has been a very tedious passage throughout. Barcella Polena fell from the fore top to the deck; killed himself instantly. My crew are getting pretty well bunged up, and I am getting well tired of this weather [92 days at sea].

Head winds, high seas and squalls continued throughout the following week; then Captain Knowles writes:

Thursday, September 4.... Ends with fresh breezes from the W.S.W. and pleasant. A rough sea from N.N.W.; reefs all out. A ship astern gaining on us. What hard luck I do have in winds. God help us. My longest passage to Valparaiso is 102 days in a slow ship.

Monday, September 8.... This is the first time for thirty days we have had all sail set.

Thursday, September 11.... Ends with hard gales from W.N.W. and very squally. In God's name when shall I get a fair wind. Over forty days since we have had one.

Saturday, September 13th. Ends with strong breezes from N.N.W. Looks like a norther. Don't I have the luck. I am quite discouraged.

Sunday, September 14th, '56. Ends with fresh gales from the west and a high sea from N.N.W.... Continuation of hard luck.

Wednesday, September 17.... Ends with fine breezes from S.S.W. and pleasant. All sail out. Going 10 knots.

235

First fair wind for 50 days. Much as ever I have had one for the passage.

Monday, 22 September, 1856. Ends with light breeze from N.N.W. and pleasant. All sail set by the wind. My luck for head winds follows me. Shall expect to get the S.E. trades from the North West. I had them from the S.S.W. on the other side. God help us.

About a month later, Captain Knowles arrived at Acapulco after a passage of 145 days. After a little more than two months in port, he set sail on December 29, 1856, for Callao. On this leg of the voyage, hard luck of another sort pursued him, for his officers had apparently not spent their shore leave so wisely as the Captain would have wished:

Thursday, 8th January, 1857.... All the officers sick in bed.

Monday, 12th January, 1857.... Mates all sick yet. I was up all last night.

Thursday, January 15th 1857.... Mates sick. *Oyster soup and green peas for dinner.*

January 26.... No one very well on board.

Friday, January 30.... All the mates sick and off duty. Fine time for me.

From Callao he went to the Chinchas for guano, and sailed thence for Hampton Roads June 19, 1857. One more entry in the log will suffice to give the tenor of the whole:

Tuesday, 28th July, 1857. Ends with strong N.N.W. winds and cloudy. *Damn the luck.*

The weary voyage ended with a short jog from Hampton Roads to New York, where he arrived in October, 1857, a year and four months after he had set sail.

Fairer fortune followed him on another passage round the Horn in the same ship about two years later. He left New York, April 7, 1859, bound for San Francisco, and one day behind him came Captain Laban Howes, of Dennis, in the Orpheus. Both men were veterans; enough has already been said about Knowles's past experiences, and as for Howes, he had taken the clipper

The Last of the Clippers

ship Electric Spark out to California on her maiden voyage in 1855 in 106 days. It was a great race. Though the days of record-breaking passages were about over, this contest was in a class with the best of them when it came to even sailing. The honors went to Laban Howes, who reached San Francisco in 114 days, followed by Knowles and the Chariot in 117 — a very different story from his 145 days to Acapulco!

Captain Knowles subsequently commanded the Agenor during the first four years of her life (1870–74), and on his last voyage in her drove her, full-bodied though she was, from Callao to San Francisco in thirty days — only one day longer than the record between the two ports made by the clipper ship Rattler. He left the Agenor to take command of another new ship, the Conqueror, which he took out to China on what was to be his last voyage. On his return, he retired to Yarmouth, where he died of a stroke of paralysis in 1875. Laban Howes afterwards had, among other commands, the bark Lizzie in the cotton trade, usually with a good proportion of Cape men with him. In the spring of 1871, for example, on a voyage in her to New Orleans out of Boston, he had Marcus Hall, of Dennis, as his chief mate; W. H. Earle, of Sandwich, as his second mate; and a number of Dennis youngsters before the mast, for not all New England boys, even at that late date, had forsaken the sea.

The year 1859 — the same that saw Knowles and Howes racing round to San Francisco, Joshua Sears tending Elkanah Crowell in Hong Kong, and Eben Linnell giving a ball on board the Flying Mist — saw also another Cape Cod shipmaster making a record for all time between Shanghai and New York. He was Captain Joseph Crocker, of Barnstable, now master of the extreme clipper ship Swordfish, and formerly mate of the blunt old Eben Preble in the East India trade. Crocker had taken command of the Swordfish in 1856 when she was five years old, and, according to clipper

237

standards, had seen her best days. For three years he had been sailing her round the world by way of the East Indies and China, never meeting with any startling adventures and never making any very fast passages. The Swordfish was not, in fact, a popular ship with officers and crew. Sharp even for a clipper, very heavily sparred, and wet even in moderate winds, she had earned for herself the name Diving Belle; but never did she so justly deserve it as during the first half of her famous voyage in 1859.

She left New York in midsummer for Shanghai, and before reaching port, went through such weather as is the sailor's nightmare. Westerly gale followed westerly gale, raising a sea in which the slender old clipper rolled her lower yardarms nearly under, first on one side and then on the other. Her decks were so deep with water that Captain Crocker ordered great holes cut in the bulwarks to let it run off before it should smash them out. The suction through the holes was so great that some of the crew narrowly escaped being carried overboard. Life lines were rigged fore and aft, for the seas came over the quarter-deck almost as freely as amidships. The cabin was no drier than the forecastle; both were flooded for weeks on end. The galley was washed away. Not a dry stitch of clothing or a dry blanket remained on board. The one good feature was that the gales were fair, and sent the ship through the water at a good rate even under bare poles. Captain Crocker brought her into Shanghai in October, 1859, where his crew deserted to a man. This, needless to say, was no record passage.

The homeward voyage, however, had a different tale to tell. The time usually given for it is eighty-two days — a record between the two ports — but in fact it was eighty days, as is shown by a journal kept by an anonymous Cape man who made the passage under Captain Crocker and later held a master's ticket himself. Here is his account of the run:

The ship Swordfish, Captain Joseph W. Crocker,

The Last of the Clippers

Master, left Shanghai December 12, 1859; was 11 days down the China Sea and out clear of Java Head; 55 days from Java Head to the Equator west of the Cape of Good Hope; becalmed about the Equator 5 days, gaining about 60 miles during the 5 days; 14 days from that point to New York and anchored in the North River at 2.30 A.M. March 2nd, 1860, 80 days from Shanghai. I have not heard of a vessel that has made any shorter run. While at anchor in Shanghai River, waiting for the tide to turn, the mail steamer with the New York and land mail passed us, but the ship [Swordfish] arrived in New York 6 days before the mail. During the passage passed 102 vessels. Sailed 16,122 nautical miles during the 80 days, and 5 of the days made only 60 miles. Someone may say we could not get by the quarantine in the night, but we did — called the Doctor at 1.00 A.M. and paid the extra fee, and he let us pass, thereby saving half a day.

A Ship-Master

Here was a magnificent climax to Captain Crocker's career. He retired after this voyage to a life of well-earned leisure in Barnstable, a town full of Crockers and fast filling with retired captains.

Dennis, during the dull years just before the Civil War, and afterwards, too, when the war had begun, was still busy and tolerably happy, in spite of the loss of her principal citizen and capitalist, Christopher Hall, who died in 1857. Fewer nobler characters are to be found in New England history. His liberality with his captains, to whom he allowed all the independence of judgment they wanted, was a byword in Dennis and Boston. His habit of selling shares in his new vessels to as many of his friends as could afford to take them, made many comfortable who would otherwise have died in poverty; and his humorous resourcefulness in bad times, when he jocosely announced his intention of going into seining or taking up the gunning business, was a fine example to his less courageous neighbors.

After his death, Prince S. Crowell, his friend and associate, took his place as the leading merchant and shipowner in Dennis, and conducted the business in much the same genial style that Hall had followed. He, too, gave his captains a free hand. When they did well, he told them so; if they lost spars, he had no fault to find, for he had been at sea himself. Above all, he avoided a trick that had become almost a formula with owners, that of telling a captain who was setting sail in an old hooker which had seen her best days, that his ship was as good as new. It was only when Crowell's captains showed poor judgment in transacting ship's business that he criticized them; then he spoke his mind plainly and with force. Most of the vessels which he owned or managed were built in East Dennis by the Shivericks, and most of the captains who sailed for him were fellow townsmen.

A notable exception, and incidentally the cause of considerable trouble to Crowell, was Captain John Dillingham, of Brewster, an able navigator and voluminous correspondent, but, as it turned out, not much of a business man. Dillingham took one of Crowell's ships, the Kit Carson, out to San Francisco in the fall of 1857, Mrs. Dillingham accompanying him. He arrived in the middle of February, 1858, and wrote to Crowell that there was no direct business for the ship, but adds:

> I have arranged a charter after serious contemplation, with Daniel Gibbs & Co.... to proceed as follows — to Puget Sound, and load up with a cargo of sawn lumber for Australia; from there to Calcutta and back to this port for the round sum of $25,000.... I can't see but what I have acted up to the highest light. Fact is, the ship is too large for the times.

He wrote again on March 20 from Port Gamble, in Puget Sound, describing the scenery, the birds and animals that were to be seen there and giving his opinion of the region. Then he continues:

> The sound is very dangerous to a perfect stranger. I had the bad luck to enter the Straits at night. Tide runs very strong, forming races at every point. Hail and snow squalls. No anchorage and dark nights make it very

disagreeable. I rode out one severe South Easter with both anchors and all the chain in 25 fathoms water. I expected to lose my anchors but am all right now. I know the road hereafter. These wild countries serve to scare up a fellow's resources all at once in the way of management. The other ships all took pilots; several offered their services to me in San Francisco, but it seemed like taking one for the Sandwich Islands. I thought of Vancouver and Sir Francis Drake and put her through, and Kit Carson's effigy done us as well as the original.

The Captain loaded his lumber and proceeded to Melbourne, where he found two letters from Crowell which show what that dignitary thought of Dillingham's proceedings. In them, Crowell acknowledges the receipt of the Captain's letter from Puget Sound, expresses pleasure at the interesting account of the natural beauties of the region, is glad to know that wild animals and birds are abundant, but intimates that it would have been quite as much to the point if Dillingham had said something about the amount of his disbursements in San Francisco, an item which the Captain had neglected to include. Crowell then continues, in regard to the second section of the proposed voyage:

> To go to Calcutta, one of the most expensive ports in the world, and take a cargo from there in the height of the N.E. monsoons at a rate equal to $8.50 per ton for a ... port in the United States, exceeds by far all the miscalculation I ever heard of since I ever had anything to do with any ships — but I suppose it is no use to cry for spilt milk.

He even offered Gibbs and Company two thousand dollars to cancel the rest of the charter, but without success.

Dillingham was hurt by this criticism. He replied from Melbourne on July 30, 1858, that Crowell's letters had been received and 'contents most critically noted in consequence of its being the first of the kind ever directed to my particular notice. I am most willing to admit that the ship is doing a poor business but am not conscious of committing an error in management up to this present date, and cannot but consider myself unjustly reprimanded.'

After a month in Melbourne, he cleared for Calcutta, where he arrived on October 20, and he sailed on November 27 for San Francisco, arriving on April 1, 1859. The length of the passage was owing in part to a typhoon which the Kit Carson ran into, and which necessitated putting in at Batavia. From San Francisco Dillingham writes cheerfully that 'the ship is in fine order, minus the damage sustained by the typhoon.' But his cheerfulness vanished when he presented the underwriters with a bill of five thousand dollars for repairs and heard what they had to say on the subject. 'Mr. Bacon,' he writes, 'and perhaps underwriters' agents generally, seem to have an idea that the usual necessities of life are luxuries, and that anything not connected with a junk store, does not belong to a ship and was never insured on.' However, the business was finally settled, and Dillingham sailed for Iquique with a cargo of gunny bags and barley. At Iquique he loaded with nitrate for Liverpool and he arrived in the Mersey on January 3, 1860.

Here another blow awaited him. Prince Crowell had been hardly better satisfied with the Captain's later proceedings than with his first charter, and had decided to relieve him of the command and send another man to Liverpool to take charge of the ship. As Crowell puts it: 'The owners would not be willing for Captain Dillingham to remain longer in the ship, as they have lost all confidence in his business capacity. We doubt not he is a good sailor.' He accordingly gave the command of the Kit Carson to Captain Josiah Gorham, of Yarmouth, with instructions to proceed to Liverpool and take her on her arrival.

Gorham was on hand to meet Dillingham and the Kit Carson when they reached Liverpool, and the somewhat delicate transaction was accomplished without undue embarrassment. Dillingham, always a gentleman, wrote to Crowell that, though many of the faults that had been found with him were quite new to him, he had no wish to remain where he was not wanted. Gorham took command and loaded the ship with coal for China.

An interesting sidelight on Crowell's views as to carrying coolies appears in his letter of instructions to the new Captain:

> The Kit Carson is insured not to carry Coolies [he writes]. Besides, we have other than pecuniary reasons for not wishing any of our ships to engage in that trade. I thought I would mention this now, for should you find a dull freight market in China, which I am a little afraid you will, a big offer of that kind might be a little tempting, and not wishing to subject you to too severe a test between a moral obligation and a pecuniary gain, I would intimate the wishes of the owners in that respect.

Gorham brought the Kit Carson back safely from this voyage, arriving home in the spring of 1861, and relinquished his command.

The Civil War, it is pleasant to relate, brought a return of fortune to Captain Dillingham. The Government wanted sailors, not business men, to man its vessels and promptly put him in command of the extreme clipper Morning Light, which had been converted into a man-of-war. But in 1863, while she was cruising in southern waters somewhere off the coast of Texas, she was surprised and captured by the Confederates. This ended Captain Dillingham's career at sea. The disagreement which he had had with Prince Crowell was soon forgotten, for both men were too big to bear malice. After the war, indeed, the Captain showed his regard for Crowell by asking him for a recommendation as United States Consul in some South American port, a post well suited to his talents; but whether or not he got the position does not appear.

When Josiah Gorham left the Kit Carson, Crowell

decided that her next captain should be a Dennis man; he had had bad luck in Brewster, and the Yarmouth incumbent had not cared to continue. He accordingly invited an East Dennis neighbor, Captain Anthony Howes, to take her. Howes was a veteran who had proved his mettle early in the fifties by taking the Amulet round the world and later by getting the Shiverick-built medium clipper Hippogriffe clear of an uncharted rock that she had run up on in the Java Sea, and bringing her safely to port. The Hippogriffe was, in fact, a notoriously crank ship and an unlucky one. The accident in connection with the rock occurred in the spring of 1858, when Captain Howes was on his way to Hong Kong. By a smart piece of maneuvering, he worked the ship off into deep water and, believing her undamaged, proceeded to Hong Kong, where it was found that a big piece of the rock had come loose and remained embedded in the ship's planking, effectively plugging the hole that it had stove. The rock was subsequently charted under the name of Hippogriffe Rock, and on that grim foundation rests the ship's one claim to immortality.

Captain Howes, after getting her patched up in Hong Kong, set sail from Singapore for London in the fall of 1858, only to run into the worst storm of his career. Tremendous seas swept clear over her; her jib boom was smashed short off, taking with it most of the foremast; the only two spars left on the stump of it were badly sprung; the main topgallant mast went over the side; the mainmast itself was sprung; almost a whole suit of sails was blown to ribbons, the running rigging was mostly gone, and the hull itself was badly strained. Howes looked his command over and set to work, as soon as the wreckage had been cut clear of the ship, to get her to rights. He fished the mainmast with spare spars and chain, and served it with a nine-inch hawser that he cut up for the purpose; he then set what sail he could on the stumps of the other two masts, replaced the lost upper masts with makeshifts cut from the rest of his spare spars, and limped into the Thames in February, 1859, no doubt heartily endorsing Prince Crowell's remark that 'the ship was getting something in years.' This voyage, at any rate, had made an old vessel of her. But he kept her until the spring of 1860, when he resigned his command to take over the Kit Carson from Josiah Gorham. He stayed in the Kit for a couple of years, chiefly rice droghing between Eastern ports, to give what Crowell called 'Jeff Davis's pirates' a wide berth, and then retired.

The command of the old Hippogriffe, meanwhile, Crowell handed to his son-in-law, Captain John H. Addy, also of East Dennis; but he did not keep her for long. Times were not improving as the war progressed; Crowell, like many another owner, was providing his captains with powers of attorney to sell their ships in the East, usually at Calcutta, and that is what Addy finally did with the Hippogriffe, getting 70,000 rupees for her — more than she had cost when new. But before she was sold, Captain Addy had some pretty tough times, for her reputation as an unlucky ship stayed with her. His first voyage as master was in April, 1860, from Philadelphia to Callao with coal. He ran into bad weather on the way out, the cargo shifted, giving the ship a dangerous list, and Addy finally had to jettison about a hundred tons of it and put in at Montevideo for repairs.

After finishing the voyage to Callao, he went over to the Chinchas for guano, where bad luck of another sort befell him. His mate, a certain unidentified Mr. Howes, turned out to be a poor lot — 'about as much use as a spruce belaying pin,' to use one of Captain Joshua Sears's expressions — and allowed three men to get into a drunken brawl while visiting the crew of the ship Kineo, of Bath, Maine. Before the rumpus was over, one of Howes's men had stabbed a member of the Kineo's crew so severely that he died the next day. But the Hippogriffe was finally loaded, and Captain Addy headed for Cork in February, 1861. Thence he went to Hamburg, where he discharged Mr. Howes and wrote to Crowell on June 8:

> The news from the States has caused a great depression on American ships in Europe.... I shall not decide on any future employment for the ship for a little while, as things cannot be worse... than they are at present.... There has been some American ships that have changed their nationality and have got Hamburg register and flag by pretended sales to Hamburg citizens.

Captain Addy, however, did not resort to this expedient. Instead he showed marked skill in nosing out cargoes here and there, sometimes carrying coal from Cardiff to Calcutta, then freighting rice locally in the East for a while until he could pick up something for Colombo, for war insurance to any port in the United States was high enough to keep vessels far from home. Then came his chance to sell her, as already stated, and he came home from Calcutta early in 1864.

Another of Prince Crowell's ships, which was also launched from the Shivericks' yard, was the medium clipper Webfoot. Her captain, Milton P. Hedge, who had her throughout her whole career under the American flag, lived only a stone's throw from Crowell. For the first few years, he kept her going round the world *via* San Francisco and the East Indies. His hardest passage out to San Francisco was in 1858, when he was over a month off the Horn, carried away sections of his bulwarks, stove a hatch, and took 146 days to reach port. Captain Hedge was humiliated and expressed his feelings strongly in a letter to Crowell. The genial reply shows the magnate of East Dennis in a characteristic light: 'Yours... at hand, together with draft for $3500 and bills of repairs etc. If you got in a bad scrape, it's no use to feel so thundering bad, as that does not mend the matter; but keep a stiff upper lip. In regard to your proceedings, we are satisfied.' The Captain obviously acted on this excellent advice, for the next year, 1859, he brought the Webfoot from Calcutta to New York in a splendid passage of eighty-

CAPTAIN PRINCE S. CROWELL

five days — one of the four or five best on record. Then followed a voyage or two with grain from San Francisco to Liverpool, and the evil days began. Just before the outbreak of the war, the Webfoot was doing what she could to pick up cargoes in our southern ports, much to the dissatisfaction of Captain Hedge, who wrote to Crowell from Savannah that the charter which had been arranged for him was an unworthy one. Again Crowell replied with excellent advice in a letter dated June 5, 1860:

> I would recommend you to look [up] the coolest place you can find in Savannah, under some shady tree, order a claret julep — a long one — and when you have become refreshed and cooled off and a fair degree of tranquility restored to your mind, you could take out your Charter Party (which is a good one) and read it over in a common sense way, and I think you will find that the ship's interests are well protected.

During the next few years, when the Alabama was making it unsafe for Yankee ships near home, Captain Hedge was busy in the old guano trade, with occasional side trips to Australia. In the spring of 1864, while entering Dunkirk, he ran the Webfoot aground, and she was badly damaged. Crowell wrote to the Captain, telling him to use his judgment regarding the next move. Hedge, finding that repairs would cost £5000, wisely sold her to the British and came home for a rest. After the war he continued to follow the sea until 1878, when he retired to East Dennis.

One of the Cape men who during these bad times was in command of an old clipper that had been a queen in her day, was Caleb Sprague, of Barnstable, master of the Neptune's Car. She was not, in fact, the finest clipper ship that Sprague had commanded, for he had already taken the Gravina through the first voyages of her career, before she was sold at Valparaiso about 1858. He took over the command of the Neptune's Car at the very end of 1859 and went out to

San Francisco in her, returning the same way. In 1861 he made another voyage out, and a terrible time he had. Off the Horn the ship ran into weather that was unusual even for those latitudes. For forty-five days she battled her way westward, and three times got round into the Pacific only to be blown back again. A number of her spars and upper masts were gone; the seas opened up the seams of the weary old clipper; the crew mutinied and refused to pump, and Sprague, with the leaders of the mutiny in irons, headed for Callao for repairs. Here he got some new men and, with his ship caulked and rerigged, started once more for San Francisco, where he arrived 186 days after leaving New York. The last commands of Captain Sprague were the bark Chipsa and the brig Ossipee. After forty-three years as master, he came back to Barnstable, where he lived quietly until his death in 1893.

It is not to be expected that all of the Cape captains who put to sea during the Civil War escaped the ubiquitous Confederates. A number of them shared the fate of John Dillingham and the Morning Light, notably another Dillingham from Brewster, Captain James, Jr., a man who had to be caught twice before they really had him. The first time came in 1863, while he was bringing the lovely old clipper White Squall home from Penang. He had rounded the Cape of Good Hope and started on the last long leg of his voyage when he sighted the auxiliary bark Tuscaloosa, which came alongside, hoisting the Stars and Stripes in reply to Dillingham's flag. Then suddenly a row of portholes in the side of the bark flew open, the Confederate flag was run up, and the Captain ordered Dillingham to heave to. Instead of obeying, he held on for a few seconds until he had got out from under the lee of the Tuscaloosa, and then, trusting to the speed that the White Squall still had in spite of her years, took off, with every stitch of canvas drawing. The Confederate, for all his auxiliary power, could not catch her, nor did any of his shots hit the flying clipper. Captain Dillingham brought his ship into New York and received from the underwriters not the traditional silver service for his exploit, but a purse of $1375.14, doubtless even more acceptable a token than a tea-set would have been. This is said to be one of the few instances when a Union ship escaped a Southern steamer that had once come up with her.

On another occasion Captain Dillingham tried the same trick, but the wind failed at the crucial moment and he was captured. What was his surprise, on being taken on board the Confederate, to find that she was his old acquaintance, the Tuscaloosa, and that her captain was the same who had commanded her in 1863. Dillingham and his captor were both Masons, a fact which accounts for the latter's courtesy in handing him a receipt for $1500 for his navigating instruments. After the war, when Dillingham turned this document in at headquarters, it was honored in full. The Captain later had command of the second Blue Jacket — a fine ship, but not the extreme clipper that the first of that name had been — and finally went into steam. He died on board his last command, the S.S. Finance, while bringing her into New York Harbor in 1883.

Another old flyer that fell a prey to the Confederates was the Southern Cross, commanded by Captain Benjamin P. Howes, of Dennis. She was burned by the Florida in June, 1863, and after the war, Captain Howes, who was shrewd enough to realize that the palmy days for clippers and voyages round the world were over, built the little brig Lubra, and, taking his wife and child with him, headed for China, intending to put his vessel to work in local trade in the East Indies and along the China Coast. In September, 1866, when one day out of Hong Kong, he was surrounded by a fleet of pirate junks. Before any guns could be got up from below, the pirates had possession of the brig. Some of the crew dived overboard; others climbed into the rigging and were shot. Captain Howes was chased to his cabin and locked in, guards being posted at the door, while for six hours the pirates looted the vessel. One of them then came into the cabin, and shot the Captain dead, as he sat on a sofa beside his wife and child. Then they all departed, after setting fire to the Lubra and smashing her boats and nautical instruments. What was left of the crew managed to put the fire out and work the brig back to Hong Kong, where Mrs. Howes and her child went ashore.

The last Cape captain that will be mentioned as a victim of the Confederacy was Edgar Lincoln, of Brewster, master of the ship T. B. Wales. She was not a clipper, and so really does not belong here, but perhaps the gentility of Lincoln, as testified to by his captor, will justify his being included among the aristocracy of the clipper captains. The Wales, on a return voyage from the East Indies, was overhauled and burned by Semmes in the Alabama. Captain Lincoln, during his enforced sojourn on board that famous vessel, made a deep impression on the Southerner. 'He had,' writes Semmes, 'few of the earmarks of the Yankee skipper about him. He was devoid of the raw-boned angularity which characterizes most of them, and spoke very good English, through his mouth instead of his nose. His pronunciation and grammar were both good — quite an unusual circumstance among his class.' If even the ranks of Tuscany could scarce forbear to cheer, Captain Lincoln must indeed have been a polished mariner! Perhaps, however, if Semmes had been fortunate enough in the course of the war to capture more than one man from Cape Cod, his surprise at their lack of boorishness would have been less marked.

No account of the later clipper-ship captains from the Cape would be complete without some mention, at least, of the Baker brothers, Ezekiel C. and Horace T. of South Yarmouth. Captain Ezekiel was the better known of the two and commanded more famous ships than Horace. Yet the two were complementary the

The Last of the Clippers

one to the other in much the same way that Oliver and John Eldridge were. Captain Ezekiel had three celebrated clippers in their later and tenderer years: the Black Hawk, the Three Brothers, and the Young America; but it was his sojourn on the quarter-deck of the last-named vessel that contributed most to his fame. She was a remarkable ship, a maker of fast passages in her youth and in her old age still seaworthy and able. When Captain Ezekiel took her in 1876, she was already twenty years old. He kept her until 1879, going out to San Francisco and back with great regularity and on his last voyage in her made a fine passage of 102 days out. His brother Horace, who had been mate under him during these years, then took command until 1882; but he never got so much out of the old ship at Captain Ezekiel had; his best run out to San Francisco, made in 1880, was 106 days.

An anecdote shows the way in which Captain Ezekiel Baker boosted his officers into promotion even at the cost of his own comfort. He had the Young America out in China on one occasion, with Charles Whelden, of West Yarmouth, as his mate.

A man came on board one morning and said to Baker, 'Where can I get a captain to take one of my ships home?'

'There he is,' replied Baker, pointing to Whelden, who was busy on another part of the deck.

'Who is he?' asked the stranger.

'Charlie Whelden, my mate. He'll get your ship home for you.'

And he did; and later became captain of the Anahuac, the Cassandra Adams, and the Sterling. Captain Baker afterwards had the J. C. Bryant and the Jabez Howes, and wound up his sea career by taking the steamer City of Columbia to Alaska with a party of prospectors bound for the Klondike.

Here, then, are some of the men from Cape Cod who rose to the top of their profession by commanding clipper ships. Only a fraction of the total number has

Shipmasters *of* Cape Cod

been mentioned, yet enough, it is hoped, to indicate the quality of the rest. No mention has been made, for example, of such men as Captain Elijah Knowles, of Brewster, who went through a bloodless mutiny in the notorious White Swallow, or of Horace Taylor, of Chatham, who brought young Neesima Shimeta home from Shanghai in the Wild Ranger, and called him Jo for short. Nothing has been said of Edwin Chase, of Harwich, who was lost with the Black Prince in 1864, or of Charles Jenkins, of West Barnstable, master of the Raven. Space has been lacking to do justice to others as well — such captains as Seth Taylor, of Yarmouth, and Franklin Bearse, of Hyannis, both of whom commanded the Robin Hood. David E. Mayo, of Chatham, had the Nightingale, the loveliest of all clippers, and so did Hiram Sparrow, of Orleans. Another Chatham man, Thomas Sparrow, had the Wild Rover, and Joseph Snow, of Brewster, the Antelope. Hiram Nye, of Falmouth, and David Kelly, of Dennis, both had the fine old Fleetwing; Asa Lothrop, of Hyannis, the Electric Spark; Christopher Lewis, of West Yarmouth, the Belle of the Sea; and Barnabas C. Howes, of Yarmouth, the Swallow. Benjamin Freeman, of Brewster, was master of the Climax and the Witchcraft; Perez Hall, of Dennis, had the Sea Serpent; another Dennis man, Thomas Prince Howes, commanded the Wild Hunter and the Southern Cross; Sumner Pierce, of Barnstable, who wore a clean boiled shirt every day and sometimes returned from a voyage with seven hundred of them to be laundered, commanded the Lightfoot and was poisoned by a mutinous crew while in command of the Sunshine. Reuben Snow, of Truro, also had the Lightfoot, and Azariah Doane, of Orleans, the Carrier Pigeon. Christopher Crowell, of Hyannis and George Matthews, of Yarmouth, both commanded the National Eagle; Benajah Crowell, Jr., of Harwich, had the Wild Rover; William B. Cobb, of Brewster, had McKay's Empress of the Seas, Ira Bursley, of Barnstable, the Snow Squall and

252

the Archer, and Frank Bursley, also of Barnstable, the Skylark.

Some day, perhaps, the logs and letters of these men will be found, and their stories written; but our tale of the clippers is told, and we must proceed to other phases of the nation's maritime activity in which Cape men were employed.

II

Non-Clippers from the Fifties to the Eighties

THROUGHOUT the fifties and sixties and later as well, solid, useful ships were plowing across this sea or that in the wake of the clippers, making few record passages, it is true, but arriving in due time; and though the careers of their captains lack the thrill that colored the lives of clipper-ship commanders, yet they contain much that is picturesque and important. A good many of these full-bodied ships went to California, for when news of the discovery of gold first reached New England, clippers were few and far between. During the first flush of the boom, therefore, a goodly number of blunt-nosed craft of the old school thrashed their way out to San Francisco with crews whose one idea in signing on was to get a free trip to the mines, and with cargoes that consisted of whatever Boston owners, in their inexperience with this new business, guessed would be wanted in a mushroom town.

One of the most interesting of the early voyages in this class was made by Captain Winslow Knowles, of Brewster, who took the Albatross out to California in 1849. It is interesting not only because it shows the difficulties of doing business in so disorganized a settlement as San Francisco then was, but also because it illustrates the mistakes that even shrewd owners made at that early date in selecting cargoes for California.

Captain Knowles was already an experienced commander. He had taken the Edward Everett to Valparaiso in 1845 and had made another voyage out there two years later in the Chile. It was with high hopes of big profits, therefore, that in August, 1849, he set sail from Boston for San Francisco in the Albatross, owned by Benjamin Bangs and loaded with a cargo that outdid in variety even the stock in trade of a general store. Among other items were bricks, nails, pork, cement, shovels, hams, stoves, cordage, raisins, rice, lard, salt-mackerel, corn meal, an iron safe, lumber, oakum, soap, an express wagon, cheese, shingles and clapboards, a thirty-foot launch, pickets for fences, sixty-five oars, a large scow, and twenty house frames, with all the doors and windows pertaining thereto. He also took a lot of clothing to sell for a Boston merchant named John Gove, and as many passengers as could be squeezed in. The lumber had been contracted for by a man in San Francisco; everything else was a speculation.

From the outset the voyage was an unlucky one. Captain Knowles reached Valparaiso late in December, after 119 days at sea, and wrote to Bangs that it had been the longest and most unpleasant passage he had ever made. 'The passengers,' he says, 'have been a great annoyance to me, especially those in the forward cabin. They come to me every day with some complaint about the fare: sometimes the provisions, they say, was cooked too much; at other times not enough.' There seems, in fact, to have been some foundation for this criticism, for the Captain was honest enough to add, 'We have not had the provisions cooked very well, I must acknowledge, owing to the cook being sick all the passage.'

Such troubles, however, were fleeting compared with those which lay ahead. Captain Knowles finally anchored in San Francisco in the spring of 1850, and received his first lesson in the business ethics of that boom town when he discovered that the man who had ordered the lumber had changed his mind and refused to take it, as lumber was a drug on the market. 'The shingles and clapboards,' writes Knowles, 'I shall have to put on board of some store ship or keep them for firewood, which will amount to about the same thing.... The pickets will not sell for anything; I shall keep them on board.' Moths had ruined the clothing which he was to sell for John Gove, so that it brought only a fraction of its cost. All his crew, with the exception of his son Winslow, deserted for the mines, and stevedores were getting six dollars a day. The house frames at this rate hardly paid for the labor of unloading them. 'A Captain of a ship has a hard time of it in this place,' writes the Captain. '... Our California voyage will turn out a losing concern.'

Knowles stayed in San Francisco throughout the spring, doing what he could to save the voyage from being completely ruinous, and finally, receiving no orders from Bangs, he took a charter on his own responsibility for Newcastle, New South Wales, to bring back a cargo of coal for a San Francisco merchant. He arrived at Newcastle in September, 1850, and in addition to the coal, took on board soap, candles, brown sugar, copper, beef, ale, porter, canary seed, senna, lime, port wine, ginger, raisins, hay, corn and barley. But on reaching San Francisco again early in the spring of 1851, he found that the man who had ordered the coal had changed his mind and would have none of it, and that the place was overstocked with all sorts of goods from every part of the world. A lawyer whom he consulted told him frankly that a lawsuit, even if it should be decided in his favor, would cost more than it would be worth. Captain Knowles, at this point, would have emphatically endorsed the pronouncement that Josiah Richardson was inspired to make on the Queen City of the West at almost exactly the same time: 'San Francisco must reform, break off from its iniquities, or God's curse will follow it.' He got rid of his Australian cargo for what it would bring, and set sail for the Chinchas to load guano for New York at ten dollars a ton. While there he wrote to his wife, under date of September 22, 1851: 'I have got to be rather nervous and my health not very good. I think it is owning to the worryment of mind and the idea of making a ruinous voyage after being such a length of time from home.' And what, indeed, was an honest shipmaster to do in a city whose merchants regarded charters with the same nonchalance that European governments nowadays show toward treaties?

For one member of Captain Knowles's crew the voyage of the Albatross to San Francisco was the beginning of an exciting and romantic life. This was young John Higgins, an East Brewster lad who had embarked with the same idea that all the rest of the crew had — that of making a fortune in the gold fields. But distant scenes loom fairest to men like Higgins. On arriving in California, he decided that the best place to dig gold was Australia; so he shipped for Sydney on the steamer Monumental City. She was wrecked, and as young Higgins crawled out of the surf to the dry land of an Australian beach, the gadfly of restlessness still buzzed in his ear that Australia was not his Mecca after all. What he wanted he did not yet know, but whatever it was, he felt sure that it lay far from the elm-shaded propriety of Brewster, Massachusetts. Another voyage might bring him to it; so he shipped as second mate on a local trading-brig. She, too, was wrecked, and Higgins was washed ashore on one of the Caroline Islands six degrees north of the Equator.

Here, at last, was what he had been searching for. The island was inhabited by a handful of childlike savages who looked on Higgins as a gift from their gods. He was adopted into the tribe, was treated like a son by the old chief, one of whose daughters he married, and he began by degrees, without spoiling the idyllic simplicity of their way of life, to teach the natives some of the comforts of civilization and a few of the simpler precepts of Christianity. Before long, thanks to his instruction, they were living in houses and carrying on a profitable trade in cocoa oil, hogs, and tortoise-shell with the whalers, who, finding that business there was conducted with some system, dropped anchor at the island with more and more regularity. On one occasion a Brewster whaling captain, Charles Freeman, came ashore for a gam, and found life so agreeable that he spent a week, giving Higgins a fine chance to talk about home and to send back letters to his family.

'But Scripture saith an ending to all fine things must be.' After ten years or so, some natives from a neighboring island, coming over perhaps on purpose for a row, got into a fight with Higgins's tribe, and Higgins, in an attempt to stop the fracas, was stabbed to death. But he died happy and, what is rarer still, contented, for he had reached his goal on the same wave that washed him ashore on the island, the sole survivor of a wrecked brig.

So much for the voyage of the Albatross and its consequences. The only other voyage of a full-bodied ship to California that is of particular interest was that of the Goddess, commanded by Zenas Crowell, of West Yarmouth. He left Boston on July 9, 1857, the same day as the clipper ship Panther. Owing partly to luck in dodging a pampero off the Platte, and partly to smart work in cutting through the Straits of Le Maire, Captain Crowell beat the Panther to port by nearly two weeks — an achievement in which he might have taken proper pride even if the Goddess had been a clipper. But his voyage must be regarded as exceptional, for the glory of the merchant marine had begun to depart.

Times were growing hard for owners and harder still for young captains. Economy was the order of the day, and economy sorts ill with the impetuosity of youth. Merchants thought twice before promoting youngsters of twenty to commands; they wisely preferred to carry

on with veterans who knew the tricks of foreign merchants in all ports from Liverpool to Shanghai and who
saw eye to eye with the owners when it came to saving
pennies. When, by good luck, a young officer was
raised to a command, he was pretty sure to receive,
along with his promotion, a paternal lecture on the
value of a dollar — a subject on which owners at all
times might justly have pronounced themselves high
authorities! Even so genial a merchant as Prince S.
Crowell held clear views on economy, and showed no
hesitation in communicating them to his captains. His
correspondence with a young fellow townsman, Daniel
Willis Howes, when he put him in command of the old
Scargo, is a good case in point.

Howes had, in fact, shown himself so lively a lad
while in subordinate positions that he could hardly
have been denied a captain's berth. He had been
mate of the Hippogriffe when she went on a rock in the
China Sea, and on another occasion, when the Captain
was sick, had quelled a mutiny on board her with a
red-hot poker held to the touch-hole of the ship's cannon. Here was a young man of parts, whom not even
hard times could hold back.

In 1859 he was in London, serving as mate of the
Scargo under Captain Nelson Crowell. She had been a
good ship in her day, but had grown tender and leaky
with the passing of the years. Crowell resigned his
command before leaving London and recommended
Howes as his successor. Prince Crowell promptly ap-
pointed the young man and sent him, along with the
appointment, a letter of advice, dated December 27,
1859, that shows clearly the trend of the times:

> Your experience as officer has doubtless qualified you
> in all things necessary for the navigation and sailing of
> the ship [he writes]... but the most important part, that
> constitutes a valuable shipmaster, is yet before you, viz
> the business of the ship, demanding your most untiring
> efforts for its successful prosecution. The first and most
> important part is to know what is — and to secure — the

best business that is going; the next is, especially in these dull times, to prosecute it with despatch and the most rigid economy, or else her whole earnings will slip away and none or little of it come to the pockets of the owners. My experience has taught me that there are many merchants and mechanics... [who] think a ship is fair game to be plundered, and knowing that in most cases the ship always pays her bills, they have little regard for her except to fleece her to any extent they will be permitted to....

It is important to look well to whose hands you fall into both as regards merchants and mechanics — especially shipwrights, the latter of which have such opportunities that the most shrewd and experienced will often get taken in by them....

When you make a charter, and the Charter Party is drawn up, take it away and read it over — and it is well to sleep on it one night before signing, as the most experienced often fail to see the full import of the conditions implied in the language used in one reading, and I have seen many Charter Parties drawn up with such adroitness for the purpose of deception as to almost deceive the very elect; in fact, I have been a victim in one instance, where it was so well done that it was not discovered by the most shrewd merchants until we had to suffer by its practical operation....

Wishing you a fair success in your new situation and a safe return at no distant day

I remain your
Obdt svt
Prince S. Crowell

This letter, one would suppose, was forcible and explicit enough, but Crowell was not satisfied. He followed it with another about a month later, after Captain Howes had sailed from London for Calcutta.

I would reiterate and impress indellibly if possible on your mind [he says] the absolute necessity of the most rigid economy, for it will be impossible to continue the ship and maintain the extravagant manner of sailing them that has generally obtained with ship masters of late.... Owners now are selecting, whenever it can be done, the older Captains of the stamp of Levi Howes and that class.

Whether it was owing to so much excellent advice or to his own native shrewdness, Captain Howes acquitted himself creditably under his new responsibilities. He got his vessel safely to Calcutta and from there to Boston, where he took a short vacation and was off again for Melbourne in March, 1861, just before war was declared. Crowell sent a letter after him telling him of the war and suggesting that it might be wise to stay out in the East if he could find profitable business for the ship.

But a different destiny was in store for Daniel Howes. When about two months out, near the island of Tristan da Cuñha, the old Scargo, already leaky, ran into a spell of such weather as would have tested the timbers of the stoutest ship and the endurance of the redoubtable Levi Howes himself. Her log shows the character of the weather and of the Captain about equally well: here are some of the entries for the week beginning May 23, 1861: 'Heavy gales and hard squalls.' 'Heavy gales and squally weather.' 'Terrific gales and frightful squalls — hove to — ship makes much water — has sprung a leak.' 'Heavy gales and hard squalls — hove to under bare poles — ship makes considerable water.' 'Heavy gales and squally weather — carried away slings of main yard — ship makes more water than usual.' 'Squally, rainy weather — ship makes much water.' A few days later comes the following entry: 'Hard gales and squally weather'; 'Heavy gales and terrific squalls,' during which the ship was again hove to. Later in the same month these remarks appear: 'Heavy gales and terrific squalls.' 'Strong gales from W.S.W. with squally weather and heavy sea on. Ship laboring very heavy and makes much water.' The next day Captain Howes found that the oakum was all out of the wood-ends on the stem, but he could not caulk them because of the high sea. As soon as it moderated, he did caulk them, but the next day, in light airs, he writes, 'Ship makes more water than usual,' and on the day following, 'The leak increases.' Even in calm weather, it took three hundred strokes an hour to keep her clear. Late in July, 1861, she arrived at Melbourne.

After lying there for a month, Captain Howes set sail for Surabaya, in Java, and promptly ran into more troubles. The beginning of them, appropriately enough, came on Friday, the 13th of September, on which day appears the ominous entry: 'Heavy gales and fearful squalls; split the fore topmast staysail into ten thousand giblets — Ends queer.' Then came a fortnight of the same sort of weather that he had had on the way out, with intervals of calm, until on September 28, the limit was reached, and he wrote: 'This is the hardest weather for this latitude that I ever had. I cannot say anything bad enough to do it justice. I never did have any luck, and I never expect to, and what is more I don't care a —— whether I do or not.' After this outburst he resumed the dreary tale of head winds and hard squalls until he picked up the southeast trades on November 3, 1861, and took a pilot for Surabaya.

After nearly three months in Java, Howes took his departure for Holland on January 22, 1862, on what was to be the old Scargo's last voyage. On March 12 came the beginning of the end, when the ship sailed into a hurricane that almost literally beat her to pieces. Here is Captain Howes's account of the storm:

At 4.00 A.M., the wind blowing a Hurricane, hove the ship to on the starboard tack. At 11 A.M. blew away main topgallant mast and close reefed main topsail and fore topmast staysail. At meridian blowing a perfect hurricane; ship lying on her beam ends; pumps constantly attended, and water gaining fast. William Child, seaman, was hove over the wheel and badly injured; Carpenter was very much hurt by being jammed with loose spars.

March 13, 1862. Commences with a fearful hurricane.

At 1.00 P.M. the ship was in the calm center with a tremendous sea from all points of the compass, and laboring fearfully. The decks were constantly filled with water. At 2 P.M. the wind hauled to the west-ward and blew with the same force that it did from the opposite point. Ship lying in the trough of the sea. At 3.00 P.M. found 7 feet in the weather pump. Found that if the ship was not got on the other tack she would sink. At 4.00 P.M. the wind moderated. Set the jib and blew it away. Set part of the topsail, and after much exertion, wore around. Found the ship to be settling very much in the water. Bulwarks on the port side mostly washed away; cabin and forecastle filled with water. Lost a number of spare spars and water casks and bbls of beef off deck. At 6.00 P.M. cut away the wreck of main topgallant mast and let it go overboard. Pumps constantly at work, but do not gain upon the water. I deemed it expedient to throw some of the cargo overboard for the safety of the ship, which we accordingly did. The ship is badly strained all over, — the rudder braces started, and the foremast very bad. Finding that we could not free the ship of water, at 6.00 P.M. bore away for Mauritius, both pumps continually at work night and day.

But the Scargo never reached Mauritius or any other port. Captain Howes abandoned her in a sinking condition and was carried to St. Helena by the British ship General Neill, of Glasgow. From there he took passage on the Yankee ship Tirrell, commanded by his friend Captain Peter Morgan, and finally reached home. Subsequently, on the advice of his uncle, Captain Ezra Nye, of packet-ship fame, he went into steam, commanding the U.S.S. John Rice during the war and afterwards the Tartar and the Catherine Whitney. His later years were spent in the employ of various marine insurance companies, investigating cases that smacked of fraud.

The war, as has been suggested, sometimes kept Cape shipmasters away from home, freighting between Eastern ports where they were safe from Confederate privateers. One such — and a particularly fortunate one — was Captain Simeon N. Taylor, of Chatham, who was making money on the China coast during the worst part of the hostilities. Captain Taylor's career is remarkable for the speed with which he rose from an inconspicuous coasting skipper to a shipmaster of such repute that owners sent out to China for him to come back to New York and superintend the building of a new ship for them — a rise that the Captain achieved between the years 1854 and 1861.

His first years at sea were not auspicious. His coasting trips, some of which used to take him past the Back Side of the Cape, were enlivened for him by a signal which his wife flew from their house in Chatham and which the Captain could sometimes see as he sailed past. He learned the coasting business on the barks Ella and Radiant before he got his master's ticket, trading chiefly to Baltimore, Philadelphia, and Charleston. Then, in 1855, he was in command of the bark Laconia, trying in vain to make money by carrying coal and pig iron from Philadelphia to Boston. 'Times are very dull,' he writes. 'I do not have anything to do but just set down in Mr. Cooper's counting room [in Philadelphia] and drink ice water and smoke cigars. Last evening Atkins and Lewis and myself went down the street and went into a Bath House. Elish' [Atkins] came very near getting into the Ladies' apartment. Think I shall leave off going to sea and buy a farm.' On another occasion he wrote to his wife from Baltimore, 'I don't know how the devil it is freights are always dull when I come here; I think I must be Jonas or something else.'

But at the end of 1855 his luck changed. Howes and Company offered him the command of the bark Ella, which was engaged in the Mediterranean fruit trade, and at one bound Captain Taylor became a foreign trader instead of a southern coaster. He enjoyed the new business far better than the old, not only because it brought in more money, but because it gave him a chance to see foreign countries, pithy comments on which he invariably wrote home. From Smyrna he writes, 'I am now about ready to leave this land of Greeks and Jews.' From Palermo he writes: 'I am now about ready to leave this place of sin and beggars. ... Tell Emma and Maria I shall have two yellow birds for them.' And from Malaga, using the same formula, he writes, 'We are now about ready to leave this place of worship.' The sacred atmosphere of Malaga seems, indeed, to have cast a slight damper on the Captain's cheerful spirits, for in another letter from that sacred city, he says, 'Not so fine times here as in Bordeaux, I tell you, Hitty.'

But these voyages had their grim side, too, particularly in winter. Here is the Captain's description of taking the Ella out of New York on the morning of December 21, 1856:

> ... We are now going down with a fair wind, and a bitter cold morning, I will assure you, Hitty. I am homesick as a dog...; our sails are all frozen and the ropes are all like iron. The mate, he is cross at the sailors.

Captain Taylor left the Ella in 1857 for the brig Granada, also owned by Howes and Company, and in her, after another voyage or so in the fruit trade, he made a trip to Matanzas with a locomotive under his hatches, a brand of cargo that gave him great concern because of the difficulty and danger of unloading it. He had never been in the West Indies before and was, as usual, quick to form an opinion of the place and to communicate it to his wife:

> MATANZAS, *February* 12, 1858
> ... I am well and hearty as ever and enjoy myself finely.... Captain Nickerson, of Dennis, of the brig J. Nickerson, is here.... Matanzas is not much of a place anyhow. We have got clear of our Locomotive all right and nobody hurt, thank the Lord.... It is fine warm weather, so that I parade on shore dressed in white.... Tell Lucy I am afraid she will not get her Bay Rum, for

they do not know anything about that kind of rum. I guess they are pretty well posted on the other kind of rum. Tell Mother if she was in Matanzas she would want to put her feet in a cooler place than the stove oven.

But Lucy got her Bay Rum after all, for a month later, on the eve of sailing for New York, the Captain says, 'Tell Lucy to be of good courage, for I have a Demijohn of Bay Rum that I got out of a vessel.'

In the spring of this year, fortune smiled yet more fairly on Captain Taylor, for Howes and Company sent him out to Bangkok in the Granada on his first East Indian voyage. He sailed in June from New York with five passengers and a cargo of heavy machinery, all of which he landed safely. 'We are nearly unloaded without any damage,' he writes. 'I tell you, Hitty, I never want another such a cargo to handle — some pieces weighing 13 tons.' On several occasions he had tea with the King, whom he describes as 'a very social sort of a chap,' and he found life novel and on the whole agreeable. Soon after his arrival he received orders from Howes and Company to stay in the East and under no conditions to bring the Granada home but to keep her busy trading locally as long as he could find freights; then to sell her and come home.

Following these instructions, he took a cargo of rice, sugar, and sappan wood at Bangkok for Shanghai, but when he was about ready to sail, his crew all deserted. There was nothing for it but to try his luck with a native crew, which he obtained easily enough, but he was startled to observe that two of them brought along their wives and children. It was also necessary, if any work was to be got out of them, to engage a native mate; his own mate, Mr. Ryder, now had to give orders to the native, and the native to the crew. However, the arrangement worked so well that the Granada reached Shanghai in sixty-two days, the fastest passage of the season. His first letter to his wife after reaching port is entertaining:

Non-Clippers from Fifties to Eighties

SHANGHAI, *March* 4, 1859

... I am obliged to associate here with the big ship Captains for there is no small ones here. I find I can blow as well as any of them. We have made the best passage that has been made from Bankok this season. Vessels have been 80 and 90 days. The old Granada is up and dressed.... Ships are loading for New York at $5.00 a ton, so you may judge times are hard; we used to get $4.00 from Baltimore to Boston.

For the next two years Captain Taylor stayed on the China Coast, keeping his brig at work with whatever offered. After a month in Shanghai, looking in vain for freights, he writes, 'I am now about ready for sea, bound I do not know where. I have laid in Shanghai until I am tired and now I am going to look somewhere else.' He made tentative trips to Amoy, Ningpo, Chin Chew, and Foo-Choo, in all of which places he found business poor. After a couple of months of it, he writes again: '[Howes and Company] say they are depending on the little brig to keep the big ships alive till their turns come. I think they will come short of their expectations.... I did think I might make some money, but it seems my dish is always bottom up.'

But by degrees, as he began to get an insight into the trend of business on the Coast, Captain Taylor worked into steady packeting in the Granada between Shanghai and Nagasaki, carrying both freight and passengers — a business for which small American craft were in demand, as the lack of a treaty prevented Chinese vessels from taking their own goods to Japan. The Captain stayed in this trade for six months or more, with plenty of time in port, and began to feel more cheerful. His leisure days in Shanghai were particularly agreeable, for he found excellent company there. In November, 1859, for example, six Cape Cod captains were in port: Bursley, two Crockers, Burgess, Baxter, and himself. 'We have quite a nice time when we all meet,' he says; 'it seems quite like home.' It is not easy to identify these men, but one of the Crockers was Captain Joseph, who was about to make a record passage home in the Swordfish. A little later Taylor fell in with Captain Seth Doane, of the Northern Light. 'He was telling me,' he writes, 'they had the best schools in Chatham that is on the Cape.'

What with sociability and diminishing worry and his trips to Japan and back, the time passed. On one occasion Captain Taylor picked up thirteen survivors on a wrecked junk, and on another he ran into a Japanese holiday, which caused him to vent a little of his spleen on Howes and Company. 'I wish I was at home,' he says, 'and Howes and Company had this *mortified* brig in their charge.... I would like for them to come here for a year or two and try their luck.... The Japanese are having a nine days Jubilee or Holidays; no business in the shipping line as long as this is in operation.'

In February, 1860, after he had been in China about a year, Taylor received a staggering blow: he heard in Shanghai that Howes and Company had failed. He had just landed from Nagasaki and writes: 'On my arrival here the first news that came to my ears was that Messrs. Howes & Co. had failed and was broke down as flat as they could be.... The news comes direct from Chatham; Captain Isaiah Hardy received a letter from his wife.... I laid awake most all night thinking of it. I wish I was in the Western Country as far as I could get and [had] a small farm. Then I should not have to think of vessels or owners.' However, he continued as if all were well (wisely, indeed, as the report turned out to be unfounded) and was smart enough to make the most of some trouble between imperialists and rebels in Shanghai by chartering the Granada to a group of Chinese merchants to store their possessions on while the hostilities lasted. This brought in $1200, and business besides was looking up very briskly. On his last trip to Nagasaki he had made $12,600, and was well pleased. This, however, was about the end of

Non-Clippers from Fifties to Eighties

his Japanese packet trade, for in December, 1860, he was back at his former business of coasting. But he felt far flusher than when last engaged in the business and sent home to his wife a trunk full of presents, including two mandarin silk coats lined with Siberian squirrel skin.

In March, 1861, Olyphant and Company chartered the Granada for a trip up the Yang-Tse-Kiang River to Nanking, and urged Captain Taylor to stay in command. This was his first experience in river work, and he had the distinction of being the first man to take a merchant vessel to Nanking. After he had spent two or three months running between Shanghai and Nanking, Olyphant and Company sent him back to New York to superintend the building of a new steamer and to take her out to China for the river run.

Captain Taylor stuck pretty close to New York during the early stages of the building of his new command, but in the spring of 1862, after she was well started, Olyphant and Company asked him to go to Montevideo and take the Mississippi, another of their steamers, out to China, returning in time to supervise the finishing touches on the new vessel. He took his wife and daughter with him and seems to have been wrecked somewhere. Details are missing, but at all events he and his family turned up at St. Helena in September, where the Captain noted a protest, and they were back in New York in November, long before his new command was completed. He took a vacation at home in Chatham until September, 1863, when his vessel was launched and christened Kin Kiang. Early in the new year, 1864, he started in her for Shanghai.

The first his wife heard of him was a letter from St. Vincent written in the Captain's usual picturesque style.... 'The Island of St. Vincent,' he says, 'I should think was the last place made in the world, and there was not enough left to finish it.' He was keeping a weather eye open for the Alabama, but was lucky enough not to fall in with her. After one more stop at Mauritius, he reached Shanghai in the middle of May, 1864, and immediately went to work on the river, running the Kin Kiang between Shanghai and Hankow, about a ten-days' trip. Business from the point of view of Olyphant and Company was not very good, but this did not prevent Captain Taylor from enjoying himself. Two of his brothers were out there — Horace and Prince — both in command of ships, and he saw one or the other of them from time to time. 'Horace is down the Sea again somewhere,' he writes; 'I have not heard from him lately.' Prince had been laid up with dysentery and had gone to Japan to recuperate.

By the end of 1864, the Captain was feeling very prosperous. 'Only think, Hitty,' he writes, 'my wages in greenbacks per month at the same rate of exchange as you sold your bill for would amount to $656.' But in 1864 greenbacks were not gold, and the Captain was really earning $250 a month. Again he remarks: 'I think we both ought to be pretty well satisfied... you being high cock a lorem of your mansion and me the same of a fine steam ship during the hard times and troubles in our country.... Today I have been in company of my brother Horace on board the Wild Rover and have talked and smoked and drunk and eat and had a first rate time.' Most of his money he sent home for his wife to do with as she saw fit, but though, like all sensible Yankees, he knew the value of a dollar, he wisely realized that the chief use of money was to spend: 'Money is no use to a man,' he used to say, 'when his wife is a widow.'

He continued to run the Kin Kiang as a river packet between Shanghai and Hankow until the fall of 1865. Then Russell and Company bought her from Olyphant to make daily trips on the Canton River between Hong Kong and Canton. Captain

Non-Clippers from Fifties to Eighties

Taylor stayed in her and took her up to Hong Kong. A letter to his wife gives a lively account of the run and of his new business in Canton.

CANTON, *December*, 16, 1865

... We left Shanghai on the 3rd of this month and made the run to Hong Kong in 58 hours, the best time that ever was made, and there was quite an excitement about it.... It was very pleasing to Messrs. Russell & Co. I was taken by the hand at once and must go and dine with the head of the House, and they think that the Kin Kiang and the Captain are all right.... The business of running on the Canton River is much better than the Yang Tse; we depart at 9.00 A.M. and arrive at 2.00 P.M. every day. The rest part I have nothing to do. We have strong opposition, but the old Kin Kiang can beat them all. The Fire Dart is our opponent. We can and do beat her one half hour on the passage easy. This afternoon I think there was 1,000 people on the dock to see us come in; gave us three cheers as we came alongside of the dock. I tell you Hitty, there is some pleasure in having a fast boat and more pleasure to have business that you like.

But soon the Captain decided that he had been away from home long enough. The war was over, and everyone believed that shipping would immediately revive. He resigned his command in April, 1866, but made one more voyage for Russell and Company, taking their steamer Plymouth Rock to Shanghai; then early in the summer he took passage for home, leaving China, which had treated him so well, forever.

While Captain Taylor was coasting between Chinese ports in the Granada, another Cape man, Captain James Jenkins, of West Barnstable, was bobbing slowly along toward Singapore in the old Chilo, of Boston, very much such a ship as Daniel Howes's Scargo in regard to age and condition. One thing, however, must be said for these tubby old craft: they had to lie in port so long before anyone would give them a cargo that their captains had ample time to look around town and report what they found.

And so it was with Captain Jenkins in the Chilo. The passage out — barring a mutiny headed by the second mate but quickly suppressed — was monotonous and wearing, for the vessel leaked badly, and a survey made in Singapore showed her to be in such bad shape that she would have to be extensively repaired or sold. While agents and brokers and shipwrights were deliberating and inspecting and reporting, Captain Jenkins amused himself by cruising round town with a Mr. Safford, of Salem, whose acquaintance he had made in port:

> I thought when I left home [he writes], I shouldn't be likely to hear any more about the wonderful city of Salem; but at this other side of the world, I am wearied with the wonders of Essex Street and the beauties of the Common and Harmony Grove. I have only said I thought it appropriately named 'a place of rest,' for after wandering about it for three hours one summer morning, I found one person astir — an old man digging clams down on the flats, and the clams were so small, Cape Cod would never have owned them.

On one of their cruises round Singapore Jenkins and Safford were caught in a shower and took shelter in the house of a Chinese merchant whom they had met. He provided them with a bamboo couch apiece, a pipe, and a supply of opium, and, ensconcing himself on a third divan, began to smoke happily, urging them to do the same. Here was a new experience for the New-Englanders. They were willing to try almost anything once, but Jenkins's Yankee shrewdness suggested to him that the genial Chinaman might be going to put them to sleep and rob them. Yet he was loath to forego the opium experiment. He accordingly suggested to Safford that one of them should smoke while the other looked out for any sinister demonstrations on the part of their host. However, as it turned out, the merchant had no evil designs. Each of the young men smoked a pipeful and was somewhat disappointed to experience no sensations at all. Their host, who was smoking pipe after pipe and was rapidly becoming insensible, assured them that they had only to continue and they would feel very happy, but they had had all they wanted. 'The stuff tasted pleasantly enough,' says Jenkins, 'but it is a good deal of trouble to smoke it.... On the whole I should say opium-smoking is less disgusting than rum-drinking, for the drunkard is an insane brute, while the opium smoker is only a happy fool.'

On his return home after this voyage, young Jenkins married and got another command, the Hoogly, which, though no flyer, was a great improvement on the Chilo. Like other war-time captains, he kept her away from American ports as much as he could, and in 1864 was making a voyage from Callao to Cork, varying the bill of fare on board by serving fresh dolphin and enlivening the monotony by rescuing all hands from the sinking British bark James Lamb, Captain Braithwaite. This adventure was a pretty close call for the Englishmen; if Jenkins had been a less conscientious man, or a less discerning one, they would all have been lost. Here is his account of the incident:

I was reading in my berth about 4.00 o'clock in the afternoon when Mr. Miller put his head in at the cabin doorway and said there was a sail on the lee bow. It was a wet, drizzly, day and nearly dark, and it was just a chance that I bothered to get up and have a look. The vessel was a long way off, but on looking thro' the glass, I thought her colors were set. Then I fancied that she was going about with her head the other way to get nearer to us. Then the fog shut down and shut her from sight altogether.

We were having the first fair wind we had had for weeks, and I didn't like to run the ship out of her course on the bare supposition of trouble; but I couldn't get over the impression that there was trouble; so I steered so as to come nearer her. Bye and bye she hove in sight, and as soon as they saw us, they began burning blue lights and making signals to attract our attention. I ran the Hoogly close to her and spoke her. The Captain said they were sinking. I asked him if his boats were ready, and he said they were. So I told him to come on board and to bring bread with him, for we were short. I hove the Hoogly to, and in half an hour the Captain, mate and crew, thirteen in all, were safe on board and the poor barque left to her fate.

Our last glimpse of Captain Jenkins shows him, still on the Hoogly, on his way from Shields to San Francisco, in 1868. His wife was with him, and in her journal she writes as follows:

January 7, 1868.... We are 17' south of the Line on this beautifully warm bright day such as we have in June at home. The reflections at sunset tonight were the loveliest I have ever seen, and the moon is nearly full. We have the doors and windows all open, my birds are happy and singing, the water is smooth, there are two or three sail in sight and we are all well and happy.

February 9, 1868.... I can look out of my window now and see Cape Horn. It has no terrors today. The sun is shining brightly on it, the wind is fair and the water is bright and very smooth. Yes, today Cape Horn is beautiful.

Another Cape man who during the war was trading locally, but far from home, was Captain Joshua N. Taylor, of Orleans. He had begun his sea career in 1850 at the age of eight, as cook of a fisherman out of Dennis, and afterwards had made a voyage to Capetown and back before the mast on the bark Sea Bird, commanded by Captain John Taylor, of Chatham, a brother of Captain Simeon. Another of Simeon's brothers, Prince Harding Taylor, was mate; thus the ship's company was pretty well exposed to Cape influence fore and aft. After completing this voyage, young Joshua Taylor took command of the little yacht Charmer, bound for Littleton, New Zealand, with a cargo of wheelbarrows, washtubs, brooms, and Yankee notions. He set sail in December,

1863, and made the 16,000 miles out to Littleton in eighty-two days.

On arriving there, the yacht's name was changed to the Canterbury and she was put under the British flag in case she might meet, even in those distant seas, one of Jeff Davis's privateers. Then, secure under his new registry, Captain Taylor spent a year or so as a South Sea trader, but always with Littleton as his home port. While he was ashore there late in 1865, a storm came up, and the Canterbury dragged her anchors and went on the rocks, a total loss. Taylor had about decided to try his luck in the gold fields of Otago, but before he could start, he received an offer from Captain James White, of the celebrated clipper ship Blue Jacket, to sign on as sailing master for a voyage to London. He accepted and got his one and only taste of sail-carrying on a clipper — an interesting and valuable experience. After seeing the sights of London, he felt like going home for a while; so he took passage for Montreal and came down from there by rail.

His next command was the bark Otago, in which he made a few voyages to Capetown and East African ports, carrying farming tools for the Boers and returning to Boston with hides, wool, and a few passengers. His last voyage in her was in 1867, when, though his own vessel was leaking badly and in a dangerous condition, he stood by the sinking British bark Blond until all her officers and crew were aboard the hardly more seaworthy Otago. Then, pumping steadily day and night, he sailed into Capetown, where, to the amazement of the local talent, he ran the Otago right up on the beach lest she should sink at her moorings. There she was condemned and sold.

Captain Taylor was at home again before the end of the year, in time to pick up a new command, the ship Dexter, which had just been launched at Quincy. This berth he got in a curious way. The ship, on her way to New York in charge of a coast pilot, to pick up her cargo for San Francisco, ran aground near Corn Field Lightship in Vineyard Sound and lost part of her keel in getting clear. Her captain, Prince Harding Taylor, of Chatham, resigned after she reached New York, thus giving his mate, Edmund Linnell, of Orleans, a chance which most men would have seized eagerly. He was thirty-four years old, had held a master's ticket for a number of years, and was apparently qualified for the position in every way. The owners of the Dexter thought so, at any rate; so did he when he accepted the promotion they offered him. But after the stevedores began to roll her cargo on board, it was found that the Dexter was leaking badly, and what was worse, that the leak had nothing to do with the accident to her keel. Here was a strange thing indeed: a new vessel strikes a shoal on her way to pick up her maiden cargo; afterwards she springs a leak in a part of her hull that had never touched bottom. It did not look right to Captain Linnell.

Idle tongues along South Street began to wag, amusing themselves by fabricating prophecies of disasters that lay ahead. Linnell had heard about unlucky ships before; nothing could break a hoodoo once it had attached itself to a vessel. He ordered an examination of the Dexter's hull, and found that no stop-water plug had been put in. The prophets of evil pounced upon this oversight with glee; she was never meant to make a prosperous voyage, they said; she was a doomed vessel. The only question was what sort of fate would overtake her. Linnell did his best to laugh at these Jeremiads, but superstition was too strong for him. He took to his bed, a victim of worry and fear, until he fell actually ill and resigned the command. It was at this point that Captain Joshua Taylor turned up, a cousin of Linnell's, but endowed with a less sensitive nature. He accepted the position of master of the Dexter, and at forty-eight hours' notice started with her for San Francisco, arriving there after a voyage of 128 days, and turned her over to Captain John Taylor, of Chatham, who was there to receive her. Edmund Linnell soon retired to his farm in Orleans, where he may have taken some satisfaction in the reports of repeated misfortune that befell the Dexter. More leaks, whirlwinds, and a collision were among her mishaps, with never a quick voyage to lift the curse. Perhaps there was sense in his superstition, after all.

Joshua Taylor next spent a year or two in the brig J. L. Bowen, carrying salt from Cadiz, and cotton and phosphate rock from South Carolina to Liverpool, but with no experiences out of the ordinary until, with the passing of the years, he turned up in command of the bark George T. Kemp on his way to Boston from Port Elizabeth, in South-East Africa. The Captain had bought, as a private speculation, a tiger, an ostrich, and a big baboon, and the baboon made trouble on the homeward passage. It was allowed on deck, but because it was a savage beast, was kept forward in a heavy wooden cage, where the sailors amused themselves by plaguing it. One of them in particular, a Swede named Swinson, took delight in tormenting the beast, and one day poked at it through the bars of its cage with the handle of a broom. The animal seized the broom and pulled it toward him. Swinson — not a quick thinker — hung on to his end until he was close enough for the baboon to reach through the bars and grab him. It was then the work of a few seconds to fasten his fangs in the sailor's throat.

At this point Captain Taylor was summoned and came running forward to see what was up. He first tried prying the beast's jaws open with an iron belaying pin, but in vain. Twisting its tail was no good either. There was nothing for it but to cut away the flesh of Swinson's neck round the fangs and release him in this way. It was a delicate operation, as may be imagined, but the Captain did it, and Swinson, unconscious and his face almost black, was carried into the cabin. Here Taylor and the mate examined the wound, and a terrible-looking thing it was. However, they washed it clean, and the Captain, rolling up his sleeves, got out his surgical kit and ordered the mate to take down the book on surgery, open to the part describing the anatomy of the neck, and read it aloud. This the mate did, and the Captain, listening to the instructions and groping his way as best he could, sewed up the wound with thirty stitches. It swelled horribly, but after three weeks Swinson was as well as ever. A circus man paid $300 for the baboon, and the proprietor of a zoölogical garden bought the ostrich and the tiger; thus Captain Taylor's flyer in wild life came to good account in the end. After leaving the Kemp and taking the ship Littleton from San Francisco to Montevideo with grain, and thence to New York with wool and hides, the Captain left the sea and spent his declining years at home in Orleans.

This is as good a time as any to say a word about Captain John Taylor, of Chatham, one of Captain Simeon's numerous brothers, who has already been mentioned in a fleeting fashion, as captain of the bark Sea Bird in Capetown and later as taking over the command of the Dexter from Joshua Taylor in San Francisco. He had a long career and on the whole a successful one, but only two items about him will be mentioned here. In 1878 he was in command of the new ship Red Cloud, which looked as much like a clipper as any ship built in the seventies did. Captain Taylor took her out to Bombay with a cargo of ice and, on arriving, wrote his brother Simeon a letter, dated August 16, 1878, giving a sketchy account of the voyage, and his opinion of the ship.

> ... She is perfect in every respect [he declares]. She is fast — will walk off her 11 knots on a taut bowline, and such an easy ship I never saw — not a roll or pitch. [He continues, by way of explaining his slow passage:] The

ship was all on her beam ends and crank as all ice ships are, and of course could not carry any sail. And then such weather *I never had on any passage I ever made:* every day squalls, and squalls.... We got becalmed for 8 days, and then squalls and torrents of rain and no observation; but am in in 103 days — not so bad after all, Sim. I have had lots of anxiety this passage, and you would hardly think me your fat brother of other days. I am a mere shadow of my former self.

If the Captain had worn himself to a shadow, one wonders what must have been the condition of the officers and crew; for John Taylor, unlike the genial Simeon, was a bundle of nerves and very particular about even the smallest details; he also expected a great deal of his officers, as young Sam Harding, of Chatham, learned in the course of a voyage as second mate under him. The first port of call was Capetown, where Captain Taylor and his wife left the ship for lodgings ashore, but gave orders that Harding, while the vessel lay in port, was to send down all her spars, unreeve her running rigging, overhaul it all, set up her shrouds, sling her spars again and reeve her running rigging — a job for a seasoned rigger. 'He thought he had me that time,' said Harding. But the youngster put the job through in so shipshape a style that not even the old man's inspection could find any fault with it.

Another pair of Cape captains who distinguished themselves in the late sixties and seventies were Captain Benjamin Bray, who was born in Dennis but moved to South Yarmouth, and his mate, Joseph Bursley, of Barnstable. They started for San Francisco late in the fall of 1869 in the fine new ship Comet, the second of the name. She was owned by the Boston firm of Howes and Crowell and was built for durability and capacity rather than for speed. She had an extra heavy oak frame, copper-fastened, a deckhouse forward for her crew, and a cabin finished in bird's-eye maple. She was, in fact, much such a ship as McKay's Glory of the Seas and was launched within a few months of the same time. On the way out to San Francisco, she had a chance to match her speed against the Golden Fleece, a medium clipper with a name for fast voyages. It was a tough race, both ships arriving after passages of 111 days, the best of the season. 'But,' says a San Francisco marine reporter, 'from the difference in models and the well-known sailing qualities of the Golden Fleece, the Comet would seem to have made the best time. She is turning out her cargo now [February 28, 1870] in splendid order.' Her mate, Joseph Bursley, was afterwards captain of the Victory, and when he left the sea served as station-master in Barnstable until his death.

The last of this group of Cape shipmasters who attracted attention in his day and for whom space must be found in this cursory account, was Captain Elijah Crocker, also a Barnstable man. His earliest claim to distinction was the discovery of an uncharted cluster of rocks in the Pacific Ocean, in the summer of 1869, when the Captain was bringing the ship Akbar from Hong Kong to San Francisco. He sighted the rocks on the direct route between the two ports, but the weather was so thick that no observation could be taken; by dead reckoning they lay in latitude 31.50 North, longitude 139.23 East, bearing N.N.W. from Smith's Island, distant forty-two miles. A contemporary reporter, on the basis of this discovery, called Captain Crocker 'one of our most intelligent and observing shipmasters.'

But he was more than intelligent and something besides observant, though it was seven years before he had a chance to show it. Then in 1876 the opportunity came for Captain Crocker to show the extraordinary determination that formed the keystone of his character.

On April 4 he left New York, bound for San Francisco in the ship Conqueror. Two weeks out he ran into such violent storms that all the iron work of the lower main topsail yard was carried away. From Rio all the way to Cape Horn the wind held south-west or west- southwest, the ship laboring heavily. Sixty days out the Captain passed Cape Horn; two days later he lost one of his men, who was killed by falling from a yard; the next day he ran into more gales, and the day after the ship sprung such a leak that the engine had to be hooked up to the pumps to keep her clear. A few days later, the gale shifted to northwest and north-northwest — dead ahead. Another seaman was killed by a sea coming aboard; some sails were blown from the bolt-ropes, and others were split; finally the lower main topsail yard was carried away, which meant that for five days no sail except a reefed mainsail could be carried on that mast. A week later there came another gale from the north-west and such a high head sea that the Captain had to keep the ship off before it, running southeast by south for one hundred miles to save his spars, the vessel leaking upwards of eight inches an hour all the while. On the 4th of July the engine on the pumps gave out and they had to be worked by hand. Through the next week the winds, though light, continued dead ahead, and even in the light airs the ship leaked seven and a half inches an hour. 'This,' writes Captain Crocker, 'is the hardest passage I ever made.'

By the 1st of August, all hands were worn out by constant work at the pumps, and the leak had increased to fifteen inches an hour. On August 5 the engine gave out again, and the Captain had to keep the ship under easy sail to prevent her from foundering. On August 7 the pumps broke, and the leak had increased to sixteen inches an hour. The pumps were repaired after a fashion, but for the last three weeks of the voyage, pumping never stopped. On the night of August 22, when the ship was off San Francisco Heads, both pumps gave out entirely, and in half

an hour there were three feet of water in the hold.
The next day she made port.

Such, briefly told, is the story of Captain Crocker's
voyage of 141 days to San Francisco. The marine
reporters of that city were used to tough passages,
but here was something exceptional, and the San
Francisco *Daily News* for August 24, 1876, came out
with the following editorial about the Captain:

> ... Here is a man who not only carried on his shoulders
> all the responsibility inseparable from such an occasion,
> but who also navigated the ship, stood his watch, worked
> the pumps, ran the engine and encouraged his men by
> his presence and example. In these efforts for the preser-
> vation of other men's property, he was well seconded by
> his officers — particularly the mate, Mr. Horn, and crew.
> We trust that action will be taken immediately by the
> underwriters, and that they will present Captain Crocker,
> his officers and crew with a substantial reward for their
> successful efforts to bring the ship to port under circum-
> stances which justified her going in in distress, if not her
> abandonment, at any time since she passed Cape Horn.

It is pleasant to report that the underwriters, following this happy suggestion, did present Captain
Crocker with a 'suitable reward,' and concluded
their letter of appreciation with the assurance that
they believed him to be 'an honest man as well as a
brave and skilful seaman.' The Captain's last command was the bark Mary S. Ames, which he had for
years. After leaving her, he retired from the sea to
his home in Barnstable, where he died in 1895 at the
age of sixty-seven.

Here, though the tale of the wartime and post-war
shipmasters has not nearly been told, we must stop.
It would be interesting to continue with anecdotes
of other captains and other ships, but space forbids.
Such far voyagers as Joshua Eldridge, of Chatham,
whom his friends called 'China Josh' because of his
many voyages there, ought not to be overlooked;
neither should Levi D. Smith, another Chatham man,

who about 1880 carried the last cargo of natural ice
to the Barbadoes on the bark Florence, and in 1892
took the coal-laden bark Xenia through a typhoon
on her way from Newcastle to Hong Kong. Captain
Seth Kingman, of Orleans, in the Stamboul, took the
first ice to Egypt that had ever been seen there;
Captain Edmund Burke, of Truro, in the Western
Islands packet Azor, rescued all hands from the
sinking ship Gratitude in 1865; David Bursley, of
Barnstable, commanded McKay's splendid new Minnehaha in 1867; few China traders were better known
than Captain Alfred Doane, of Orleans, master of
the ship Endeavor. The two fine ships Conqueror
and Agenor were commanded on most of their voyages
by Cape men: Captain Ansel D. Lothrop, of Barnstable, had both at one time or another; so did Captains John H. Frost, of Hyannis, and Nathaniel Gould,
of Orleans. Some mention, too, should be made of
Captain John Turner Hall, of Barnstable, who, while
in command of the ship Abelino, shook hands with
Fremont in California, and of Captains Atkins Hughes,
of North Truro, and David Annable, of Barnstable,
who had the Briggs's second Southern Cross. Captain Freeman Lincoln, of Brewster, father of Joseph C.
Lincoln, whose novels have brought hundreds of visitors to the Cape, distinguished himself after the Civil
War. So did Captain Francis Hinckley, of Barnstable,
master of the ships Star of Peace, Arabia, and Leading
Wind. He it was who was directed by the owners of
the Arabia to use thinner note-paper in writing from
New Zealand in order to save postage!

The ladies of the Methodist Sewing Circle in Orleans
prevailed upon three of the shipmasters of their town
to address them after a church supper held on March
8, 1870. They were Captains Lewis Smith, James
Prince, and Abijah Mayo, and any one of them would
undoubtedly have preferred to take his ship through a
typhoon rather than to harangue the ladies; but they
all went through with it. Unfortunately, their re-

marks are not preserved. No one knows, either, why a mysterious bright red steamer appeared off Agulas Bay in the sixties, sailed three times round Captain George Matthews's ship National Eagle, and then took her departure without answering the Captain's hail. But the incident is still told in Yarmouth, where he came from. And so it goes. In the face of such numbers it is idle to continue; the line stretches out to the crack of doom; and besides, the Mediterranean fruit trade — about the last branch of foreign voyaging that can be put into a category of its own — is awaiting our attention.

12

The Mediterranean Fruit Trade

THE fact that the Mediterranean fruit-traders are here placed in a group of their own does not signify, by any means, that they were exempt from the lean years that rolled along the whole Atlantic seaboard before, during, and after the Civil War. It means only that they had a clearer idea of where they were going and when they might expect to return than the shipmasters whose voyages took them to South Africa, India, or China. Hard times were shared by all and hung on so persistently that a good many of the wisest Cape captains began to furl their sails for good and try their luck ashore. The Barnstable *Patriot* for October 26, 1869, reflects the alarm that thoughtful citizens on the Cape, who had always depended on the sea for their prosperity, were now feeling for the future of their towns:

> Chatham is continually losing its prominent families [says the writer]. During the last winter Captain Moses Nickerson and Captain Heman Smith have found homes elsewhere. People begin to inquire... 'Where are these things going to stop?' If we must suffer our business men to go to the cities, our sea captains to decrease in number and our capital to betake its way to business outside of shipping, what is to save our village?

Moreover, the author of this article, instead of being an alarmist, was, in fact, behind the times, for

Chatham had begun to suffer several years before.
Mrs. Simeon Taylor, writing to her husband under
various dates in the year 1865, gives a good idea of
the exodus that was already under way. 'Saw Captain Adolphus Ryder,' she says. 'He told me he
thought he should try to get his living on land;
he intends to try his luck in Chicago. Many have
gone from Brewster [and] have become independent.'
'It is very dull in regard to Captains getting business.
Captain D[avid] Harding says, "Tell Sim to come
home and go out West with him in the pork business
or keeping hotel"; but I think you Captains would not
be much in business on the land unless you are very
saving.' Again she writes: 'All the Captains seem to
be getting business on the land. Captain Ryder has
gone to Chicago and gone into the fish business;
Captain Stephen Bearse has gone into the boot and
shoe business in Boston; Captain D[avid] Harding
has gone to Chicago.' 'The war is over,' says another
letter, 'but business is rather dull. Many captains
are out of employ.'

Nor were the misfortunes of Chatham unique; the
same story might be told for a dozen other towns on
the Cape. But because it was hard for veterans to
believe that the old signs had really failed, some of
them continued to sail away as bravely as ever into
the twilight; and prominent among this diminishing
company were the Mediterranean fruit-traders. Their
business was by no means a new one. Osborn Howes
had been at it as early as 1831, and Simeon Taylor's
first foreign voyages had been for fruit. But the trade
continued after most others had failed; and a full
history of it would be a long story. The business was
carried on chiefly in little barks, a fact which meant
hardship on the return voyages, for like the British
tea-clippers racing from China to the Thames, the
fruit-carriers also raced home to win the bonuses that
owners paid for first arrivals, and crowding sail on a
light bark for a trans-Atlantic beat against the pre-

The Mediterranean Fruit Trade

vailing westerlies meant wet decks and lost spars. As Captain Samuel Harding, of Chatham, put it, 'We always used to come home under water.' The trade consisted, 'strictly speaking, of two branches, dry and green. Raisins from Spain and figs from Smyrna comprised the dry cargoes; oranges and lemons from Messina and Palermo, the green. But as often as not, Captains had to take both kinds to make up their cargoes and sometimes even then had room to spare for a few bales of rags.

Two hard-working fruit-carriers were the Nickerson brothers, James W. and Augustus, of Harwich, one or the other of whom commanded Joseph Holmes's little bark Abby as long as she was afloat. Captain James had her first, taking command in 1854, when she was launched, and setting sail from Boston in December with a cargo for Constantinople. He brought back fruit and rags from Smyrna and was off again early in the summer of 1855, trying his hardest to beat another of Holmes's vessels, the bark Fruiter — but in vain. 'I shall never try again to beat the Fruiter,' he writes, 'until I have something to compete with her. I never tried harder to beat a vessel than I have this voyage to beat the Fruiter, and I begin to think the harder a man tries, the slower he gets along oftentimes. When I arrived and found she was there, my courage was all gone.'

Captain Nickerson need not have felt so concerned about his defeat, for the rival bark was almost twice the size of the Abby and was one of the fastest vessels in the fruit trade. After this voyage, he turned the Abby over to his brother Augustus and went into cotton-carrying in the ship Nathan Hannau. Captain Augustus made some voyages to South America and the West Indies and then in 1856 took a charter in New York for a round trip to Malaga for fruit. Holmes was displeased with Nickerson's bargain, and the Captain, determined, it is supposed, to make the voyage pay, drove the little bark so hard on the way home that she went down with all hands.

It would be interesting to follow the fortunes of Captain Joseph A. Lavender, of Provincetown, who in 1856 commanded the Fruiter that James Nickerson tried so hard to beat, and who later had the Sicilian, an equally celebrated vessel in the same trade. James H. Arey, of Orleans, who made fruit voyages for twenty-five years and then retired to run a grist mill, act as selectman, and serve on the School Committee, was another captain worth knowing about. So was Solomon Smith, of Barnstable, who had the Sicilian in the trade for a time. But information about these men is not at hand. One anecdote, to be sure, is told about another commander of the Sicilian, Captain Daniel W. Percival, of Barnstable. In the winter of 1869–70, while in Messina, he bought a wild goldfinch which he put in a cage and kept like a canary. The next spring, while he was taking the Sicilian coastwise from Philadelphia to Boston, the bird escaped and perched on the spars of the Five Fathom Lightship. Captain Percival continued the voyage without it, and thirty-six hours later was off Long Island, one hundred and twenty miles from the Lightship, and surrounded by a fleet of vessels — some thirty in all. A bird appeared, heading for the Sicilian, and came aboard; to the surprise of all hands, it turned out to be the lost goldfinch, but a goldfinch, it would seem, with a drop or two of homing pigeon blood in its veins!

Then there was Captain William Chipman, of Barnstable, who made voyages to the Mediterranean in the barks Azof and Isaac Jeanes, and whose wife presented a Spanish nobleman with the first rocking-chair ever seen in Spain. But Captain Chipman loaded with salt more often than with fruit, and so he hardly belongs among the fruit-traders. Captain Zenas Nickerson, Jr., and his mate, Starks Nickerson, both of Chatham, were wrecked off Plymouth in October,

The Mediterranean Fruit Trade

1867, at the end of a voyage from Smyrna in the bark Velma. Fortunately neither was drowned. About 1878, Captain Zenas Gould, also of Chatham, had a fine chance to draw comparisons between nation and nation in the course of a voyage from Messina to Boston with oranges and lemons in the brig R. M. Heslin. About nine hundred miles off Boston his vessel was struck by a whirlwind and completely dismasted. A gale followed, and what with one thing and another, the brig was upwards of three months covering the nine hundred miles to port under jury rig. During this time, Captain Gould spoke two vessels — a Dutchman, who, when asked for water and provisions, bluntly suggested that Gould first turn over the brig to him for salvage, and then they would see about supplies. Finding that the Yankee captain held other views, the Dutchman presented him with a peck of barley and went his way, but not until the mate, who had at least a drop of the milk of human kindness, had given them some tobacco. 'So much,' thought Captain Gould, 'for a Dutchman.' Later they fell in with a Nova Scotian, whose captain, though low on supplies himself, readily handed over half of what he had to the Heslin. 'And that,' thought Captain Gould, 'is a Nova Scotian,' and he took his opinions with him to his grave.

But the most dramatic of all fruit voyages was that of the bark Amy, begun by Alexander Nickerson in 1864 and finished by his mate, Captain Joseph Harding, in 1865. Both men, and most of the crew as well, were of Chatham. On the voyage out to Smyrna, Captain Nickerson, so Harding reports, seemed depressed, and his low spirits continued in spite of there being a number of Cape shipmasters out there to keep him company. Two of them, Captain Daniel Howes and Captain Sylvester Hamilton, of the bark Armenia, called on him as soon as the Amy arrived, and the next day they rowed over again for a chat. But before they had come alongside, Joseph Harding

289

leaned over the rail and hailed them with the news, 'The Captain has blowed his brains out.' They climbed on board and made their way to the cabin. From the way the body lay, it looked as though Captain Nickerson had stood in front of the mirror and watched his own suicide. The motive, so his friends believed, was bad luck in his voyages the preceding year; he had been heard to say that he should not care to live if it were not for his wife and children.

Young Joseph Harding assumed command, the Chatham boys in the crew rallied round in loyal style, and the spirits of all on board rose rapidly with the elasticity of youth after the shock of the tragedy. The Amy finished loading her figs for Boston, and the Captain, planning to stop at Gibraltar for supplies, headed westward with his first command. No vessel, so said Clarendon Freeman, one of the Chatham boys before the mast, ever had a sweeter sail the length of the Mediterranean. She entered the Straits of Gibraltar under a full moon, with a fresh fair breeze, and every stitch of canvas drawing, while the water swished musically aft from her cutwater. 'We'll be home in two weeks, men,' said the Captain. 'Keep her as she is; we've got no time to stop for stores.' And they all agreed, for youth, in its impatience, is confident that it can perform miracles.

About the time that the Amy took her departure from Smyrna, Captain Sylvester Hamilton also set sail in the Armenia, homeward-bound. Week followed week, and no word of either vessel reached Chatham. Two months passed with no tidings, and then three. At last in January, 1865, more than one hundred days from Smyrna, Hamilton and the Armenia put into Holmes's Hole, battered and leaking, with tales of a dreadful passage, hard gales and high head seas. Of the Amy and her crew of Chatham boys, nothing had been heard.

And perhaps it was just as well, for if their families

could have known what that ship's company was going through, it would have done little to allay their fears. The little bark, when hardly clear of the Straits, met the first of a series of heavy westerlies that prevailed throughout the passage. The first gale started a leak; the second, which followed hard on its heels, increased it. But the boys were strong and willing to pump; when the wind flattened out, they said, or shifted to fair, the seams would come tight again. But the wind neither flattened out nor did it come fair. Week after week the westerlies blew on, while the Amy, too light to compete with such head seas as had blown even the great Chariot of Fame backward, gained scarcely a mile. Supplies grew lower and lower until even rationing could not make them go round, and the famished youngsters fell upon the cargo of figs. They pumped until they dropped from exhaustion; then woke to pump again, while their beards grew long on faces that were young no more, and the figs, without nourishing bone or sinew, bloated their lean bodies with fat. The sea had transformed them from a crew of likely looking Yankee sailors into a group of sunken-eyed and bearded horrors. Two months passed. Then one day somewhere in mid-Atlantic, they were aroused from their dazed mechanical routine of pumping and dropping asleep, by finding a bottle of wine among the ship's stores. Captain Harding poured it into as many cups as there were men on board, and handed one to each. 'What shall we drink to?' asked one of them. 'To Eternity,' answered the Captain. 'We shall never see Chatham again.' The toast was drunk, and the pumping resumed. But the Captain was wrong, for youth conquered after all, and in January, 1865, brought the Amy, leaking and battered into port, after nearly four months — 'the hardest passage ever made across the Western Ocean,' according to Clarendon Freeman, who went through it at the age of sixteen.

Shipmasters *of* Cape Cod

Why, one may ask, did they not put back? And to a generation of yachtsmen the question is a fair one. Harding was no Allen Knowles, seasoned by Atlantic winters to slam ahead through anything, nor was his command a great McKay packet like the Chariot of Fame, heavy enough to hold her own against all but the worst weathers. He was a youngster of twenty, and his vessel was a bark of perhaps eight hundred tons that could do nothing against the great gray seas that the westerlies rolled up before them. By wearing ship and letting her run before it, Captain Harding could have made any one of half a dozen European ports in a week; there he could have bought the supplies that he should have taken on at Gibraltar and could have had the Amy made seaworthy once more. But though he was no veteran captain in experience, he was a veteran by tradition and inheritance. His father, Captain Hiram Harding, had trodden a quarter-deck before him, and the son throughout his boyhood had in imagination commanded a hundred ships, had fancied himself a dozen times in just such a predicament as had finally overtaken him, and had a dozen times hung on and brought his ship to port. So the experience was not new; its only novelty lay in the fact that reality had taken the place of imagination. And this, I suppose, is the meaning of being bred to the sea.

But the end of America's carrying trade was in sight. Young Cape men, if they were prophets enough to read the signs of the times, turned seaward no longer, while veterans who were too old for untrodden paths went home to the Cape at last, their voyages behind them and their day's work done. Until 1890 or so, enough of them were still alive to keep the Cape villages alert and broad-minded, for in each of them lived a score of men who had caught something of the breadth of the notched horizons which their eyes had so often scanned. Here were

292

The Mediterranean Fruit Trade

men who had lived in foreign cities for months on end, weathered typhoons, put down mutinies, smashed records, and taken tea with kings. They had seen life in half the seaports from St. Petersburg to Hong Kong; they had shivered through February snow-storms on the North Atlantic and sweltered through pongee and pith helmets in Ceylon. They had dined with Chinese merchants whom they had learned to trust and had been shamelessly cheated by Yankees whom they believed to be their friends. They had eaten caviar in Russia, drunk claret in Bordeaux, and smoked opium in Singapore. And when they came back to Brewster or Yarmouth or Orleans, they brought with them something more than camphor-wood desks and strangely inlaid card tables; they brought a perspective so true that they could distinguish between the important and the unimportant and could laugh at much that loomed large in the narrower minds of the few of their brethren who had stayed at home.

Such were the men of Cape Cod, who before the sun had set on our great days of sail, were ambassadors of their nation in the seaports of the world: a handful of mariners in Colonial days, when the Cape was too busy to go to sea; coasting skippers who skirted the Atlantic seaboard from Nova Scotia to the West Indies in their blunt-bowed brigs and schooners; the North-West fur-traders, the most daring and romantic of them all; their contemporaries in the tangled trade of warring Europe; later European traders in the easier days, who varied their voyages with an occasional flyer to the East Indies; the grim routine of the Liverpool packets; the glory of the clipper ships, that were born, flourished, and faded from sight in a single decade; other voyagers from the fifties through the eighties, in an era of lengthening shadows; and finally the fruit-traders, with their little vessels and stout hearts — about the last real sailors to keep our flag afloat. Along all these lanes of commerce sailed the captains of Cape Cod — no insignificant part of the history of a nation. A few men only and a few voyages have been mentioned in comparison with all that there were — a slender representation of what the full company would have been. But the representatives who have been chosen are, it is hoped, such as will show that the Cape Cod shipmaster made his way early into the front rank of the sailors of the world and stayed there as long as there were ships to sail.

Acknowledgments

WITHOUT the help of three generations of their descendants, this book about Cape Cod shipmasters could hardly have been written. Only through the kindness of granddaughters and grandsons would it have been possible to obtain the letters, logs, sea-journals, account-books, and pictures without which these pages would have held little but statistics.

From first to last, Stanley W. Smith, Esq., of Boston and South Orleans, has been a more than staunch ally. His own collection of manuscript documents, his books and his time have always been at my disposal. His wide acquaintance among the citizens of Chatham, Harwich, Orleans, and Eastham has thrown open doors at which I should never have been wise enough to knock uninstructed, and his unfailing confidence in the importance of the pursuit has been a support during the not infrequent moments when enthusiasm seemed to have pushed perspective from its throne. My debt to him is very great.

To the extreme kindness of Mrs. Chandler Bullock and Mrs. Arthur Nye, of Worcester, I am indebted for a large number of logs and letters of Captain Josiah Richardson, as well as for pictures of him and two of his commands. On this material — together with some supplied by E. B. Worrell, of Dorchester — is based all of Chapter V in this volume. I am equally indebted to Mrs. Louisa M. Crowell, of East Dennis, for permission to examine a large collection of logs, letters, and papers of Captains Prince S. Crowell and Joshua Sears, and to Mrs. Minerva Wexler, granddaughter of both these distinguished shipmasters, for her great helpfulness in making them immediately available. Allen H. Knowles, of Yarmouthport, has been of the greatest assistance, not only in furnishing logs and account-books of Captains Winslow Knowles and Allen H. Knowles, but also in supplying charts

Acknowledgments

and photographs. A desk full of the same sort of data in regard to Captain Eben Linnell and his commands was placed at my disposal through the kindness of Henry Cummings, of Orleans, and his sisters, Miss Mary Cummings and Mrs. E. H. Sprague.

My information about Captain Daniel C. Bacon comes from the manuscript account of his life written by Miss Julia Bacon and lent to me by Mrs. W. S. H. Lothrop, of Boston, to whom I am also indebted for valuable suggestions in regard to other sources of information. Louis Bacon, Esq., of Boston, further helped to complete the story of Captain Bacon by lending me the log of the Atahualpa and numerous photographs. To Mrs. Roger Warner, of Boston, I am indebted for access to the original journal kept by William Sturgis on his first voyage, and for his manuscript lectures on the Indians of the North-West Coast. The picture of the Indian village on the Queen Charlotte Islands is reproduced from Sturgis's journal by the kind permission of Mrs. Warner. Further material about Captain Sturgis was supplied by Mrs. Algernon Coolidge, of Boston. His photograph was furnished through the kindness of Mrs. Ward Thoron.

Miss Elizabeth Jenkins, of West Barnstable, contributed a number of letters, written by her father, Captain James Jenkins, and extracts from his wife's sea-journal. George P. Matthews, late town clerk of Yarmouth, not only compiled for my use a list of sixty deep-water shipmasters of his town, but gave me some lively anecdotes about many of them as well. Information about a number of Orleans and Eastham captains was supplied by George Austin Smith, of Eastham. Without the interest and helpfulness of W. Sears Nickerson, of East Harwich, one of the soundest authorities on early Cape history, I should never have heard of that picturesque branch of short-voyage coasting known as 'corn-cracking' or have learned the names of some Harwich corn-crackers.

Acknowledgments

The entire account of Captain Sturgis Crowell is based on letters, logs, and similar documents lent by his daughter, Miss Annie Crowell, of Hyannis.

Miss Mona Howes, of East Dennis, supplied much valuable information about her father, Captain Daniel Willis Howes, as well as the very interesting log of the Scargo's last voyage. Miss Aimee Sears, of Sandwich, placed at my disposal letters and other documents written by Captains Daniel Howes and Ezra Nye, as well as pictures of both. To Robert Munroe, of Longmeadow, Massachusetts, I am indebted for a box full of letters which Captain Simeon Taylor wrote home from foreign ports and some of Mrs. Taylor's replies, containing very useful information about affairs in Chatham in the sixties. Francis W. Sprague, of Barnstable, very kindly furnished documents relative to his grandfather, Captain Caleb Sprague, and to his uncle, Captain Elijah Crocker. John Kendrick, of South Orleans, showed great courtesy in allowing me to examine the letters and papers of his ancestor, Captain John Kenrick. I owe much to Mrs. Henry Allen and to Miss Caroline Dugan, of Brewster, for their help in supplying information about Captain Elijah Cobb.

Without the kindness of Mrs. J. A. Godoy, of Brookline, who allowed me to examine a scrapbook kept by her grandfather, Captain Rodney Baxter, and who furnished pictures of two of his commands, the account of that distinguished shipmaster would have been sadly inadequate. The courtesy of Mrs. H. H. Freeman, of Boston and Sandwich, curator of the Sandwich Historical Society, made it possible for me to spend hours in the rooms of the Society, examining the journals of Mrs. William Burgess and other valuable manuscripts, as well as to secure pictures of the clipper ship Whirlwind, and the Collins liner Pacific. Richard Hopkins, of Orleans, showed great kindness in allowing me to copy extracts from logs in his possession. To Miss Elizabeth Reynard,

Acknowledgments

of the faculty of Columbia University, I am indebted for the authentic account of the trial of Ansell Nickerson for piracy. Russell Fessenden, Esq., of Boston, supplied most of the facts about the Bursleys, of Barnstable, especially those relating to his grandfather, Captain Ira, and to his great-uncle, Captain Allen Bursley.

A number of anecdotes about Captains John, Asa and Oliver Eldridge, and photographs of the first two, were furnished by their nephew, Asa Eldridge Goddard, of Cambridge. Further information about this great trio, as well as interesting facts about Captain Otis White and a photograph of Captain Oliver Eldridge, were given me by Miss Edith White, of Yarmouthport. Mrs. Nathan Allen, president of the Osterville Historical Society, supplied a bundle of manuscripts pertaining to Captain Benjamin Hallett, and another Osterville lady, Mrs. Ellen Scudder, showed the greatest kindness in lending me a rare book on the same Captain Hallett as well as giving me permission to reproduce a picture of him and his family. I have to thank Mrs. S. Alexander Hinckley, of the Hyannis Library, for many helpful contributions, not the least of which was in directing me to the door of Mrs. Scudder. To Leslie F. Jones, of Barnstable, I am indebted for a number of items about local coasting captains and deep-water shipmasters, many of whom he remembers well. Homer P. Clark, Esq., of Brewster, Massachusetts and St. Paul, Minnesota, was particularly gracious in allowing me to examine manuscripts dealing with Captains Isaac Clark, Jeremiah Mayo, and Bailey Foster as well as a long manuscript account of early days in Brewster by Augusta Mayo. I am indebted to L. D. Baker, Esq., of Boston and Wellfleet, for particulars in regard to his father, Captain Lorenzo D. Baker. Osborne Howes, Esq., of Chestnut Hill, Massachusetts, very kindly lent me a copy of the autobiography of his grandfather, Captain Osborn Howes.

Acknowledgments

The late Captain Thomas F. Hall, of Omaha and East Dennis, who was the last clipper-ship officer from Cape Cod, supplied much information about the shipmasters of his town and in particular about the clipper, Belle of the West. To Captain Samuel Harding, of Chatham, one of the few deep-water shipmasters still alive on the Cape, I am indebted for facts about the Mediterranean fruit trade, in which he was long engaged. Ansel Preston Howes, of East Dennis, and Seth Taylor, of Yarmouth, both of whom made voyages in their youth, have contributed many items about ships and captains. Elwin Smith, of Greenfield, New Hampshire, furnished me with the names of many Chatham captains and accounts of their voyages, in particular those of his father, Captain Levi D. Smith, with whom he sailed as a boy.

I have also to thank Mrs. George Evelyn, of South Yarmouth, for information about her uncles, Captains Ezekiel and Horace Baker. To the late Percival H. Lombard, of Brookline, first president of the Bourne Historical Society, I am indebted for valuable suggestions as to sources of information. Mr. and Mrs. John Smart, of Eastham, were extremely helpful in supplying a photograph of Mrs. Smart's uncle, Captain Freeman Hatch, and details of his life. A number of items about Barnstable captains are taken from a scrapbook in the possession of Miss Louisa Cobb, of Barnstable, which she kindly permitted me to examine. Without the able and very intelligent co-operation of L. B. Robbins, of Harwich, who, working sometimes under the greatest difficulties, made most of the photographs in this volume, the book would have lacked one of its most valuable features. I am further indebted to Mr. Robbins for obtaining access for me to some collections of documents in Brewster, notably that of Mrs. F. T. Cleverley. The authorities of the Yale University Press kindly allowed me to quote freely from their book, *Elijah Cobb, a Cape Cod Skipper*.

Acknowledgments

From the beginning of the work to the end of it, my father, George Lyman Kittredge, has helped me in every way — by solving problems of arrangement, by advice in regard to omissions, and by transcribing long extracts from letters and logs. He also waded through the entire manuscript, pencil in hand. Without his wisdom and enthusiasm, many of the difficulties connected with the book would never have been overcome.

BARNSTABLE, *July* 16, 1933.

Bibliography

PUBLICATIONS

Albion, Robert G.: 'Yankee Domination of New York Port,' *New England Quarterly*, Vol. V, No. 4, Oct., 1932.

Bartlett, John: Narrative of Events in Life of. Reprinted in *The Sea, The Ship, and the Sailor*, Salem, 1925.

Baxter, Captain Rodney: Communications to *Boston Investigator*, *Cape Cod Item*, and *Yarmouth Register*.

Bray, Mary Matthews: *A Sea Trip in Clipper Ship Days*, Boston, 1920.

Briggs, L. Vernon: *History of Shipbuilding on the North River*, 1640–1872, Boston, 1889.

Buell, Augustus C.: *Paul Jones, Founder of the American Navy*, New York, 1903.

Chase, Alexander B.: *Old Shipmasters*, Library of Cape Cod History and Genealogy, No. 16, C. W. Swift, Yarmouthport.

Choules, John O.: *The Cruise of the Steam Yacht North Star*, *etc.*, Boston, 1854.

Clark, Arthur H.: *The Clipper Ship Era*, New York, 1910.

Cobb, Elijah: *Autobiography*, Yale University Press, 1925.

Congdon, Charles T.: *Captain Rowland R. Crocker*. (Twenty-First Annual Report of Trustees of New Bedford Free Public Library, New Bedford, 1873.)

Crosby, Katherine: 'When the Cape Built Clipper Ships,' *Cape Cod Magazine*, Aug. 16, 1926.

Cutler, Carl C.: *Greyhounds of the Sea*, New York, 1930.

Dana, Richard Henry, Jr.: *Two Years Before the Mast*, Boston, 1911.

Davenport, G. L. and E. O.: *Genealogy of Families of Cohasset*, Boston, 1909.

Davis, William T.: *Plymouth Memories of an Octogenarian*, Plymouth, 1906.

Deyo, Simeon L. (ed.): *History of Barnstable County, Massachusetts*, New York, 1890.

Doane, Alfred Alder: *The Doane Family... and Their Descendants*, Boston, 1902.

Dulles, Foster Rhea: *The Old China Trade*, Boston, 1930.

Freeman, Frederick: *Freeman Genealogy*, Boston, 1875.

Freeman, Frederick: *History of Cape Cod*, Boston, 1858.

Bibliography

Goodwin, E. S.: Account of Wreck of Schooner Almira and Death of Captain Josiah Ellis. (From *The Token and Atlantic Souvenir*, Boston, 1833.)

Hall, Thomas F.: *Shipbuilding in East Dennis*, Library of Cape Cod History and Genealogy, No. 11, C. W. Swift, Yarmouthport.

Hallett, Captain Alvin S.: Letter to Barnstable *Patriot*, Oct. 11, 1853.

Hawthorne, Julian: *Hawthorne and His Circle*, New York, 1903.

Howay, F. W.: 'John Kendrick and His Sons,' *Oregon Historical Quarterly*, Vol. 23, No. 4, Dec., 1922.

Howe and Matthews: *American Clipper Ships*, Salem, 1926.

Howes, Osborn: *Osborn Howes: An Autobiographical Sketch*, edited by his children, Boston, 1894.

Jarvis, Russell: *A Biographical Notice of Commander Jesse D. Elliott, etc.*, Philadelphia, 1835 (privately printed).

Jones, Henry M.: *Ships of Kingston*, Plymouth, 1926.

Knowles, Captain Josiah N.: Diary, giving account of wreck of Wild Wave, 1858. (From *Stories of the Sea*, edited by E. E. Hale, Boston, 1880.)

Loring, Charles G.: *Memoir of William Sturgis*, Massachusetts Historical Society Proceedings, VII.

Lubbock, Basil: *Colonial Clippers*, Glasgow, 1921; *The Down Easters*, Boston, 1929; *The Western Ocean Packets*, Boston, 1925.

McKay, Richard C.: *Some Famous Sailing Ships and Their Builder, Donald McKay*, New York, 1928.

Marvin, Winthrop L.: *The American Merchant Marine*, New York, 1919.

Matthews, Frederick C.: *American Merchant Ships*, Salem, 1930.

Mayo, Charles (ed.): *Mortuary Record from Gravestones in Old Burial Ground in Brewster*, Yarmouthport, 1898.

Morison, Samuel Eliot: *Maritime History of Massachusetts*, Boston, 1921.

Otis, Amos: *Genealogical Notes of Barnstable Families*, Barnstable, 1888.

Paine, Josiah: *Edward Kenwick*, Library of Cape Cod History and Genealogy, No. 35, C. W. Swift, Yarmouthport.

Palfrey, J. G.: 'The Barnstable Boy.' (From Introduction to *American Common School Reader and Speaker*, Boston, 1845.)

Bibliography

Phinney, Julia: *Historical Notes on Centerville*, Old Home Week Celebration, Centerville, Mass., 1904.

Pratt, Enoch: *Comprehensive History ... of Eastham, Wellfleet, and Orleans, etc.*, Yarmouth, 1844.

Rich, Shebnah: *Truro, Cape Cod, or Land Marks and Sea Marks*, Boston, 1884.

Sears, J. Henry: *Brewster Ship Masters*, Yarmouthport, 1906.

Semmes, Raphael: *Service Afloat, etc.*, Baltimore, 1887.

Simpkins, John: *Sketch of Brewster*, Massachusetts Historical Society Collection I, 10, p. 77.

Smith, Nancy W. P.: *The Provincetown Book*, Brockton, 1922.

Smith, William C.: *A History of Chatham, Massachusetts*, Hyannis, 1909–1913.

Sprague, Francis W.: *Barnstable and Yarmouth Sea Captains and Ship Owners*, 1913 (privately printed).

Sprague, Leavitt: *List of Sailings from New England to San Francisco, 1849–1856*. (Bound with *Barnstable and Yarmouth Sea Captains and Ship Owners*.)

Sturgis, Julian: From the Books and Papers of Russell Sturgis, Oxford University Press (privately printed).

Swift, Charles F.: *Cape Cod*, Yarmouth, 1897; *Old Yarmouth*, Yarmouthport, 1884.

Taylor, Captain Joshua N.: *Sea Yarns: Being the Reminiscences of Captain Joshua N. Taylor.*

Whidden, Captain John D.: *Old Sailing-Ship Days*, Boston, 1925.

Anonymous Publications

Memories of a Grandmother, by a Lady of Massachusetts, Boston, 1854.

Half-Centennial Celebration of the Yarmouth Institute, Yarmouthport, 1893.

Celebration of the 200th Anniversary of Incorporation of Town of Falmouth, Mass., Falmouth, 1887.

Records of Superior Court of Judicature, Boston. Dockets 13642, 13615, 144633, 52105.

Registry of Deeds, Barnstable County.

'State Aid Granted': Report of Joint Committee of Senate and House. Massachusetts Senate No. 100, March 25, 1857.

State Street Trust Company, Calendar of 1929, with account of Captain Isaac Freeman and ship Bethel.

Bibliography

Old Shipping Days in Boston, State Street Trust Company, Boston, 1918.

Some Merchants and Sea Captains of Old Boston, State Street Trust Company, Boston, 1918.

Other Merchants and Sea Captains of Old Boston, State Street Trust Company, Boston, 1919.

Some Ships of the Clipper Ship Era, State Street Trust Company, Boston, 1913.

Gleason's Pictorial, Dec. 30, 1854; Sept. 4, 1852; Sept. 20, 1851; Aug. 9, 1851; Aug. 30, 1851.

Spirit of the Times, Aug. 14, 1852.

Along the Line, Jan., 1932.

Chatham Celebration, 1712–1912. Report of the 200th Anniversary of Incorporation of Town of Chatham, Mass., 1913.

NEWSPAPERS

Alta Californian, Aug. 24, 1876.

The Barnstable Patriot.

Boston Advertiser, May 22, 1847.

Boston Globe, Oct. 22, 1905.

Boston Journal, March 17, 1883; Jan. 17, 1854.

Boston Transcript, Jan., 1919; Feb. 20, 1904.

Cape Cod Advocate and Nautical Intelligencer, Sandwich, April 26, 1861.

Hong Kong Daily Press, Nov. 26, 1859.

Sandwich Observer, March 2, 1850.

San Francisco Daily News, Aug. 24, 1876.

Worcester Daily Transcript, Feb. 2, 1854.

Yarmouth Register.

MANUSCRIPTS — LOGS AND JOURNALS

Log of ship Atahualpa: Captain Daniel C. Bacon, 1810 ff.

Abstract Log of ship Boston Light, Captain Sturgis Crowell, 1861 ff.

Diary and Journals of Mrs. William Burgess, 1853 and 1854, ashore and on ship Challenger.

Log of ship Chariot of Fame, Captain Allen H. Knowles, 1856, 1857.

Log of ship Chatham, Captain Josiah Richardson, 1840–41.

Journal of ship Eliza, Captain William Sturgis, 1798.

Journal of ship Herbert, Captain William H. Burgess, 1851.

Bibliography

Log of schooner Ocean, Captain Abner Hopkins, 1833 ff.
Sea Journal on the ship Orissa, Mrs. Joshua Sears, 1850.
Abstract Log of ship Orpheus, Captain Sturgis Crowell, 1865–70.
Account-book of ship Santa Claus, Captain Bailey Foster, 1857–61.
Log of ship Scargo, Captain Daniel W. Howes, 1861–62.
Journal of voyage of ship Staffordshire, Captain Josiah Richardson, 1852.
Log of ship Staghound, Captain Josiah Richardson, 1851.
Abstract Log of ship Volunteer, Captain Sturgis Crowell, 1863–64.
Log of ship Walpole, Captain Josiah Richardson, 1847 f.
Log of ship Webfoot, Captain Milton P. Hedge, 1856–58.
Log of ship Western Star, Captain Allen H. Knowles, 1852.
Journal of ship Whirlwind, Captain William H. Burgess, 1852–54.
Log of ship Wild Hunter, Captain Joshua Sears, 1857 ff.

MISCELLANEOUS MANUSCRIPTS

Bacon, Julia: Captain Daniel C. Bacon, 1899.
Hallett, Benjamin F.: Life of Captain Benjamin Hallett, Osterville Historical Society.
Lovell, Adeline: Life of Captain Benjamin Hallett, Osterville Historical Society.
Mayo, Augusta: Narrative of early days in Brewster.
Sturgis, William: Lectures on North-West Indians, etc., Massachusetts Historical Society.
Letters of Eben Bacon to his son, Daniel C. Bacon.
Miscellaneous Papers and Clippings in regard to Captain William H. Burgess, Sandwich Historical Society.
Job Chase Papers.
Captain Isaac Clark Papers (photostat).
Captain Prince S. Crowell Papers.
Captain Sturgis Crowell Papers.
Captain Thomas F. Hall Letters.
Cargo List of ship Webfoot, Captain Milton P. Hedge, 1857 ff.
Captain Daniel Howes Papers, 1792 ff.
Captain James Jenkins Letters.
Captain John Kenrick Papers, 1804 ff.
Captain Winslow L. Knowles Papers and Account-Books.
Captain Eben H. Linnell Papers.

Bibliography

List of captains in Barnstable village, compiled, 1926, by Captain Ansel Lothrop.

Miscellaneous Papers, owned by W. Sears Nickerson.

Captain Ezra Nye Letters.

Inscriptions from old Orleans Cemetery.

Original Registers, issued by Joseph Otis, Collector of Barnstable, 1801.

Bills for inspecting incoming vessels at various Cape towns, sent by local inspectors to Joseph Otis, Collector of Cape District, 1804, etc.

Josiah Richardson Letters.

Joshua Sears Letters.

Captain Nehemiah Smith Papers.

Miscellaneous Papers, owned by Stanley W. Smith.

Captain Caleb Sprague Letters.

Captain Simeon N. Taylor Letters.

Index

Abbott W. Lewis, schooner, 35
Abby, bark, 287
Abby Pratt, ship, 187
Abelino, ship, 283
Abigail, schooner, 11
Acapulco, 235 ff.
Adams, John, 12
Addy, Capt. John H., 245 f.
Adriatic, steamship, 134
Africa, 86 ff., 95 f.
Agenor, ship, 237, 283
Agulas Bay, 284
Ainsworth, John, 154
Akbar, ship, 153, 280
Akyab, 208 f., 213
Alabama, Confederate cruiser, 247, 250, 270
Alaska, 251
Albatross, ship, 227, 254 ff.
Albert, schooner, 19
Alden, Joseph, 116 ff.
Aldinga, steamship, 203
Alert, ship, 65
Algerian Pirates, 74
Algoa Bay, 170
Alicant, 90
Allen, Capt. John, 29
Alligator, schooner, 32
Almira, schooner, 23 f.
Alphea, schooner, 84
Amazon, schooner, 22
Amelia Strong, brig, 22
America, steamship, 171
American Belle, schr., 144 ff., 187
American Navigation Club, 68
Ames, Henry, 182
Amethyst, ship, 124, 126
Amoy, 267
Amsterdam, 90
Amulet, ship, 244
Amy, bark, 289 ff.
Anahuac, ship, 251
Andrew Jackson, clipper ship, 183
Angelique, ship, 223
Anjer, 59, 63, 153, 156
Annable, Capt. David, 283
Antelope, clipper ship, 185, 209, 252

Antwerp, 144, 150
Appotesi, 54 f.
Arab, bark, 185
Arabia, ship, 283
Araminta, 72
Archangel, 41, 72 f.
Archer, clipper ship, 186, 253
Arctic, steamship, 131, 133 f.
Arey, Capt. James H., 288
Arey, Capt. John, 221
Ariadne, frigate, 93
Arklow Bank, 139
Armenia, bark, 289 f.
Arthur Seitz, schooner, 35
Asa Eldridge, clipper ship, 184
Aspinwall (now Colon), 190
Atahualpa, ship, 53 ff., 58 ff.
Atkins, Capt. Daniel, 72
Atkins, Capt. Elisha, 264
Atlantic, steamship, 131, 196
Atlas Steamship Line, 34
Atwood House, 10
Atwood, Capt. Joseph, 10
Aurelius, ship, 150
Australia, 198, 204, 240, 247, 257
Autoleon, bark, 150 ff.
Azof, bark, 288
Azor, bark, 283
Azores Islands, 10, 211, 283

Bacon, Capt. Almoran, 36
Bacon, Capt. Daniel C., 54, 57 ff., 138, 152, 196
Bacon, Edward, 12
Bahama Islands, 90
Baker, Capt. Ezekiel C., 250 f.
Baker, Capt. Horace T., 250 f.
Baker, Capt. Isaiah, 22
Baker, J. & Co., 26, 221
Baker, J. G., 223
Baker, Capt. John, 221
Baker, Capt. Joshua, 26
Baker, Capt. Judah P., 111 f., 165
Baker, L. D. & Co., 34
Baker, Capt. Levi, 27 f.
Baker, Capt. Lorenzo Dow, 33 f.
Baker's Island, 202, 222 f.
Bald Eagle, clipper ship, 185

Index

Baltic, steamship, 131, 195
Baltimore, 21 ff., 92, 125, 179, 264, 267
Bangkok, 266 f.
Bangs, Benjamin, 18, 255 f.
Barbadoes, 283
Barnstable, 5 ff., 12 f., 23, 35 f., 38, 40, 47, 54, 57, 61, 63, 65 f., 69, 122, 137, 139, 147 f., 154, 156, 169 f., 177, 179, 190, 205, 237, 239, 247 f., 252 f., 279 f., 282 f., 288
Barnstable, ship, 152
Barnstable County, 138
Barnstable County Peace Convention, 85
Barnstable *Patriot*, 285
Barrell's Sound, 43, 45
Barrington, 119
Bartlett, J. H., 228 ff.
Bashee Islands, 155
Bass River, 26, 84
Bassett, Cyrus, 197
Batavia, 59, 170, 226, 242
Bath, 245
Baxter, Capt. Rodney, 144 ff., 187 ff.
Bay de Chaleur, 12
Bay of Bengal, 159
Bearse, Capt. Allen H., 35
Bearse, Capt. Franklin, 35, 186, 252
Bearse, Capt. Orren B., 178
Bearse, Capt. Richard, 187
Bearse, Capt. Robert, 147
Bearse, Capt. Stephen, 286
Bearse, Capt. Warren H., 187
Belle of the Sea, clipper ship, 252
Belle of the West, clipper ship, 183 f.
Belvedere, ship, 226 f.
Berlin, ship, 178
Berlin Decree, 71 f., 84
Bethel, ship, 10
Billingsgate Point, 20
Black Ball Line, 122, 138
Black Cross Line, 122
Black Hawk, clipper ship, 171, 251
Black Prince, clipper ship, 252
Black Star Line, 122
Blackwater Bank, 139
Blue Jacket, clipper ship, 275
Blue Jacket, ship, 249
Bluff Harbor, 202 ff.

Boardman, William, 95 ff.
Boeroe Bay, 155
Bombay, 160, 188 f., 225, 278
Bonaparte, Julian, 70
Bonaparte, Napoleon, 70 f., 93, 123
Bonita, clipper ship, 170
Bordeaux, 91 f., 148, 265
Boston, 4, 6, 10, 15 ff., 19, 22 f., 26, 29 ff., 33 ff., 40 ff., 45, 52, 55, 58, 61, 63, 66 f., 73 f., 78 f., 81 f., 84, 89, 94, 101, 103 ff., 111, 114, 116 f., 120, 122, 124, 137 f., 142 ff., 147, 149, 153 ff., 160, 162, 165 ff., 169 ff., 175, 179 f., 184 f., 187, 194, 199, 205 ff., 213, 233, 237, 239, 255, 258, 261, 264, 267, 275, 277, 279, 288 ff.
Boston Fruit Co., 34
Boston Harbor, 140
Boston Light, clipper ship, 189 f., 216, 221 ff.
Boston–Liverpool Packet Co., 122
Bounty, ship, 228
Bounty Bay, 230
Bradford, Capt. Gamaliel, 90
Bray, Capt. Benjamin, 279
Brazil, 107 f., 143, 198
Breck, Capt., 51
Bremen, 22
Bremerhaven, 150, 210
Brest, 74, 76 f.
Brewster, 4, 6 f., 18, 31, 33, 41, 72 ff., 78, 84 ff., 89, 92 f., 111, 160, 165, 172, 180, 185, 197, 199, 215, 230, 233 f., 240, 244, 248, 250, 252, 254, 257 f., 283, 286
Brewster Ship Masters, 199
Brewster, Capt. William E., 168
Briggs Brothers, shipbuilders, 283
Bristol, Eng., 40
British Blockade of Cape Ports, 14, 19
Brooklyn, 135
Brown & Bell, 125, 131
Brown, William, 131
Bryant, John, 55
Bryant & Sturgis, 55
Buena Vista, ship, 153 f., 199
Burgess, Capt. William H., 160, 172 f.
Burgess, Mrs. William H., 172 ff.
Burke, Capt. Edmund, 283
Burmah, ship, 157 ff.

Index

Bursley, Capt. Allen, 122, 137 ff.
Bursley, Capt. David, 138, 283
Bursley, Capt. Frank, 253
Bursley, Capt. Ira, 122, 138 f.
Bursley, Capt. Ira, 2d, 139, 252
Bursley, Ira, Jr., 139
Bursley, Capt. Isaac, 138
Bursley, Capt. Joseph, 279 f.
Burlsey, Capt. Samuel, 138
Bush & Wildes, 213 f., 225

Cabinet, ship, 153, 199
Cabot, schooner, 144 ff., 186
Cádiz, 74, 83 f., 90, 144, 277
Caiganee, 51
Calcutta, 114, 138, 153 f., 157 ff.,
  164, 167, 170 f., 184, 187, 189 f.,
  199, 205, 224 f., 227, 240 ff.,
  245 f., 260 f.
Caldera, 201
Caldwell, Capt. A. H., 185 f.
California, 166, 177, 184, 198, 201,
  205, 217, 237, 254, 257 f., 283
California Dry Dock Co., 197
California gold rush, 35 f., 105, 164,
  200, 254
Callao, 173, 186, 218, 227, 236 f.,
  245, 248, 273
Cambridge, ship, 138 f.
Camden, Me., 35
Campobello, 94
Candace, ship, 153
Canterbury, yacht, 275
Canton, 41 ff., 47, 52 ff., 58 f., 62 ff.,
  110, 153, 156, 162, 214, 270 f.
Cape Cod Bay, 20 f.
Cape Cod Canal, 39
Cape Haytière, 99
Cape Henry, 17 f.
Cape Horn, 42, 48, 107, 115, 164 ff.,
  175 f., 181, 186, 198, 219, 221,
  224, 233, 235 f., 246, 248, 274,
  281
Cape of Good Hope, 41, 156, 164,
  189, 248
Cape St. Roque, 166
Capetown, 274 f., 278 f.
Cape Verde Islands, 42
Capitol Gas Co., 197
Cardiff, 170, 211 ff., 246
Carolinas, the, 22 f., 92
Caroline, ship, 52, 79
Caroline Islands, 257

Carribean Sea, 31
Carrie Reed, ship, 223
Carrier Pigeon, clipper ship, 252
Case, Capt. Willis L., 35
Cassandra Adams, ship, 251
Catherine Whitney, steamship, 263
Cavanas, 31
Celestial, clipper ship, 175 f.
Centerville, 38, 98 f.
Ceylon, 211
Chadwick, Capt. Watson, 122
Challenger, clipper ship, 173 f.
Charger, clipper ship, 205, 233
Chariot of Fame, clipper ship,
  140 f., 234 ff., 291 f.
Charles H. Lawrence, schooner, 34
Charleston, 33, 264
Charlestown Navy Yard, 67
Charlotte, ship, 185
Charmer, yacht, 274
Chase, Capt. Edwin, 252
Chase, George, 200 f., 203
Chase, Horatio W., 35
Chase, Capt. James, 22
Chase, Job, Sr., 22
Chase, Job, Jr., 21 ff.
Chase, Capt. Job, 3d, 22 f.
Chase, Capt. Jonathan, 22 f.
Chase, Capt. Otis D., 35
Chase, Ozias, 22
Chase, Capt. Sears, 22
Chase, Theodore, 154, 200 f.
Chatham, 10 ff., 25 f., 29, 37, 96 f.,
  99, 166 f., 252, 264, 268 f., 274,
  277 ff., 282, 285 f., 287 ff.
Chatiqua, 49
Chelsea, Mass., 195
Chesapeake Bay, 92, 201
Chicago, 286
Child, William, 262
Childs, Capt. Edward, 13
Childs, Capt. Josiah, 13
Chile, 201
Chile, ship, 255
Chilo, ship, 271 ff.
China, 41 ff., 45, 47, 52 f., 58 ff., 61,
  64 f., 97 f., 121, 142 ff., 152 ff.,
  177, 184, 196, 199 f., 205, 208,
  225 f., 237 f., 243, 249, 251, 264,
  267 ff., 283
China Sea, 159
Chincha Islands, 173, 176 ff., 198,
  205, 222, 236, 245, 257

309

Index

Chin Chew, 267
Chipman, Capt. William, 288
Chipsa, bark, 248
Cipher, brig, 143
City of Columbia, steamship, 251
Ciudad Bolivar, 33
Civil War, 28, 39, 157, 195 f., 199, 224, 233, 239, 243, 245, 248 f., 261, 263, 273, 275, 283, 285
Clark, Capt. Isaac, 41, 86 f.
Clark, Capt. Kimball, 90 f., 93
Clark, Kimball, Jr., 87 f.
Clark Winsor, schooner, 30
Climax, clipper ship, 180 f., 186, 252
Clipper Ship Era, 68, 98, 105 ff., 162 ff.
Coasting trade, 11 f., 14 ff., 92, 143, 150, 264
Cobb, Capt. Elijah, 73 ff., 93 ff., 97
Cobb, Matthew, 148
Cobb, Capt. Scottow, 73
Cobb, Capt. William B., 186, 252
Coenties slip, 145
Collins, Edward K., 126 ff., 141, 180
Collins, Mrs. Edward K., 133
Collins, Capt. John, 122, 129 f., 132 ff., 141, 180
Collins Line, 122, 130 ff., 184, 195 f.
Colombo, 246
Colon (formerly Aspinwall), 190
Columbia, ship, 41 ff.
Columbia River, 61, 104
Comet, clipper ship, 170
Comet, ship, 279 f.
Commercial Wharf, 147, 155
Competitor, clipper ship, 174, 180 f.
Connecticut, 144
Conqueror, ship, 237, 280, 283
Constantinople, 287
Constellation, brig, 72
Constitution, frigate, 66 f.
Contest, clipper ship, 168 f.
Cook, Capt. James, 41
Copenhagen, 79, 82
Coquette, bark, 162 f., 196
Cork, 80 f., 147, 222, 245, 273
Corn-cracking, 25
Corn Field Lightship, 276
Corunna, 92
Cosmos, schooner, 29
Costa Rica, 34

Cotton trade, 99, 129, 149 ff., 153, 198 f., 226, 237, 277, 287
Cow (Indian chief), 49
Cowes, 190
Cressy, Capt. Josiah P., 113
Creture, schooner, 73
Crimea, 196, 198
Crocker, Capt. Elijah, 280 ff.
Crocker, Capt. James B., 154 ff.
Crocker, Capt. John, 51
Crocker, Joseph, 61
Crocker, Capt. Joseph, 154, 237 ff., 267 f.
Crocker, Capt. Josiah, 169 f.
Crocker, Capt. Rowland R., 122 ff.
Cronstadt, 22, 41, 99
Crosby, Capt. Joshua, 185
Crosby, Josiah, 84
Crosby, Sally, 92
Crosby, Capt. Solomon, 90
Crosby, Sylvanus, 31 ff.
Crosby, Capt. Tully, 185 f.
Crosby, Capt. Zenas, 186
Crowell, Capt. Allen, 144 ff., 186
Crowell, Capt. Benajah, Jr., 252
Crowell, Capt. Christopher, 252
Crowell, Capt. Edward E., 30 f.
Crowell, Capt. Elkanah, Jr., 189, 215 f., 221 ff., 237
Crowell, Mrs. Elkanah, 222
Crowell, Hannah, 143 f.
Crowell, Capt. Isaiah, 89, 94
Crowell, Capt. Isaiah, Jr., 144
Crowell, Nathan, 144
Crowell, Capt. Nelson, 259
Crowell, Oris, 223
Crowell, Capt. Prince S., 146 f., 150 ff., 162, 184, 207, 229 ff., 259 ff.
Crowell, Capt. Simeon, 37
Crowell, Capt. Sturgis, 223 ff.
Crowell, Capt. Zenas, 258
Cuba, 66, 99
Cummaquid, brig, 148
Cunard Line, 126, 130 ff.
Cunneau (Indian chief), 49
Curtis, James, 199
Cutler, Carl, 7, 128
Cyclone, clipper ship, 221

Dana, Richard Henry, Jr., 61, 174
Darien, 22
Dauntless, clipper ship, 168

Index

Davis, Jefferson, 223, 245
Dean, frigate, 15
de Bodisco, A., 108
Dedham, 142
Defiance, clipper ship, 177 ff.
Delano, Amasa, 47
Delano, Warren, 196
Delano, Warren, Jr., 69
Delight in Hope, schooner, 21
Dennis, 6, 13, 24, 72, 89, 94, 122, 142, 151, 154, 180, 183, 215, 223, 236 f., 239, 244, 249, 252, 265, 274, 279
Deposit, schooner, 150
Derby, Capt. Charles, 52
Despatch, ship, 51 f.
Dewey, Capt. Samuel W., 67
Dexter, ship, 275 ff.
Dillingham, Capt. James S., Jr., 248 f.
Dillingham, Capt. John, 240 ff., 248
Dillingham, Capt. John, 3d, 87
Dillingham, Mrs. John, 240
Discovery, ship, 46
Dispatch Line, 26
Doane, Capt. Alfred, 283
Doane, Capt. Azariah, 252
Doane, Capt. Joseph, Jr., 11 f.
Doane, Capt. Justus, 166 ff.
Doane, Capt. Seth, 168, 170 f., 268
Dodge, Capt. Thomas, 37
Donegal Bay, 146
Dorothy Palmer, schooner, 35
Dover, 123
Dover, ship, 138
Draco, brig, 33
Drake, Sir Francis, 241
Dramatic Line, 122, 127 ff., 141, 191
Dublin, 80, 90
Dunkirk, 148, 247
Duxbury, 99
Dwight, Rev. Timothy, 73

Eagle, clipper ship, 175 f.
Eagle Wing, clipper ship, 154, 199 ff., 205
Earle, W. H., 237
East Boston, 68, 105, 162
East Brewster, 257
East Dennis, 150, 152, 154, 157, 183 ff., 202, 206, 220, 240, 244 ff.

Eastham, 8, 10, 16 f., 19 f., 95, 167, 170, 180, 205, 227
East Harwich, 11, 25
East Indies, 98, 121, 142 ff., 153 ff., 160, 171 f., 183 f., 226, 238, 246, 249 f., 266
Eastport, 94
Eben Preble, ship, 154 ff., 163, 237
Eclipse, clipper ship, 109
Ecuador, 149
Edward Everett, ship, 255
Edwin, schooner, 150
Egypt, 283
Eldredge, Samuel, 11
Eldridge, Capt. Asa, 122, 125, 133 ff., 137, 141, 175, 180, 191 ff.
Eldridge, Mrs. Asa, 191 f.
Eldridge, Capt. John, 122, 135, 138, 175, 180, 195 f., 251
Eldridge, Capt. Joshua, 282
Eldridge, Capt. Oliver, 122, 135 ff., 162 f., 175, 180, 196 f., 251
Electric Spark, clipper ship, 237, 252
Eliza, ship, 47
Eliza and Ella, ship, 215
Elizabeth B., schooner, 35
Ella, bark, 264
Ellen Brooks, ship, 150 ff.
Elliott, Capt. Jesse, 67
Ellis, Josiah, Jr., 23 f.
Ellis & Loring, 93
Elphingstone, Lord, 189
Elsinore, 41, 72
Embargo of 1807, 58, 71, 83, 94
Empress of the Seas, clipper ship, 186, 252
Endeavor, ship, 283
Engelina, brig, 35
Erin go Bragh, 130
Espindola, bark, 136 f.
Essex Street, Salem, 272
Eternity (Indian chief), 49
Eunice P. Newcomb, schooner, 34
Euridice, sloop-of-war, 232

Fair Wind, ship, 222 f.
Falkland Islands, 6, 13, 42
Falmouth, sloop, 10
Falmouth, Eng., 35, 209 f.
Falmouth, Mass., 16, 51, 122, 252
Faneuil Hall, ship, 198
Fannie Palmer, schooner, 35

Index

Fanny, privateer, 42
Feather voyages, 12 f.
Finance, steamship, 249
Financier, ship, 41
Fire Dart, steamship, 271
Fisheries, 9, 12, 90
Five Fathom Lightship, 288
Fleetwing, clipper ship, 252
Flora, bark, 143 f.
Florence, bark, 283
Florida, Confederate cruiser, 249
Flying Cloud, clipper ship, 112 f., 183
Flying Dragon, clipper ship, 112, 165
Flying Fish, clipper ship, 166 f.
Flying Mist, clipper ship, 154, 201 ff., 215, 237
Flying Scud, clipper ship, 187 ff.
Foo-Choo, 200, 267
Forbes, John M., 69
Formosa, 174
Foster, Capt. Bailey, 215
Foster, Mrs. Bailey, 215
Foster, Capt. Freeman, 72
Foster, Capt. Isaac, 41
Franklin Haven, ship, 198
Frazar, Capt. Samuel, 99
Freeman, Capt. Benjamin, 186, 252
Freeman, Capt. Charles, 258
Freeman, Clarendon, 290 f.
Freeman, Frederick, 6
Freeman, Capt. Isaac, 10 f.
Freeman, Capt. Joshua S., 234
Fremont, John C., 283
French Revolution, 70
Frost, Capt. John H., 283
Fruiter, bark, 287 f.
Fruit trade, 284 ff.
Fugitive Slave Law, 26 f.

Galatea, ship, 223
Game Cock, clipper ship, 68
Garnet, schooner, 130
Garrick, ship, 127 f.
General Neill, ship, 263
Geneva, ship, 157
Genoa, 143, 227
George M. Barnard, ship, 175
George Porter, ship, 41
George Rogers, ship, 178
George S. Homer, steamship, 223

George T. Kemp, bark, 277 f.
Georges Banks, 130
Georgia, 22
Gerard C. Tobey, bark, 223
Gibbs, Daniel & Co., 240 f.
Gibraltar, Straits of, 74, 82, 90, 94, 143, 290 f.
Glasgow, 202, 263
Glidden & Williams, 116
Glory of the Seas, clipper ship, 233 f., 280
Gloucester, 5
Goddess, ship, 258
Godfrey, Capt. David, 26, 96
Godfrey, Mrs. David, 96
Golden City, clipper ship, 175
Golden Fleece, clipper ship, 280
Golden Gate, steamship, 233
Gonaives, 30
Gorham, Capt. Francis, 205
Gorham, Capt. Josiah, 242 f., 245
Gotenburg, 92
Gould, Capt. Nathaniel, 283
Gould, Capt. Zenas, 289
Gove, John, 255 f.
Granada, brig, 265 ff., 271
Grand Banks, 84, 117
Gratitude, ship, 283
Graves, David, 174
Gravina, clipper ship, 247
Gray, Capt. Robert, 42 ff.
Greyhounds of the Sea, 7, 128
Griffeths, John, 162
Grinnell, Hon. Henry, 127
Grinnell & Minturn, 125
Gross, Capt. Jazzaniah, 72
Guadeloupe, 23
Guano trade, 173, 176 ff., 198, 202, 205, 218 f., 222, 236, 245, 257
Guernsey, 81
Gulf of Guinea, 86 f.
Guyaquil, 148 f.

Halifax, 119, 139
Hall, Capt. Christopher, 150 ff., 183 f., 206, 239 f.
Hall, Capt. John Turner, 283
Hall, Marcus, 237
Hall, Capt. Perez, 252
Hall, Samuel, 68, 162, 166
Hall, Capt. Thomas F., 183, 206 f.
Hallett, Capt. Alvin S., 175 ff.
Hallett, Capt. Bangs, 160 f.

Index

Hallett, Capt. Benjamin, 15, 67
Hallett, Capt. Franklin, 116, 122, 140, 156 f.
Hallett & Carman, 223 f.
Hamburg, 75, 77 f., 81 f., 150, 246
Hamilton, Capt. Sylvester, 289 f.
Hampton Roads, 150, 186, 222, 236
Hancock, ship, 51
Hankow, 270
Harding, Capt. David, 286
Harding, Capt. Hiram, 292
Harding, Capt. J. Clement, 35
Harding, Capt. Joseph, 280 ff.
Harding, Capt. Nehemiah, 23, 72
Harding, Capt. Samuel, 279, 287
Hardy, Alpheus, 37
Hardy, Capt. Isaiah, 268
Harmony Grove, Salem, 272
Harriet, schooner, 72
Harriet Irving, ship, 174
Harris, Capt. Thomas, 36 f.
Hartford Convention, 85 f.
Harwich, 21, 23, 25, 29, 39, 41, 95, 252, 287
Hatch, Capt. Freeman, 167 ff., 171, 180
Havana, 144
Havre, 72, 93, 99, 150,152, 170, 173, 227
Hawaiian Islands, 44 ff., 48, 52, 232, 241
Hawes, Capt. Joseph, 37, 41
Hawthorne, Julian, 182
Hawthorne, Nathaniel, 182
Hebe, brig, 143 f.
Hedge, Capt. Milton P., 246 f.
Helsingfors, 109
Henry Clay, ship, 125, 141
Herbert, ship, 160, 172
Heroine, 37
Hetty Thom, schooner, 99
Higgins, John, 257
Higgins, Capt. Simeon, 16
Highland Light, 158
Hinckley, Capt. Francis, 283
Hingham, 47, 148 f.
Hippogriffe, clipper ship, 244 f., 259
Hippogriffe Rock, 244
Hog Island, 222
Holland, 53, 262
Holmes, Joseph, 287
Holmes's Hole, 290

Honduras, 10
Hong Kong, 109, 159, 164, 166, 171, 174, 200 ff., 214 f., 217, 221 f., 225 f., 237, 244, 249 f., 270 f., 280, 283
Hong Kong *Daily Press*, 202
Honolulu, 166, 222, 224, 232
Hoogly, ship, 273 f.
Hope, schooner, 21, 86 f.
Hope, ship, 59
Hope's Delight, schooner, 21
Hope and Hannah, schooner, 21
Hope's Lady, schooner, 21
Hope Mary Ann, schooner, 21
Hope for Peace, schooner, 21
Hope and Phœbe, schooner, 21
Hope and Polly, schooner, 21
Hope for Success, schooner, 21
Hope and Susan, schooner, 21
Horn Pond, 57
Hoskin's *Narrative*, 45
Hottinger, ship, 138 f.
Howes, Allen, 154
Howes, Capt. Allison, 183 f.
Howes, Capt. Anthony, 244 f.
Howes, Capt. Barnabas C., 252
Howes, Capt. Benjamin P., 215, 249
Howes, Mrs. Benjamin P., 250
Howes, Calvin Clark, 215
Howes, Capt. Daniel (Mediterranean Fruit Trader), 289
Howes, Capt. Daniel (neutral trader), 72
Howes, Capt. Daniel Willis, 259 ff., 271
Howes, Capt. Elisha, 142 f.
Howes, Capt. Ezra, 13
Howes, Capt. Frederick, 180 ff., 201
Howes, Mrs. Frederick, 182
Howes, Capt. Jabez, 122
Howes, John C., 154
Howes, Capt. Laban, 236 f.
Howes, Capt. Levi, 151 f., 160, 183 ff., 212, 261
Howes, Capt. Moses, 180 ff.
Howes, Capt. Osborn, 142 ff., 286
Howes, Capt. Thomas Prince, 252
Howes, Capt. William F., 183 f.
Howes & Co., 264 ff.
Howes & Crowell, 144, 279
Howes topsail rig, 181 f., 201

313

Index

Howland, Capt. William, 109 f., 112
Huckins, James, 169 ff.
Huckins, Thomas, 8
Hughes, Capt. Atkins, 283
Huntsville, ship, 128
Hurd, Capt. Luther, 205
Hurricane, clipper ship, 170
Hyannis, 26, 35 f., 144, 175, 178 f., 186, 252, 283

Ice trade, 153 f., 157, 278 f., 283
Inagua, 30
Independence, ship, 125
Independent, schooner, 35
Industry, ship, 90
Ingles, Capt. Moses, 58
Iquique, 242
Ireland, 80, 144 ff., 186
Iris, brig, 31 ff.
Isaac Jeanes, bark, 288
Isabelle Blythe, bark, 158
Isle Sables Galley, schooner, 10

Jabez Howes, ship, 251
Jackson, Andrew, 66 f.
Jacob Westervelt, ship, 116
Jamaica, 16, 33 f.
James Lamb, bark, 273
James River, 152
Jane, brig, 74 f.
Japan, 44, 267 f.
Jason, frigate, 84
Java, 262
Java Head, 59, 239
Java Sea, 244
J. C. Bryant, ship, 251
Jefferson, Thomas, 71
Jenkins, Asa, 61
Jenkins, Capt. Charles, 252
Jenkins, Capt. James, 271 ff.
Jessie Stephens, bark, 126
Jesus Maria y Joseph, ship, 10
Jewel Line, 122, 124
J. L. Bowen, brig, 277
John Adams, schooner, 232
John Bertram, clipper ship, 109
John Gilpin, clipper ship, 166 f.
John Rice, U.S.S., 263
John Wade, clipper ship, 187
Jones, Walter, 106
Joshua Bates, ship, 200
Judith, snow, 10

Kauai, 44 ff.
Keith, Minor C., 34
Kelly, Capt. David, 252
Kelly, Heman S., 207
Kelly, Capt. Isaac, 22
Kelly, Capt. Nehemiah, 23
Kemp, Capt. Samuel W., 34
Kendrick, Capt. John, 41 ff., 49
Kendrick, John, Jr., 42 f.
Kendrick, Solomon, 42 f.
Kenrick, Capt. John, 31, 72
Kent, William, 11
Kineo, ship, 245
Kingfisher, clipper ship, 185 f.
Kingman, Capt. Seth, 283
Kingston, Mass., 5
Kin Kiang, steamship, 269 ff.
Kit Carson, ship, 240 ff., 245
Klondike, 251
Knowles, Capt. Allen H., 122, 140 f., 227, 234 ff., 292
Knowles, Capt. Elijah, 252
Knowles, Capt. Joshua, 130
Knowles, Capt. Josiah N., 227 ff.
Knowles, Capt. Thomas, 227
Knowles, Capt. Winslow L., 19, 227, 254 ff.
Knowles, Capt. Winslow L., Jr., 227
Königsberg, 143

Labrador, 12 f.
Lacon, schooner, 147
Laconia, bark, 264
Lady Hope, brig, 21
Lady Washington, brig, 41 ff.
Langdale, ship, 234
La Sylphide, brig, 108 f.
Lavender, Capt. Joseph A., 288
Lawrence, Capt. David, 40
Lawry, schooner, 92
Leading Wind, ship, 283
Leander, brig, 99
Leda, bark, 144
Lee, William Coleman, 31
Leghorn, 90
Lennox, Lord William, 125
Leonidas, schooner, 22 f.
Leonore, 72
Lewis, Capt. Christopher, 252
Lewis, Capt. Nathaniel, 16
Lewis, Capt. Orrin, 30
Lewis Wharf, 111

Index

Lightfoot, clipper ship, 252
Lightning, clipper ship, 187
Lima, 179
Lincoln, Capt. Edgar, 250
Lincoln, Capt. Freeman, 283
Lincoln, Henry, 67
Lincoln, Joseph C., 283
Lincoln, Capt. Warren, 31, 33
Lincoln, William, 67
Lincoln, William & Co., 185
Linnell, Capt. Eben H., 153 f., 160, 180, 199 ff., 215, 237
Linnell, Capt. Edmund, 276 f.
Lintin, 155
Lion, ship, 137
Lisbon, 22, 72, 79, 92, 94
Littleton, 275 f.
Littleton, ship, 278
Liverpool, 35, 58, 62, 72, 98 f., 101 ff., 116 f., 124 ff., 134, 137 f., 140, 149 f., 162, 171, 182, 194 f., 197 f., 226, 233 f., 242, 247, 277
Liverpool, ship, 135 ff.
Liverpool Packet, ship, 72
Liverpool Packets, 98, 111, 115 ff., 121 ff., 149, 156, 164, 191, 227
Lizzie, bark, 237
London, 79, 129, 170, 189, 200, 202, 205, 244, 259 f., 275
Long Island, 288
Loo Choo, ship, 156 f.
Loring Brothers, 149
Loring, George, 149
Lothrop, Capt. Ansel D., 283
Lothrop, Capt. Asa, 252
Lothrop, Samuel, 21
Lovell, George, 26
Lovely Hope, schooner, 21 f.
Low, A. A., 127
Low, George, 190
Lübeck, 82
Lubra, brig, 249 f.
Luconia, 208
Lucy Gibson, schooner, 35
Lyman, Theodore, 53, 55, 63 ff.

Macao, 165
Macao Roads, 54, 57
McKay, Donald, 5, 68, 105, 111 f., 128, 141, 166, 177 f., 185 f., 200, 224, 233, 252, 280, 283, 292
Madison, James, 85 f.
Madras, 158

Mail, sloop, 69
Maine, 34 f.
Majestic, British warship, 19
Malaga, 82, 90, 148 f., 265, 287
Mameluke, clipper ship, 208
Mandarin, ship, 55
Mandarin, clipper ship, 170
Manilla, 100 f., 109, 153, 156, 171, 201
Manterola, Martin, 201
Marblehead, 5
Marianne, privateer, 42
Marley Hill, steamship, 198
Marquesa Islands, 232
Marseilles, 72, 90, 94, 99, 143, 187, 196
Martínez, 43, 45
Martinique, 23
Mary, bark, 33
Mary, brig, 79
Mary L. Sutton, clipper ship, 183
Mary S. Ames, bark, 282
Matanzas, 32 f., 265
Matchless, clipper ship, 175
Matthews, Capt. George, 135, 252, 284
Matthews, Capt. Richard, 175
Mauritius, 158, 188, 219, 224, 263, 270
Mayflower, ship, 180
Mayo, Brewster, 31
Mayo, Capt. Abijah, 283
Mayo, Capt. David E., 252
Mayo, Capt. Freeman, 31 ff.
Mayo, Capt. Jeremiah, 89 ff.
Mayo, Capt. Joseph, 86 ff.
Mayo, Capt. Matthew, 19 f.
Medford, 172, 199
Mediterranean, 72, 90
Mediterranean fruit trade, 264 f., 284 ff.
Melbourne, 187, 198, 204, 241 f., 261 f.
Memnon, clipper ship, 196
Messina, 287 ff.
Mexico, 129
Milan Decree, 71 f., 84
Minerva, schooner, 16
Minnehaha, ship, 283
Mississippi, steamship, 269
Mississippi River, 128
Mobile, 135
Monomoy Shoals, 26

Index

Monsoon, ship, 80 f.
Monterey, ship, 185, 245, 269, 278
Montreal, 275
Monumental City, steamship, 257
Morgan, Capt. Peter, 263
Morlaix, 91 f.
Morning Light, clipper ship, 243, 248
Morning Star, sloop, 25
Mount Hope, schooner, 21
Mt. Vernon, ship, 73

Nagasaki, 267 f.
Nancy, sloop, 37
Nanking, 269
Nantucket, 21, 187
Nantucket Sound, 12
Napoleon, see Bonaparte
Nathan Hannau, 287
National Eagle, clipper ship, 252, 284
N. C. Hall, schooner, 27 f.
Neptune's Car, clipper ship, 247 f.
Neutral trade, 70 ff., 89 ff.
Neversink, 130, 145
Newark, 127
Newburyport, 23, 25, 27, 124
Newcastle, 256, 283
Newcomb, Elisha, 11
Newfoundland, 133
New Hazard, brig, 62
New Hope, schooner, 21
New Orleans, 23, 31, 34, 72, 101, 103, 127 ff., 150 ff., 179, 195, 198, 237
New South Wales, 256
New York, 15 f., 19, 22 f., 26, 33 f., 41, 59, 63, 67 f., 98, 101, 103, 105, 110, 122, 125 ff., 128 ff., 134, 136, 138, 144 ff., 147, 153, 155, 162, 168 f., 171, 173, 175 ff., 179, 184 ff., 190, 193 f., 196, 200 ff., 206, 219 f., 222 f., 225 f., 232 f., 235 f., 237 ff., 246, 248 f., 264 ff., 269, 275 f., 278, 280, 287
New Zealand, 202, 274, 283
Ney, Marshall, 93
Nickels, Capt. Edward, 166 ff.
Nickerson, Capt. Alexander, 289 f.
Nickerson, Ansell, 11 f.
Nickerson, Capt. Augustus, 287
Nickerson, Capt. David, 81, 86 ff.
Nickerson, Capt. James W., 287 f.

Nickerson, Capt. Moses, 285
Nickerson, Capt. Nathan, 22 f.
Nickerson, Sparrow, 11
Nickerson, Capt. S. S., 37
Nickerson, Starks, 288
Nickerson, Capt. Thomas, 11
Nickerson, Capt. Warren, 25
Nickerson, Capt. William, 35
Nickerson, Capt. Zenas, Jr., 288
Nightingale, clipper ship, 252
Ningpo, 267
Nootka Sound, 42 f.
Norfolk, 27, 97
Norfolk Island, 229
Norman, ship, 153
North American Review, 56
North Bend, ship, 147 f.
North Dennis, 180, 215
Northern Light, clipper ship, 167 ff., 268
North River, 239
North Star, steam yacht, 191 f., 194
North Truro, 283
North-West Fur Trade, 40 ff.
North Wind, clipper ship, 171
Nova Scotia, 10
Nukahiva, 232
Nye, Capt. Ezra, 122, 124 ff., 141, 180, 206, 263
Nye, Mrs. Ezra, 133 f.
Nye, Capt. Hiram, 252
Nye, Joseph, 127

Oeno Island, 228 f., 232
Ohevahoa Island, 232
Ohitahoo Island, 232
Old Colony, brig, 185
Old Hope, schooner, 21
Old South Shoal, 187
Oliver, Capt. James, 23
Olyphant & Co., 269 f.
Oporto, 92
Orbit, brig, 99
Orders in Council, 71, 82 f., 94
Oregon, 41, 48, 52, 56, 97
Orinoco River, 33
Orissa, ship, 157 ff., 163
Orleans, 21, 29, 72, 95, 153, 168, 170, 180, 199 ff., 252, 274, 276 ff., 283, 288
Orpheus, ship, 138, 184, 226, 236 f.
Ossipee, brig, 248
Osterville, 15, 26, 67

Index

Otago, bark, 275
Otis, ship, 123 f.
Owhyhee Harbor, 6
Owhyhee, brig, 99
Oxnard, ship, 156 f.

Pacific Mail Co., 196 f.
Pacific, steamship, 126 f., 131, 133 f.,
    137, 140 f., 184, 195
Packet, ship, 61 ff.
Packets, local, 4, 15, 69
Page, Capt., 59
Paine, Joshua Caleb, 130
Palermo, 150, 265, 287
Palfrey, J. G., 7, 9
Palmer, Capt. Nathaniel, 128, 175
Panther, clipper ship, 258
Paragon, ship, 86
Paris, 75 ff., 93
Peak, Capt. Myron, 35
Peaked Hill Bars, 26
Pelew Islands, 171
Penang, 248
Penhallow, Capt., 178
Pequot, topsail schooner, 26
Percival, Capt. Daniel W., 288
Percival, Capt. F. M., 29 f.
Perkins, James & Thomas H., 47
Perkins, Thomas H., 69
Pernambuco, 198
Peru, 176 f.
Perua, bark, 36
Phantom, clipper ship, 175 ff.
Philadelphia, 33, 36, 58, 170, 245,
    264, 288
Phinney, E. S., 38
Phinney, Sylvanus B., 177
Phœbe, sloop, 13
Pico, brig, 36
Pierce, Capt. Sumner, 252
Piracy, 54 f.
Pirates, 11, 31 ff., 74, 249
Pitcairn Island, 228 ff.
Platte River, 258
Plymouth, Eng., 227
Plymouth, Mass., 7 f., 19, 24, 185,
    288
Plymouth Rock, steamship, 271
Point de Galle, 213 f.
Polena, Barcella, 235
Polly, sloop, 16 f., 22
Pomona, 72
Pook, Samuel, 194

Port Antonio, 33 f.
Port au Prince, 30
Port Elizabeth, 277
Port Gamble, 240
Port Morant, 33
Port Patrick, 137
Portsmouth, N.H., 152
Pratt, Rev. Enoch, 19
Prince, Capt. James, 283
Prince's Island, 86 ff.
Providence, 25, 59
Provincetown, 34 f., 140, 180, 288
Puget Sound, 240 f.

Queen Charlotte Islands, 41, 43 f.,
    62
Queen of the Seas, clipper ship, 173
Queen of the West, ship, 116, 140,
    156
Queenstown, 198
Quincy, 36, 275
Quincy, Josiah, Jr., 12

Radiant, bark, 264
Ragget, Commodore, 19 f.
Railroad, Old Colony, 34
Rambler, schooner, 38
Rangoon, 214
Rattler, clipper ship, 175 f., 237
Raven, clipper ship, 169 f., 252
R. B. Forbes, clipper ship, 166
Red Cloud, ship, 278
Red Cross Line, 122
Red Jacket, clipper ship, 125, 191,
    194 f.
Red Star Line, 122
Reign of Terror, 70, 74, 78
Reindeer, privateer, 26
Renown, clipper ship, 174
Reporter, clipper ship, 183
Resolution Bay, 232
Revolutionary War, 14 f., 21, 42
Rice Plant, brig, 72
Rich, Capt. Obadiah, 73
Rich, Shebnah, 37
Richardson, Capt. Ephraim, 98
Richardson, George, 99, 114
Richardson, John, 98
Richardson, Capt. Josiah, 98 ff.,
    137, 140 f., 165, 256
Richmond, 17, 23, 150
Rider, Capt. Samuel, 72
Ringleader, clipper ship, 174 f.

Index

Rio de Janeiro, 99, 107, 109, 143 f., 165, 176, 221, 281
Ripolo, 224
Rival, ship, 220
R. M. Heslin, brig, 289
Robespierre, 70, 74, 77 f.
Robin Hood, clipper ship, 187, 252
Rockland, 194
Romance of the Seas, clipper ship, 183, 200
Ropes & Pickman, 61
Rosa Wing, schooner, 38
Rosario, bark, 148 f.
Roscuis, ship, 127, 129 f., 133, 141
Rosebud, schooner, 22
Rotterdam, 79
Rowan, Capt. James, 47 ff.
Russell & Co., 270 f.
Russia, 36, 55 f., 72 f., 99, 101
Ruth, schooner, 73
Ruth N. Atwood, schooner, 33
Ryder, Capt. Adolphus, 286

Sable Island, 119
Sagamore, 174
Sailor's Rights, 197
St. Helena, 263, 269
St. Jago, 99
St. John's, 84, 94, 103 f., 117, 119
St. Lucia, 16
St. Michaels, 72
St. Petersburg, 22, 79, 101
St. Thomas's, 23, 29, 88
St. Vincent Island, 269
Salem, 5, 41, 52, 62, 272
Salem, brig, 90
Sally, brig, 93
Sally, ship, 90
Sally and Mary, brig, 81 ff.
Salt Keys, 23
Salt Works, 20
Sampson & Tappan, 105, 109, 112, 159, 205
Samuel Lawrence, ship, 175
Sand Heads, 160, 205
Sandalwood, 44 ff.
Sandalwood Islands, 155
Sandwich, 6, 8, 23, 34, 122, 124 f., 127, 172, 180, 206, 237
Sandwich Historical Society, 174
Sandy Hook, 219
Sandy Neck Lighthouse, 135
Santa Claus, clipper ship, 215

San Domingo, 21 f., 30 f.
San Francisco, 36, 106 f., 111 ff., 115, 154, 164 f., 167 ff., 180 ff., 185 ff., 197 ff., 201 f., 205, 207 f., 217 f., 221 ff., 226 f., 232 ff., 236 f., 240 ff., 246 ff., 251, 254 ff., 274, 276, 278 ff.
San Francisco, clipper ship, 175
San Francisco Daily News, 282
San Sebastian, 90 f.
Savannah, 150, 152, 247
Scargo, ship, 259 ff., 271
Scilly Islands, 81
Scituate, 8
Scotia, bark, 130
Seacomb & Taylor, 194
Seaman's Devotional Assistant, 155
Sears, Capt. Ebenezer, 41
Sears, Ezra F., 208
Sears, Capt. J. Henry, 6, 197 ff., 226, 233
Sears, Capt. Joshua, 154, 156 ff., 180, 182 ff., 202, 206 ff., 222, 225, 237, 245
Sears, Capt. Stephen, 72
Sea Bird, bark, 274, 278
Sea Flower, schooner, 95
Sea Serpent, clipper ship, 109 f., 112, 252
Sea Witch, clipper ship, 166
Seal Island, 118
Seal Island Light, 118
Semmes, Capt. Raphael, 250
Shakespeare, ship, 127, 129
Shanghai, 159, 170 f., 185, 187, 200, 208, 237 ff., 252, 266 ff.
Sheridan, ship, 127 f.
Shields, 274
Shimeta, Neesima, 252
Shiverick, Asa, David, and Paul, shipbuilders, 35, 183, 201, 206, 240, 244, 246
Shooting Star, clipper ship, 112 f., 165
Shore whaling, 9
Shrewsbury, 99
Siamese Twins, 66
Sicilian, bark, 288
Siddons, ship, 127 f.
Silas Richards, ship, 138
Simpkins, Rev. John, 7
Singapore, 114, 201, 207 f., 210, 214 f., 244, 271 f.

Index

Skylark, clipper ship, 253
Sligo, 142, 144 ff., 187
Small, Capt. Jonathan, 22
Smith, Capt. Heman, 285
Smith, James, 96
Smith, John, 23 f.
Smith, Capt. Levi D., 282
Smith, Capt. Lewis, 283
Smith, Capt. Nehemiah, 17 f.
Smith, Capt. Soloman, 288
Smith's Island, 280
Smyrna, 142 ff., 265, 287, 289 f.
Snow, Capt. Ephraim, 72 f.
Snow, Capt. Henry, 72 f.
Snow, Capt. Joseph, 252
Snow, Capt. Nathaniel, 26
Snow, Capt. Reuben, 252
Snow Squall, clipper ship, 252
Soldam, schooner, 150
Somerset, British warship, 14
Southampton, Eng., 192
Southern Cross, clipper ship, 154,
    199, 215, 249, 252, 283
South America, 287
South Carolina, 277
South Chatham, 35
South Orleans, 31, 41, 72
South Side of Cape Cod, 26, 38
South Yarmouth, 215, 227, 250, 279
Spain, 70, 72, 92, 149, 287 f.
Sparrow, Capt. Hiram, 252
Sparrow, Capt. Thomas, 252
Speedwell, schooner, 73
Spencer, British warship, 19, 21
Spitfire, clipper ship, 175, 183, 221
Sprague, Capt. Caleb, 147 ff., 160,
    247 f.
Sprague, Francis, 5, 37
Spring Valley Water Works, 197
Staffordshire, clipper ship, 111 ff.,
    137, 140 f., 165
Stag Hound, clipper ship, 105 ff.,
    111 f.
Stamboul, ship, 283
Starlight, clipper ship, 184
Star of Peace, ship, 283
State Street Trust Co., 5
Steers, George, 131
Sterling, ship, 251
Stetson, Jotham, 195
Stevens, Capt. Levi, 154, 199
Stockton Gas Co., 197
Stonington, 25

Straits of Banca, 159
Straits of Belle Isle, 90
Straits of Le Maire, 258
Straits of Sunda, 100, 155, 200
Sturgis, James, 55
Sturgis Library, 57
Sturgis, Capt. Russell, 127
Sturgis, Capt. William, 47 ff., 85, 97
Sturgis, Capt. William, Sr., 47
Success, schooner, 95 ff.
Sullivan, Governor, 92
Sunda Islands, 155
Sundstrom, Capt., 108
Sunset Telephone Co., 197
Sunshine, clipper ship, 252
Superb Hope, schooner, 21
Surabaya, 262
Surinam, 73, 185
Swallow, clipper ship, 252
Swallow Tail Line, 122, 125, 135,
    138
Swatow, 205
Swinerton, Capt. David, 190
Swordfish, clipper ship, 237 ff., 268
Sydney, 225, 234, 257

Tahiti, 230, 232
Talisman, clipper ship, 183
Tampico, 22
Tartar, steamship, 263
Taylor, Capt. Horace, 252, 270
Taylor, Capt. John (1794), 95 f.
Taylor, Capt. John, 274, 277 ff.
Taylor, Capt. Joshua N., 274 ff.
Taylor, Capt. Prince, 270, 274, 276
Taylor, Capt. Seth, 252
Taylor, Capt. Simeon N., 264 ff.,
    274, 278 f., 286
Taylor, Mrs. Simeon N., 264 f., 286
T. B. Wales, ship, 250
Telegraph, schooner, 33 f.
Telemachus, brig, 185
Ten Brothers, brig, 72
Ten Sisters, coaster, 15
Terry, General Alfred H., 195 f.
Texas, 243
Thatcher, H. C., 6
Thomas, George, 194
Thomas W. Sears, ship, 152 f., 162
Thompson, Capt. William C., 127
Three Brothers, clipper ship, 251
Three Friends, schooner, 31
Tirrell, ship, 263

Index

Titan, clipper ship, 196 ff., 226
Title Insurance & Trust Co., 197
Tobacco trade, 150
Tonnigen, 91
Tonquin, ship, 158
Toronto, ship, 178
Townsend, ship, 103 ff.
Trade Wind, clipper ship, 168 ff.
Train, Enoch, 111, 116, 122
Tremont Line, 144
Trieste, 143
Tristan da Cuñha, 261
Trumbull, ship, 59
Truro, 6, 26, 37, 72 f., 122, 127, 129 f., 132, 154, 180, 252, 283
Tsar, ship, 159
Tuscaloosa, Confederate cruiser, 248 f.
T Wharf, 147

Ulysses, ship, 51 f.
Uncondo, Peter, 201
United Fruit Co., 34
United States Hotel, 220
Upton, George, 105

Valparaiso, 106, 108, 149, 173, 179, 201, 227, 231, 247, 255.
Vancouver, 41, 45 f., 241
Vancouver, brig, 63 ff.
Vancouver, George, 46
Vandalia, sloop-of-war, 232
Vanderbilt, Cornelius, 191 ff.
Velma, bark, 289
Vera Cruz, 127, 130
Victory, ship, 280
Vigo, 92
Vineyard Sound, 276
Virginia, 26 ff., 72, 78, 83, 92
Volunteer, ship, 225

Waldoboro, Me., 35
Walpole, ship, 104
War of 1812, 19, 21, 62 f., 84 ff., 92 ff., 129, 142
Warren, ship, 73
Waterloo, 93
Waterville, 120
Webfoot, clipper ship, 246 f.
Webster, Daniel, 6, 108
Wellfleet, 34, 72
Wells, Fargo Co., 197
West, Capt. Fred, 39

West Barnstable, 160, 252, 271
West Dennis, 35
West Harwich, 21
West Indies, 22 f., 28 ff., 47, 72, 74, 87, 95 f., 99, 262 f., 287
West Sandwich, 174
West Yarmouth, 189, 215, 251 f., 258
Western Islands, see Azores
Whampoa, 109, 153, 155, 166
Whelden, Capt. Charles, 251
Whirlwind, clipper ship, 172 f.
White Diamond Line, 122
White, Capt. James, 275
White, Capt. John, 175
White, Capt. Otis, 174
White Sea, the, 41
White Squall, clipper ship, 248
White Swallow, clipper ship, 252
Wild Hunter, clipper ship, 157, 160, 202, 206 ff., 252
Wild Pigeon, clipper ship, 168
Wild Ranger, clipper ship, 198, 252
Wild Rover, clipper ship, 252, 270
Wild Wave, clipper ship, 227 ff.
William, ship, 55
William Tell, ship, 83 f.
Williams, Capt. George, 34
Wilmington, North Carolina, 23
Windsor, Capt. Phineas, 223
Wing, Josiah, 31
Winged Arrow, clipper ship, 186
Winged Racer, clipper ship, 205
Winsor, Henry, 173
Witch of the Wave, clipper ship, 170
Witchcraft, clipper ship, 186, 252
Wixon, Capt. Barnabas, 13
Wood, Capt. George, 215
Woo Sing, 159, 200
Wright, William, 160

Xenia, bark, 283
Xenophon, ship, 58

Yang-Tse-Kiang River, 269, 271
Yankee, bark, 232
Yarmouth, 6 ff., 21, 26 f., 37 f., 41, 69, 72, 91, 94, 122, 133 ff., 140, 143, 156, 160, 162, 174 f., 180, 184, 196 f., 237, 242, 244, 252, 284
Young America, clipper ship, 251
Young Brander, ship, 195